Straight Studies Modified

Straight Studies Modified

Lesbian Interventions in the Academy

edited by
Gabriele Griffin and Sonya Andermahr

CASSELL
London and Washington

For a catalogue of related titles in our
Sexual Politics/Global Issues list
please write to us at an address below

Cassell
Wellington House
125 Strand
London WC2R 0BB

PO Box 605
Herndon
Virginia 20172

First published 1997

British Library Cataloguing-in-Publication Data

A catalogue record for this book is available from the British Library.

Library of Congress Cataloging-in-Publication Data

Straight studies modified: lesbian interventions in the academy / edited by Gabriele Griffin and Sonya Andermahr.
p. cm.
Includes bibliographical references and index.
ISBN 0-304-33633-5 (hardcover).—ISBN 0-304-33630-0 (pbk.)
1. Gay and lesbian studies—Great Britain. 2. Lesbian college teachers—Great Britain. 3. Lesbians—Education (Higher)—Great Britain. 4. Homosexuality and education—Great Britain.
I. Griffin, Gabriele. II. Andermahr, Sonya.
HQ75.16.G7S77 1997
305.9'0664—dc21 97-1949
CIP

ISBN 0-304-33633-5 (hardback)
0-304-33630-0 (paperback)

Typeset by Ben Cracknell Studios
Printed and bound in Great Britain by Biddles Ltd, Guildford and King's Lynn

Contents

Notes on Contributors

Sonya Andermahr is Senior Lecturer in English and Women's Studies at Nene College, Northampton, UK. Together with Terry Lovell and Carol Wolkowitz she co-authored *A Glossary of Feminist Theory* (Edward Arnold, 1997). Her other publications include 'Separatist Politics and Lesbian Utopian Fiction' in S. Munt (ed.), *New Lesbian Criticism* (Harvester Wheatsheaf, 1992); 'The Worlds of Lesbian/Feminist Science Fiction' in G. Griffin (ed.), *Outwrite: Lesbianism and Popular Culture* (Pluto, 1993); and 'A Queer Love Story? Madonna and Lesbian and Gay Culture' in D. Hamer and B. Budge (eds), *The Good, the Bad and the Gorgeous* (Pandora, 1994).

Yvon Appleby has recently completed her PhD on lesbian women and education at Sheffield University. She has published several articles based on this research. Currently she is taking women's studies out into the country in her work with the WEA.

Rosemary Auchmuty is Associate Head of the School of Law, University of Westminster, UK. Her teaching and research interests include feminist history, lesbian studies, property law, women and law, and girls' school stories. Her publications include two chapters in the Lesbian History Group's *Not a Passing Phase: Reclaiming Lesbians in History* (The Women's Press, 1989); *A World of Girls: The Appeal of the Girls' School Story* (The Women's Press, 1992) and *Women and the Family Home: Legal and Social Change in Postwar England* (Dartmouth, 1996).

Lynda Birke is a biologist at the Centre for the Study of Women and Gender at the University of Warwick, UK. She has a particular interest in the feminist study of science. Her recent books include *Feminism, Animals and Science* (Open University Press, 1994) and, with Ruth Hubbard, *Reinventing Biology* (Indiana University Press, 1995).

Jill Davis is Senior Lecturer in Drama at the University of Kent, UK. She teaches and publishes in the field of feminist and gender theory and theatre, with a particular interest in lesbian theatre. She has served on a number of theatre management committees and arts funding bodies, including the Arts Council and South East Arts.

Julia Erhart is a lecturer in the Department of Screen Studies at Flinders University, Adelaide, Australia. She has been involved with the topic of lesbianism and film since she helped organize Brown University's first lesbian and gay film festival in 1986. She has published on Hollywood film, independent cinema and lesbian/gay studies. She is currently working on a book on sexuality and cultural memory in contemporary feminist cinema.

Jane Gardner and **Sarah Oerton** are both lecturers in sociology and women's studies at the University of Glamorgan, South Wales. Jane Gardner's research interests include young women's identity in relation to their use of popular music and she has written articles in this area. Sarah Oerton has researched and published in the field of gender, work and organizations; family, kinship and household labour; and sexuality (including lesbian and gay sexualities). Her most recent book, *Beyond Hierarchy: Gender, Sexuality and the Social Economy*, is published by Taylor and Francis. Jane and Sarah live in Bristol with their (blood) sisters.

Ali Grant is a PhD student in the Department of Geography at McMaster University, Hamilton, Canada where she is completing her thesis on the importance of location and transgression in the development and regulation of organized anti-violence activism in place. Her thesis is entitled *Geography of Oppression and Liberation: Contesting the Reproduction of the Heterosexual Regime.*

Gabriele Griffin is Professor of Women's Studies at Leeds Metropolitan University, UK. Her most recent publications include *Gender Issues in Elder Abuse* (co-authored with Lynda Aitken; London: Sage, 1996); *Feminist Activism in the 1990s* (London: Taylor and Francis, 1995); *Stirring It: Challenges for Feminism* (edited with M. Hester, S. Rai and S. Roseneil; London: Taylor and Francis, 1994) and *Heavenly Love? Lesbian Images in Twentieth-Century Women's Writing* (Manchester: Manchester University Press, 1993).

Sheila Jeffreys teaches in the Department of Political Science at the University of Melbourne, Australia. She was a founding member of London Women Against Violence Against Women (WAVAW); of the London Lesbian Archive; and of the London Lesbian History Group. She has published widely on lesbian feminism and is author of *The Lesbian Heresy: A Feminist Perspective on the Lesbian Sexual Revolution* (London: The Women's Press, 1994); *Anticlimax: A Feminist Perspective on the Sexual Revolution* (London: The Women's Press, 1990); and *The Spinster and Her Enemies: Feminism and Sexuality 1880–1930* (London: Pandora, 1985).

Celia Kitzinger is Director of Women's Studies in the Department of Social Sciences at Loughborough University, UK. She is author of *The Social Construction of Lesbianism* (Sage, 1987) and co-author, with Rachel Perkins, of *Changing Our Minds: Lesbian Feminism and Psychology* (New York University Press, 1993). Her edited books (jointly with Sue Wilkinson) include *Heterosexuality* (Sage, 1993), *Feminism and Discourse* (Sage, 1995) and *Representing the Other* (Sage, 1996).

Alison Oram is Principal Lecturer in Women's Studies at Nene College, Northampton, UK. She has published extensively on women teachers and the history of feminism, most recently *Women Teachers and Feminist Politics 1900–39* (Manchester University Press, 1996). She co-taught the first lesbian history course in London from 1985, was a founder member of the Lesbian History Group and a contributor to *Not a Passing Phase* (The Women's Press, 1989). She is currently working on a source book on lesbian history.

Julia Penelope resigned her academic position in 1987 and now earns her living as a freelance editor and proofreader. In addition to her collaborations with Susan Wolfe, she is author of *Speaking Freely: Unlearning the Lies of the Fathers' Tongues* (Pergamon Press, 1990), *Call Me Lesbian* (a collection of her essays; Freedom, CA: Crossing Press, 1992) and *Crossword Puzzles for Women*. She lives in Lubbock, Texas.

Margrit Shildrick was Co-ordinator of Women's Studies at the University of Leeds, UK, in 1995–96 and taught courses on feminist epistemology, the body and sexuality. She has published several articles in the field of postmodern feminist philosophy, especially in the area of subjectivity. Her first book, *Leaky Bodies and Boundaries: Feminism, Postmodernism and Bioethics* (Routledge, 1997) will be followed by an edited collection (with Janet Price) that explores the implications of postmodernist theory in the substantive discourse of biomedicine.

Linda Stepulevage is a senior lecturer in the Department of Innovation Studies at the University of East London, UK. Her research and teaching deal with women's relationship to science and computing, and the development of technical skills such as database design. Her classes are taught within two interdisciplinary degree programmes: BSc (Hons.) Women and New Technology and BA (Hons.) Women's Studies.

Tamsin Wilton is Senior Lecturer in Health and Social Policy at the University of the West of England in Bristol, UK. Her publications include *Antibody Politic: AIDS and Society* (New Clarion Press, 1992), *Lesbian Studies: Setting an Agenda* (Routledge, 1995), *Immortal, Invisible:*

Lesbians and the Moving Image (Routledge, 1995), *Finger-Licking Good: The Ins and Outs of Lesbian Sex* (Cassell, 1996) and (edited with Lesley Doyal and Jennie Naidoo) *AIDS: Setting a Feminist Agenda* (Taylor and Francis, 1994). She is currently writing a lesbian health handbook for Cassell, to be published in 1997, and is keen to hear about any research on lesbian health that is going on!

Susan J. Wolfe is Professor and Chair of English at the University of South Dakota. In addition to her publications in linguistics, she has co-edited four books with Julia Penelope (Stanley): *The Coming Out Stories* (Watertown, MA: Persephone Press, 1980), *The Original Coming Out Stories* (Freedom, CA: Crossing Press, 1989), *Lesbian Culture: An Anthology* and *Sexual Practice, Textual Practice: Lesbian Cultural Criticism*. She is now finishing a book on feminism and linguistics for the University of South Dakota Press.

Introduction

Gabriele Griffin and Sonya Andermahr

Is she or isn't she? Lesbians in academe in the 1990s

1. 'I don't know how to mark this. I don't even know *if* I want to mark this.' Exasperation as subtext, as one of us, in her capacity as External Examiner, receives a piece of work on lipstick lesbianism by a young dyke from a lesbian colleague in another institution who teaches lesbian studies. 'Where *are* their politics?'
2. A young lesbian colleague is propositioned by a mature male student. We discuss if she should come out to him (by way of deterrent) or if she needs to handle this in some other way.
3. Unease in the classroom when attempts are made to discuss lesbianism in cultural production. They (the students) don't mind *reading* (about) it but are a lot less sanguine when it comes to *talking* about it (see Jane Gardner and Sarah Oerton's piece in this volume).

The 1990s (and are they really in this respect any different from previous decades?) have been a period of contradiction for lesbians – or maybe not. On the one hand, there's been the rise of the mainstreaming of lesbian chic (remember kd lang and Cindy Crawford – and what did *that* mean?!); on the other, there's been much debate about lesbians' political activism/activity or inactivity. Do we all really just want to go shopping and play with gender? Maybe for the first time in lesbian history there is a strong awareness of acknowledged generational differences among lesbians, with 'out' lesbians of diverse age groups adopting, discussing and defending divergent positions around identity, difference and politics. The discourses have grown very sophisticated (for example, Grosz, 1995; Doan, 1994; Jeffreys, 1994; Smith, 1994; Fuss, 1991), the sentiments strong – and that must surely be a good sign, for debate is one vehicle for change.

In the 1990s lesbians are more visible in British academe than they have ever been. Not only, as this volume clearly shows, in subjects in which they have traditionally been found (out) – the arts and humanities (games don't count here for the moment) – but also in areas such as geography, law, biology and indeed computing, where we have not had much of a lesbian say in the past. Lesbian scholars are becoming more visible and more articulate/d about the specificity and impact of lesbian knowledge and experience on and in academic disciplines. It seems clear that there are more out lesbian academics – and at senior levels – than ever before. Time to take stock then, to take a snapshot of how it is for us now.

In the 1990s in the UK lesbian scholarship has achieved visibility through a variety of avenues, which include lesbian studies (still mostly available only as one module within – usually – a women's studies course), women's studies, gender studies, cultural studies, theatre studies, film studies, sometimes sociology and occasionally other subjects where 'the lesbian' appears fleetingly within particular courses – now you see her, now you don't. The interesting issue about the subject areas where lesbian work has been most prominent is that these are almost all fairly recent additions to the academic spectrum (at least in the UK) – few of the contributors to this volume, for example, will have had the opportunity to study such subjects – and that they are characterized by a strongly multi- or interdisciplinary as well as an overtly theorized stance, in which the centre of enquiry is the construction of the subject (subject here in the sense of personhood and agency rather than academic discipline). Lesbian scholarship is transgressional. Without a straight [*sic*] history, it has been able to engage across academic disciplines, regulated less by boundaries of subject areas than by issues of subjecthood.

The long history of coming-out stories which make up lesbian history, the questions of subjectivity and identity that lesbians must routinely deal with as part of our life experiences propel us in academic directions which enable the engagement with, and theorization of, these questions. This is evident in the chapters in this volume. It is also clear that in this pursuit we come up against the limitations of what academe, in terms of disciplines, institutions, people, etc., will bear. Susan Wolfe and Julia Penelope's chapter, for instance, bears/bares the marks of a discipline, linguistics, which may be too patriarchal to influence, as they admit: 'the lesbian subversion of linguistic theory remains no more than a remote possibility'. Similarly, Lynda Birke declares: 'It's tricky being a lesbian biologist.' In our quest for contributors to this volume we found that as we moved away from the subject areas such as film, women's or cultural studies, for example, in which well-known out lesbians publish academic work with an overt lesbian content, it became more difficult to identify contributors. Despite, for instance, a concomitant rise of feminist and lesbian work in geography during the 1980s and 1990s, there are still fairly few out lesbian geographers writing on lesbians and space as Ali Grant does in this volume. And many of the lesbian interventions that have taken place in relation to the law have, as Rosemary Auchmuty demonstrates, occurred through the work of lesbian/feminist pressure groups outside academe rather than within it, although it is worth noting that the move towards policy orientation in higher education from the 1970s onwards has facilitated the integration of lesbian interventions, aimed at changing policy and practice, into the academy. Lesbians are present in many disciplines, more than are represented in this wide-ranging volume, but in the more traditional subjects they remain mostly invisible and are less likely to be 'out' or to work on overtly lesbian subject matter. It also seemed much harder for such lesbians to think about 'lesbian interventions in the academy', present but silenced as they are. We might well have included a chapter on that – on absence, or silence, or refusal of lesbians in academe. That could have been very interesting indeed. But our intention was to pay tribute to and explore what *is* rather than what isn't.

And what *is*, is in fact fairly spectacular. One need only look at publishers' catalogues since the early 1990s, to see evidence of the rise of lesbian scholarship. Many major publishers now have lesbian (and gay) studies sections, as indeed do major bookstores, which in some respects places them well ahead of what is going on in UK higher education where to date such courses exist only in severely limited form. Indeed, one might almost argue that current debates in lesbian scholarship take place within the pages of publishers' catalogues rather than in the British classroom or at the small, albeit increasing, number of academic conferences that focus on lesbian scholarship. Publishers' decisions, inevitably driven by market considerations, necessarily reflect the size of the readership of such works – for, let's face it, if it didn't sell it wouldn't be published. Quite a testimony, then, to the lesbian scholarship which now exists and its impact both inside and outside of academe. A testimony also, maybe, to the power of the pink pound.

On the point of the impact lesbian scholarship has (had) in academe our contributors are equivocal. How much difference have we made? Who is our audience? What is our project? During a recent programme on BBC radio a Jewish gay man discussed going to a non-conformist church because concealing his true sexuality to attend synagogue meant that he could not be 'fully himself'. In 'Dyke in Academe (II)' Paula Bennett describes going to a private girls' school which, on the surface, did not have Jewish pupils. She writes:

> My experience [there] colors everything I have to say about being a lesbian in academe or anywhere else where one cannot feel free to be fully and publicly oneself. It is the experience of the closet, of a void created by fear on one side and silence on the other. It produces a form of oppression that comes not from the things people do, *but what they do not do*. (1982, p. 4)

Implicit here is a demand for engagement, a suggestion that being 'fully oneself' requires the practice/s demonstrated in 'Dyke in Academe'. The demand for a lesbian-specific content and practice in academe within that volume reflects one major position in relation to lesbian scholarship associated with a strong sense of lesbian identity as *lesbian* rather than as feminist or queer. In current higher education in the UK this sits side by side with a position which is at once more playful, less certain and more interrogative of what 'lesbian' means. This pluralism reflects the range of lesbian thinking now available, a pluralism we need to engage with even as we – or, indeed, so that we can – more fully develop our perspectives on lesbian lives and experiences now.

The relationship between lesbian and feminist theory

The relationship between lesbian and feminist theory has been central to the development of lesbian studies since the early 1970s, both as an independent discipline and within diverse subject areas. As editors, we were interested to see how individual contributors would negotiate this relationship. Not surprisingly, chapters both explore and exhibit the tensions and dis/continuities between lesbian and feminist positions. Some of the chapters are clearly anchored in feminism, and the insights contained in them are identified by contributors as stemming from a feminist rather than a specifically lesbian critique. Examples include the work on sexist language cited by Susan Wolfe and Julia Penelope, and the feminist critique of biology discussed by Lynda Birke. In many cases gender is privileged as an analytic category and in some, for example Sheila Jeffreys's chapter, there is a close identification, if not an elision, between feminist and lesbian critiques. In relation to film studies, Julia Erhart argues that feminism laid the groundwork for lesbian research and that feminist and lesbian perspectives are largely in synch. From her point of view, the feminist critique of sexism facilitates the lesbian critique of heterosexism.

In contrast, other chapters articulate a specifically lesbian critique of heterosexism in their discipline, and reveal a significant divergence between lesbian and heterosexual feminist accounts. Linda Stepulevage argues that the field of computing may be attractive to lesbians for the very reasons that it alienates heterosexual women and girls, and that the image of the 'hacker' may appeal to lesbians marginalized from a culture of femininity. Like Yvon Appleby, she emphasizes the strongly conservative and conserving character of her discipline where sexuality is concerned. Both chapters point to the essentialist construction of women as hetero-gendered in much feminist literature – even in the 1990s when theories are supposedly more open to differences among women.

It seems therefore that contributors perceive feminist theory as being more or less resistant to lesbian appropriation. Lynda Birke believes that despite biology's resistance to feminist and lesbian perspectives, the work carried out by feminists in the discipline exhibits less heterosexism than other areas of feminist research. This suggests the interesting paradox that the most unreconstructed disciplines – for example, science – may be in some ways more amenable to lesbian perspectives than those areas traditionally identified with feminist work, such as the arts. It may also be the case that certain highly speculative areas of science render it amenable to lesbian appropriation, much like the discourse of science fiction, which lesbian writers have been successfully reworking since the 1970s. Birke's engagement as a biologist with queer theory has affinities with Donna Haraway's exploration of cyborg feminism; both demonstrate the interconnections between politics, sexuality and science.

Other chapters, most notably Margrit Shildrick's, move beyond a self-identified 'feminist' and/or 'lesbian' position and consciously mobilize a queer discourse which aims to intervene by subversion rather than modification of the discipline. Shildrick addresses a key question which some recent work in lesbian studies attempts to answer: 'What is at stake in the lesbian articulation of queer?'

The debate about postmodernism and queer theory

The emergence of queer theory in the late 1980s has transformed the field of lesbian studies. While contributors agree that it has led to the decentring of lesbian feminism, they disagree as to whether it has mainly positive or negative implications for lesbian scholarship. For example, Shildrick's enthusiasm for postmodernist perspectives contrasts both with Jill Davis's qualified welcome of performance theory and with Sheila Jeffreys's outright rejection of the category 'queer'. For Jeffreys the term 'queer' excludes lesbian existence and perspectives and she points to the lack of a feminist input in gay and queer politics. She sees lesbians' and gay men's interests as different, indeed at times conflicting, and exhorts lesbians to engage in a 'fight to overturn both a "gay" and a "straight" paradigm' (1994, p. 5).

While Jeffreys sees its impact as almost wholly negative, others believe 'queer' has done much to sharpen the specificity of lesbian criticism by foregrounding the importance of sexuality independently of gender and challenging feminist paradigms that assume heterosexuality. Queer's deconstructive approach has facilitated the destabilizing of binary oppositions – such as hetero/homosexual; inside/outside – which perpetuated the 'othering' of lesbianism. Such oppositions have also structured the identity politics on which lesbian critiques of hetero-patriarchy have been based. Margrit Shildrick argues for the deconstruction of the sign 'lesbian' as an oppositional identity in favour of its deployment as a discursive signifier which 'queers' academic master narratives. She argues that queer theory proposes 'a disruption that enacts agency in the plasticity and performativity of (be)coming lesbian where desire is neither straight nor gay' and that 'the point is to decentre everything'.

We would agree that queer has given lesbian interventions in the academy a new critical edge and that there is a need to problematize, as queer does, the binary opposition between assimilation and opposition. Yet queer theory, in disarticulating sexuality and gender, undermines the centrality of gender as a category of (lesbian feminist) analysis. While lesbian studies can perhaps cope with the relativizing of gender, it cannot survive its abandonment. In privileging the concept of sexual difference, queer undermines the concept of structural inequality that has animated lesbian research. Lesbian studies, by contrast, eschews a politics of difference and keeps hold of the simultaneous focus on sexism and heterosexism, providing a critique of both which has nevertheless been sharpened in the 1990s by anti-essentialism.

Gauging the success of lesbian interventions

Since the 1970s an important goal of lesbian political intervention has been to gain 'visibility' for lesbians. Most contributors to this volume like Alison Oram acknowledge the historical importance of 'the politics of recognition' to lesbian theory and practice, but many also highlight its limitations as a strategy in the 1990s. Yvon Appleby points to the importance of visibility issues in the context of disciplines struggling to articulate a minimal lesbian presence; Celia Kitzinger argues strongly from a radical feminist perspective against visibility as a form of 'acceptance' in the academy; and Shildrick critiques the binary opposition between visibility and invisibility that has structured and limited debates.

The contributors also raise a number of interesting questions about their discipline's potential for lesbian appropriation. For example, is it the case that there is a relationship between the degree of 'scientificity' of the discipline and its hostility to (social constructionist) lesbian perspectives? Appleby argues that the more vocational and 'applied' the discipline, the more difficult it is to establish a lesbian presence. She comments that education as a discipline has not shared the general and increasing levels of academic interest in the topic of sexuality, and argues that the high theory site of much lesbian work makes the radical transformation of 'applied' areas such as education more difficult to envisage. Is it possible that fields like education are perceived as 'unsexy' and unappealing to lesbian and queer theorists working with critical theory? And does the increasing density of lesbian theory go hand in hand with a withdrawal from 'practice' as many lesbians fear? In our view, the mobilization of diverse discourses by lesbians, including radical feminism, social constructionism and queer, suggests that 'theory' *as* 'practice' has become more visible in the academy and has widened rather than narrowed the range.

We would argue that the development of lesbian studies has to be seen in the context of shifts in academic culture. Undoubtedly it has benefited from the expansion in higher education and from the growth in new disciplinary fields and departments since the mid-1980s. We don't think it is coincidental, either, that the growth of lesbian studies has accompanied the increased profile of postmodern discourses in the academy. These two developments have encouraged an academic opportunism which is characterized by an ideology of simultaneous tolerance and conservatism. Lesbian work is tolerated, indeed positively welcomed, in so far as it meets the criteria of research funding bodies, assessment exercises and academic publishing companies. Cleansed of identity politics, it becomes so many points on a research rating. The status of lesbian interventions in the academy is therefore something of a postmodern paradox. Nevertheless, it is no good hankering after a more 'authentic' form of lesbian intervention; the context in which we work delimits the type of intervention we make but does not negate it. Given the academy's increasing importance as a site for the dissemination and practice of feminist ideas and its relationship to information technologies and cultures, it is imperative that lesbians develop strategies which move beyond simple opposition and find ways of mobilizing lesbian perspectives and critiques. In our view, it is no longer a question of 'in' or 'out' of the closet, 'inside' or 'outside' the academy, but of being 'inside otherwise'. And, judging from the contributions to this volume, there are many reasons to be cheerful: lesbian studies, in an increasing variety of forms, *is* in the academy.

References

Bennett, P. (1982) 'Dyke in Academe (II).' In M. Cruikshank (ed.) *Lesbian Studies: Present and Future*. City University of New York: The Feminist Press, pp. 3–8.

Doan, L. (ed.) (1994) *The Lesbian Postmodern*. New York: Columbia University Press.

Fuss, D. (ed.) (1991) *Inside/Out: Lesbian Theories, Gay Theories*. London: Routledge.

Grosz, E. (1995) *Space, Time and Perversion*. London: Routledge.

Jeffreys, S. (1994) *The Lesbian Heresy: A Feminist Perspective on the Lesbian Sexual Revolution*. London: The Women's Press.

Smith, A.M. (1994) *New Right Discourse on Race and Sexuality*. Cambridge: Cambridge University Press.

1

'There's Nowt So Queer as Folk': Lesbian Cultural Studies

Sonya Andermahr

If, as Raymond Williams (1958) states, culture is ordinary, then lesbian cultural studies would appear to be something of a misnomer, for in the popular imagination the lesbian is an *extra*ordinary figure, by definition on the margins of culture. Yet, lesbian cultural studies, virtually unknown before 1970, has grown exponentially since the mid-1980s, to the extent that it is one of the areas of contemporary lesbian scholarship where lesbians have had most impact, in both institutional and theoretical terms.

What accounts for the success of lesbians in cultural studies? First, like modern lesbian identity, it is a relatively recent invention which has made it easier for lesbians to create an impact. Second, it is an interdisciplinary field (drawing on sociology and cultural theory among others) and lesbians, like Gloria Anzaldúa's (1987) new *mestiza*, have a talent for border crossing. Third, it is theoretically driven and lesbians have been in the forefront of the production of cultural theory in the 1980s and 1990s. Given also that cultural studies expresses a profound curiosity about the complex and powerful ways in which cultural texts shape us and make us the (queer) folk we are, it provides a framework for the special preoccupation of lesbian (and gay) subjects with their cultural construction.

Defining lesbian cultural studies is no easy task. Like cultural studies, it draws on and seeps into sociology, history, literature, film and theatre studies, and it is also centrally concerned with theorizing the materiality of the cultural realm.[1] But lesbian cultural studies is not just a subset of mainstream cultural studies, it is also part of lesbian studies which, like women's studies and gay studies, is fundamentally interdisciplinary and has strong ties to the social movements of feminism and gay liberation. In postmodern times, lesbian cultural studies is heterogeneous and its boundaries are fluid. Indeed, lesbian cultural studies as a discipline that isn't discrete is strongly influenced by postmodernism, the theory that isn't a theory. It has also been powerfully shaped by radical feminism, social constructionism, cultural materialism and, of course, queer theory. Although lesbian cultural studies has developed alongside feminist cultural studies on the one hand, and lesbian and gay studies on the other, there is a specificity to the lesbian project in that it focuses on sexist and heterosexist oppression simultaneously, a critical double axis frequently lacking in its more powerful and established siblings. Lesbian cultural studies therefore involves a dual focus: it provides a cultural critique of the sign 'lesbian' and a lesbian analysis of culture.

Unlike history, cultural studies does not have to address the problem of whether 'we existed *then*'; however, it does have to grapple with contemporary contestations of the sign 'lesbian' which are every bit as complex and ontologically challenging. Which lesbian subculture are we constructing and analysing? Is it the political lesbian challenge to heteropatriarchy or is it the phenomenon of 'lipstick lesbianism'? Both lay claim to the sign 'lesbian'. And what of the lesbian-like women who repudiate it in the name of an ostensibly more radical queer *à la* Judith Butler?

From the movement to the academy: the development of lesbian cultural studies

During the 1970s, the first generation of lesbian activists and scholars created the basis for lesbian studies. A number of titles emerging from the gay liberation and the lesbian feminist movements anticipated and inspired the work of later cultural theorists. Examples include Sydney Abbot and Barbara Love's *Sappho Was a Right-On Woman* (1972), Jill Johnston's *Lesbian Nation: The Feminist Solution* (1973), Ti-Grace Atkinson's *Amazon Odyssey* (1974), Karla Jay and Alan Young's *Lavender Culture* (1978) and, in the early 1980s, Cherrie Moraga and Gloria Anzaldúa's *This Bridge Called My Back: Writings by Radical Women of Color* (1981). Most of this work eschewed neat disciplinary categories for two important reasons: it was strongly movement-based and its lesbian character encouraged if not necessitated an interdisciplinary approach.

Although lesbians were doing their own version of cultural studies in the 1970s with radically interdisciplinary accounts of lesbian existence, a 'lesbian cultural studies' with an academic profile was slower to emerge than gay (men's) studies, which had more resources in the academy and was able to build on the work of theorists such as Foucault (1979). In the 1980s much lesbian theory contributed to debates about the politics of sexuality. Two texts, *Powers of Desire: The Politics of Sexuality* (1983), edited by Ann Snitow, Christine Stansell and Sharon Thompson, and *Pleasure and Danger: Exploring Female Sexuality* (1984), edited by Carole Vance, contain important work by lesbian and queer writers, in part taking issue with feminist theories. At the same time, lesbian cultural studies in its contemporary academic form began to appear in academic journals and book chapters. The explosion of journals catering for the new interdisciplinary work, such as *Genders, differences* and *Discourse,* provided sites for the development of lesbian scholarship.

Significantly, both these developments, namely debates about sexuality and the growth of lesbian cultural studies, were accompanied by an increasing discontinuity between feminist and lesbian perspectives. The work of Gayle Rubin (1993) and Joan Nestle (1987) in particular promoted the disarticulation of the two positions. Within lesbian studies, both theoretical and empirical analyses exemplified the increasing specificity of lesbian research. For example, Sue-Ellen Case's now famous essay 'Toward a Butch-Femme Aesthetic' (1993) contributed to heated debates about lesbian sexual practice – the so-called 'sex-wars' – and lesbianism's location in feminism.

By the late 1980s, enough material had emerged for Diana Fuss, in *Essentially Speaking* (1989), to map the field of lesbian and gay studies. Fuss suggested a number of avenues for research – including relations between homophobia and heterosexism, and the place of homosexuality in theories of sexual difference – and warned against the emergence of a lesbian/gay binarism in homosexual theory and politics. The field really got going, however, in the 1990s when a number of important journal issues and anthologies was published. 1991 was a bumper year for lesbian work: it included Diana Fuss's *Inside/Out: Lesbian Theories, Gay Theories* and an issue of *differences* edited by Teresa de Lauretis, entitled 'Queer Theory: Lesbian and Gay Sexualities'. Two books contributing to lesbian theories of culture were also published: *Stolen Glances: Lesbians Take Photographs*, edited by Tessa Boffin and Jean Fraser, and *How Do I Look? Queer Film and Video* edited by Bad Object Choices. A number of essay collections – Munt (1992); Griffin (1993); Hamer and Budge (1994); and Gibbs (1994) – examined a wide range of lesbian cultural practices and/or explored the relationship between lesbianism and popular culture.

The most significant anthology of the 1990s to date is *The Lesbian and Gay Studies Reader* (1993), which collects together some of the most influential work of the preceding decade, half of which is by lesbians or on lesbian topics: Judith Butler's 'Imitation and Gender Insubordination'; Gayle Rubin's 'Thinking Sex: Notes for a Radical Theory of the Politics of Sexuality'; Marilyn Frye's 'Some Reflections on Separatism and Power'; Monique Wittig's 'One Is Not Born a Woman'; and Adrienne Rich's 'Compulsory Heterosexuality and Lesbian Existence' all feature in it. While many of these contributions, like so much lesbian scholarship, do not fit neatly into the category of cultural studies, they have been crucial to its developing literature. The collection demonstrates the richness and diversity of lesbian work, much of which has an eccentric or marginal relation to the academy. In so far as contributions draw on a wide range of theories and political perspectives, the *Reader* also points to the limiting nature of typologies and classification systems which polarize positions in an unhelpful manner.[2]

More recently, Tamsin Wilton's *Lesbian Studies: Setting an Agenda* (1995) is the first full-length analysis of lesbian studies to follow Margaret Cruikshank's (1982) pioneering resource book. In the chapter on cultural studies, Wilton looks at the visual arts – painting, cartoons, photography – film and music, considers the implications of a lesbian desiring gaze for these media, and undertakes an important critique of feminist and mainstream theories' erasure of lesbianism.

Two paradigms: radical feminism and queer?

Since the emergence of second wave feminism in the 1960s there has been a vigorous – and sometimes rancorous – struggle for the sign 'lesbian' and it has become commonplace to rehearse the distinction between two critical paradigms in lesbian cultural studies: radical feminism (in anglophone and francophone forms) and queer theory. Historically, so the story goes, the radical feminist strand dominated the period from the 1970s to the mid-1980s and underwent a decentring by 'queer' in the late 1980s. While the former emphasizes identity politics and either the mainstreaming of lesbian culture to include all women or the lesbian challenge to heteropatriarchy, the latter foregrounds difference, subversion and marginality.

Within feminist theory two models of lesbian identity have predominated: the lesbian as everywoman and the lesbian as not-a-woman. These positions are exemplified in Rich's (1993) concept of the 'lesbian continuum' and Wittig's (1986) notion of the 'guerrilla'. They provide contrasting answers to the questions 'are lesbians basically the same as other women, or different?' The former registers the pull of the category 'lesbian' towards 'woman', the latter represents her symbolic distance from categories of conventional gender. Both have profoundly influenced lesbian subculture and lesbian cultural studies. As Arlene Stein comments: 'Through its encounter with feminism, lesbianism straddles . . . "minoritizing" and "universalizing" strategies, between fixing lesbians as a . . . minority group and seeking to liberate the "lesbian" in every woman' (1992, p. 38). While opposed in how they define 'lesbian', both models turn on definitions of *gender*; and both are destabilized by the emergence of queer theories which displace gender as a significant factor in favour of the multiplication of *sexualities*. The explosion of cultural theory engaging with the concept of postmodernism has provided lesbian theorists, among others, with a new and exciting theoretical space. Judith Butler's (1993) 'queer' lesbian subject is exemplary of those who sport there. *Two* paradigms thus become *three* moments in lesbian theory exemplified by the work of Rich, Wittig and Butler.

In fact, the delineation of the two-paradigm – or the three-moment – model has often served to obscure the complexity and variety of the work produced by lesbian critics. Work by Marxist-oriented and/or black lesbian theorists – such as Audre Lorde and Barbara Smith – or even radical feminists cannot be easily fitted into one or the other. Monique Wittig's (1992) work, for example, is both anti-essentialist and politically 'modernist'. An important strand of lesbian research has been strongly influenced by the materialist tradition of British cultural studies. Elizabeth Wilson's contributions to *Feminist Review* are significant here. Danae Clark's (1993) fascinating analysis of lesbian consumerism and commodification in the USA builds on this tradition to critique both feminist and postmodern approaches. Lesbian cultural studies, then, has drawn on diverse strands in constructing cultural analyses. Its relation to lesbian feminism is a complex one characterized by an oscillation between two key categories: identification and difference.

The politics of identification and difference

In the 1970s and 1980s, the attempt to create an autonomous lesbian culture known as Lesbian Nation was closely tied to the political project of lesbian feminism which aimed to forge 'a stable collective identity around the category "lesbian" and to develop institutions which would nurture that identity . . . it sought to use those institutions as a base for the contestation of the dominant sex/gender system' (Stein, 1992, p. 37). According to this model, lesbian culture is the authentic expression of a homogeneous lesbian community. Lesbian art is that which is produced by a person with a woman's body who does not sleep with men. Films, plays and art are judged against a standard of woman-friendliness; only those practices and artefacts which are deemed authentically 'lesbian' gain acceptance (Dixon, 1988). On the one hand, lesbian community demanded a strong sense of identification as the basis for its politics; on the other, notions of lesbians' difference from other groups became more fixed (see Ardill and O'Sullivan, 1989, for an account of this period). By the late 1980s the excessive boundary-setting of this form of identity politics contributed to the implosion of lesbian feminism.

Lesbian cultural studies as much as lesbian feminism has been shaped by the ongoing negotiation of the categories of identification and difference, by turns foregrounding and critiquing identity politics. However, lesbian cultural studies has never been simply the cultural wing of the political movement. The disciplinary tools of cultural studies provide an analytical approach to forms of culture and allow for the critique of the notions of authenticity and experience upon which identity politics is based. The analysis of lesbian subculture inevitably raises issues of authorship, readership and mediation. And any form of analysis which seeks to retrieve subaltern voices raises important issues of agency: lesbian cultural studies, like cultural studies generally, has had to negotiate a path between the rock of structure and the hard place of agency. As a result, cultural readings tend to exhibit one of two attitudes which correspond roughly to culturalist and structuralist paradigms in cultural studies: either celebratory and affirmative (exemplified by some 'queer' work such as Madonna studies) or critical and pessimistic, tending to see lesbianism as always already recuperated and often overlooking the possibilities of deviant readings (a position frequently articulated by the radical feminist journal *Trouble and Strife*).

Within lesbian cultural studies theories of identification and difference have been concerned with three main types of analysis: of lesbian icons, of lesbian (sub)culture and of cultural representations of lesbianism. The identification of lesbian icons is characteristic of work concerned to promote lesbian visibility. It is closely connected to the gay movement strategies of achieving visibility, of 'naming and claiming', or publicly affirming lesbian or gay identity and, more recently, of 'outing' celebrities believed to be lesbian or gay. In recent years candidates for icon status have included Madonna, kd lang, Sandra Bernhard and Jodie Foster. Many of the essays in recent collections edited by Hamer and Budge (1994), Griffin (1993) and Munt (1992) focus on the cultural construction of lesbian icons and their meanings for lesbian audiences. Similarly, analyses of lesbian subculture set out to explore the relationship between lesbian communities and the forms of their cultural and aesthetic practices such as art, music and theatre. Stein's (1993) recent collection contains examples of this approach, including essays on lesbian community and marriage, butch-femme identity, AIDS awareness, lesbian 'zines, popular music and lesbian sex debates.

By the 1990s, a discernible shift had taken place away from identifying and analysing an autonomous lesbian culture towards examining the diverse cultural meanings of the sign 'lesbian' and lesbian appropriations of popular culture. As my title suggests, critics began examining the 'queerness' of the mainstream. This shift is registered in the subtitles of many recent collections: 'popular culture's romance with lesbianism', 'lesbianism and popular culture' and 'the new lesbian criticism'. Importantly, this strategy reconnects cultural studies with lesbian and gay men's popular histories of appropriating mainstream cultural forms, a concern that is shared by film studies work on gay icons such as Garbo, Dietrich, Liza Minnelli, Doris Day, etc. Munt's (1992) collection, for example, examines the importance of public lesbian spaces such as the lesbian bar and the Greyhound bus station to the evolution of lesbian popular culture, and the popular appeal of lesbian texts such as Jeanette Winterson's *Oranges Are Not the Only Fruit*. Griffin's (1993) collection includes essays on popular genre fiction, as well as cinema and representations of lesbian sexuality. Hamer and Budge's (1994) volume contains essays on lesbians on television, lesbians' relationship to country/popular music and analyses of the lesbian meanings circulating around icons such as Madonna, Martina Navratilova and Jodie Foster. It also examines the phenomenon of 'lesbian chic', questioning the extent to which lesbianism is represented as fashionable and desirable. This focus is shared by the seductively titled *Sexy Bodies* (1995) edited by Elizabeth Grosz and Elspeth Probyn. In this volume, Barbara Creed's essay 'Lesbian Bodies: Tribades, Tomboys and Tarts' examines popular stereotypes of the lesbian, arguing that while 'within homophobic cultural practices the lesbian body is constructed as monstrous in relation to male fantasies', lesbians themselves, through representation, gesture and play, are constructing bodies that are 'going places' (1995, p. 87).

The strategies of appropriation and parody which many of these analyses both examine and employ are closely connected with postmodernism. They frequently accompany a celebration of the creativity and exuberance of lesbian cultural readings which have led to the discovery of lesbian meanings in the most unlikely – or queerest – places. Just about any example of pop culture from girl bands to *The Girlie Show* can be seen as a form of subversive camp parody. Critics of this trend, however, warn against over-eager ascriptions of lesbian agency regardless of the context. Danae Clark, while arguing that 'lesbians *as lesbians* have developed strategies of selection, (re)appropriation, resistance, and subversion in order to realign consumer culture according to the desires and needs of lesbian sexuality, subcultural identification, and political action' (1993, p. 199), cautions against 'the "affirmative" character of a cultural studies that tends towards essentialist notions of identity at the same time as it tends to overestimate the freedom of audience reception' (p. 198). In 'Commodity Lesbianism', Clark examines the relationship between lesbianism and capitalism, focusing on the American media targeting of lesbians as fashion consumers. She argues that while postmodern theories present fashion as a site of female resistance, capitalism's ability to recuperate transgressive self-representation as a trendy commodity calls into question the possibilities of agency that resistance implies. So-called 'gay window advertising appropriates lesbian subcultural style, incorporates its features into commodified representations, and offers it back to lesbian consumers in a packaged form cleansed of identity politics' (p. 197). On the other hand, according to Clark, lesbian consumers' appropriation of media images as lesbian-coded subverts heterosexual feminist analyses which portray women as passive objects for straight male consumption:

> As long as straight women focus on the relation between consumer culture and women in general, lesbians remain invisible, or are forced to pass as straight, while heterosexual women can claim for themselves the oppression of patriarchal culture or the pleasure of the masquerade

> that offers them 'a longed for place outside the humdrum mainstream'. On the other hand, straight feminists may simply fear that lesbians are better shoppers. (p. 199)

Whereas earlier theories had posited the fundamental identity of lesbians and their difference from other groups, by the 1990s lesbians were increasingly represented in cultural analyses as a heterogeneous group whose cultural practices continually cross over into the mainstream. For Arlene Stein, these cultural shifts are a product of structural changes and challenges which led to the decentring of lesbian feminism in the mid-1980s. These include the ageing of members of the original movement, the challenge from groups within the movement, particularly lesbians of colour, working-class lesbians, younger lesbians and sexual minorities, and the emergence of a new form of lesbian and gay politics that insists on the relative autonomy of gender and sexuality, sexism and heterosexism. The latter

> suggested that lesbians shared with gay men a sense of 'queerness', a non-normative sexuality which transcends the binary distinction homosexual/heterosexual to include all who feel disenfranchised by dominant sexual norms – lesbians and gay men, as well as bisexuals and transsexuals. (1992, p. 50)

As a result, the politics of identity and difference entered a new phase in which lesbians either rejected identity as a basis for politics or reshaped identity politics to acknowledge multiple affiliations and the partial nature of lesbian identity.

Queering the lesbian

'Queer' represents a radically different conception of the subject to that of lesbian feminism. Unlike the sign 'lesbian', 'queer' functions not as an oppositional identity category but as a sexual signifier of difference, representing sexuality 'otherwise'. As Mary McIntosh states, it transforms the political landscape:

> Queer theory has no time for disputes about whether bisexuals are really gay or transsexuals really women; it has no time for hierarchies of oppression or for all the divisiveness of identity politics that beset the movement in the 1980s . . . Queer is a form of resistance, a refusal of labels, pathologies and moralities. It is defined more by what it is against than what it is for. Its slogan is not 'get out of my face' (let alone 'gay is good'), but rather, 'in your face'. (1993, p. 31)

The impact of queer on lesbian cultural studies has been dramatic and in many ways positive. Whereas lesbian and gay studies initially tended to assume a hetero/homosexual dyad and to generate accounts of homosexual resistance to dominant cultural oppression, 'queer' theory reconceptualizes the subject. It represents a rethinking of categories and the whole process of categorization that beleaguered identity politics. Instead of focusing on the authenticity of the lesbian/gay subject and looking for evidence of homosexuality in culture, queer offers an interpretive strategy which focuses on the construction of 'the normal', allowing us to trace the shifting boundaries of 'deviance'. It loosens identity categories, enabling us to ask different kinds of questions and to retrieve stories from 'across the border' (Anzaldúa, 1987).

As Margrit Shildrick's chapter in this volume demonstrates, there are considerable gains to be made in adopting a postmodern model of lesbianism as a sign in discourse: in foregrounding lesbianism as an interpretive strategy, queer facilitates the deconstruction of (hetero)sexuality in mainstream cultural discourses. Mandy Merck's (1993) 'deviant readings' are a good example of such queer practice. Her analysis of *Portrait of a Marriage* doesn't ask whether any of the characters depicted in the television production are authentically lesbian or gay, but what the film says about the dominant culture's ambivalent attitude towards sexuality *per se* and heterosexual marriage in particular. In a similar vein, the Boffin and Fraser (1991) collection contains some wonderful examples of perverse reading including Sue Golding's eccentric 'James Dean: The Almost-Perfect Lesbian Hermaphrodite'. By emphasizing lesbian appropriations and interventions at the level of discourse, thereby overcoming the sometimes silencing question of whether there are any 'real' dykes to be seen, deviant or perverse reading represents one of the most versatile and useful strategies to have come out of queer theory.

Recent collections are increasingly marked by an appeal to queer notions and the postmodern imaginary. Arlene Stein's (1993) volume, significantly aimed at and produced by a younger generation of lesbian writers, activists and theorists, reflects the editor's contention that lesbian feminism has been decentred by postmodernism and queer. Laura Doan's (1994) collection represents the most developed analysis to date of the relationship between postmodernism and the sign 'lesbian'. As well as essays on postmodern – and even post-lesbian! – icons, it includes theoretical work on performance theory and queer theory, and discussions of transsexuality, cross-dressing, lesbian pornography and Barbie as a teaching aid! (a list which is sure to ring alarm bells for an older generation of lesbian feminist). As well as usefully tracing the terrains of postmodern and lesbian theory, the volume is also valuable for its analysis of the intersections between sexuality and ethnicity, and includes consideration of the work of Gloria Anzaldúa, Michelle Cliff and Luce Irigaray among others.

Performance theory, associated above all with the work of Judith Butler, has been arguably the most influential strand of the new 'queer' lesbian theory. Butler (1990, 1993) elaborates performance theory as a critique of determinist psychoanalytical approaches to gender theory. Her essay 'Imitation and Gender Insubordination' (1993) posits gender not as a core identity or essence that pre-exists self-expression but rather as a social construct created in the practice of relating to others. As the subject performs gender, she plays with a repertoire of gendered symbols which create the illusion of gendered subjectivity. Butler's work has been taken up by Sue-Ellen Case among others in the context of lesbian performance. Both Butler and Case argue that practices such as butch/femme and drag provide the basis for a cultural politics that can replace a failed identity politics, since they subvert the illusion of a core gender identity. Performance theory is the basis of the highly prolific and high camp field of Madonna studies which includes *The Madonna Connection* (1993), edited by Cathy Schwichtenberg, and *Madonnarama* (1993), edited by Lisa Frank.

Much of this work is refreshing and stimulating; it both captures lesbians' enthusiastic engagement *with* culture and represents an intervention *in* culture. However, there is a danger that some of it may overstate the degree of agency available to lesbians as cultural subjects. As Danae Clark comments of postmodern theories of media: 'in our desire and haste to attribute agency to the spectator and a means of empowerment to marginal or oppressed social groups, we risk losing sight of the interrelation between reading practices and the political economy of media institutions' (1993, p. 195).

Unequal difference and the limits of performance

If queer opens up a space for the positive proliferation of differences, it also frequently works to mask certain inequalities. Teresa de Lauretis, in her now famous introduction to the queer issue of *differences*, explains how the discursive shift from the umbrella term 'lesbian and gay' to the term 'queer' represented an attempt to rectify the elisions of sexual specificity and gender difference produced by the former term:

> The term 'queer' was arrived at in the effort to avoid all these fine distinctions in our discursive protocols, not to adhere to any one of the given terms, not to assume their ideological liabilities, but instead to transgress and transcend them – or, at the very least problematize them. (1991, p. v)

But, is 'queer' really any less problematic than 'lesbian and gay'?[3] Donna Penn expresses the concern that

> queer might flatten the social, cultural, and material distinctions and liabilities confronting each type of queer and the different stakes for

> each. While, in theory, queer invites the possibility of building alliances based on our common identity on the fringes, it is equally possible that it performs the same elision it was intended to remedy. (1995, p. 33)

Of those social, cultural and material distinctions, 'class' more than most has been a casualty of the postmodern turn in cultural studies. In a recent essay, Diana Coole examines the occlusion of class in discourses of difference.[4] She asks whether a common language of difference, otherness and marginality actually allows for the articulation of class as 'a difference that makes a difference' or whether the logic of discourses of difference necessarily suppresses economic difference. She concludes:

> Class is relational, but its dynamics cannot be understood according to the structures of linguistics (as a play of *différance*), as mobile and open. No matter how fragmented, it can never be reduced to a play of multiple and endlessly deferred differences . . . class itself is not a postmodern (or liberal) phenomenon in that it will not and cannot resolve itself into either simple diversity or a mosaic of incommensurable but equally valuable differences . . . [And it] is equally problematic if it is presented in postmodern terms as performative. For, perhaps unlike gender, it cannot be reduced to its performances. Performing certain tasks and roles can be halted – for example, by striking or rioting – but it is the consequences of the activity, not the subversion of a style of performance, that is important. Unlike gender, class cannot be reduced to surface inscriptions of ritual and repetition, and it cannot be subverted by parody. It does not need denaturalizing since everyone agrees it is conventional. (1996, p. 23)

This seems to me to represent an exceptionally thoughtful analysis. But, while Coole suggests that gender (and 'race', perhaps?) lends itself to discourses of difference, I would argue that this isn't necessarily the case. In an intelligent critique, 'Do Clothes Make the Woman?: Gender, Performance Theory, and Lesbian Eroticism', Kath Weston (1993) argues that postmodern theories of gender as a performance foreground clothing and gesture at the expense of other phenomena such as gendered divisions of labour and sexual acts. In an ethnographic analysis of lesbian identities performed at Prom night in San Francisco, Weston found that the gendering of identity within same-sex relationships was much more rigid than postmodern theories had led her to expect. Her study demonstrates not only that essentialism is alive and well in sophisticated urban lesbian subcultures, but more importantly, that there are material structures and processes which delimit the shape our identities take, so that while identities are not fixed, neither are they completely unanchored. In most situations they are structured in and through power relations and are relatively stable and cohesive. For Weston, neither seeing gender as a 'core self' nor as 'artifice', neither identity nor difference, represents an adequate theorization:

> If gender can no longer be reduced to self-evident identities (Woman or Man), neither can it be conjured away as the compelling but ultimately illusory product of performance. Gender no more resides in gesture or apparel than it lies buried in bodies and psyches . . . *Social relations* are gendered, not persons or things. (p. 17)

Contrary to most postmodernisms, there is no such thing as pure difference; difference is always relative and usually unequal. Indeed to be politically significant difference must needs possess some notion of both inertia and inequality.

Queer, with its emphasis on the sexual (difference), does not seem well equipped to address the non-sexual aspects of lesbian cultural identities and unlike lesbian or gay male theory, it is not gender specific. Like them, queer also needs to be continually 'raced'. While in principle its strategies may appear alive to the nuances of ethnic and other differences and its focus on regimes of the normal would lend itself to a critique of ethnocentrism, as black contributors to Smyth's *Lesbians Talk Queer Notions* (1992) point out, it is not necessarily any more racially aware than its predecessors. Writing in *The Lesbian Postmodern* from a position not unsympathetic to queer, Sangri Dhairyam comments that '"Queer Theory" comes increasingly to be reckoned with as critical discourse, but concomitantly writes a white queerness over raced queerness [and] domesticates race in its elaboration of sexual difference' (1994, p. 26). She argues for the necessity of examining 'race' through sexual identity in order to 'force whiteness to confront its bloodless, because invisible, body that sucks race dry' (p. 43). Thus, while the invocation in cultural analyses of 'gender, race and class' has frequently been problematic, cumbersome and/or superficial, the categories as descriptions of underlying inequalities are still relevant.[5]

Queer, productive of much valuable theory as it is, has constructed a revisionist account of sexual history which incorrectly represents lesbian feminisms as essentialist and anti-sex, indeed, as 'straight'. In the process it has committed a form of what Bourdieu (1984) calls symbolic violence. And there is a sense in which contemporary post-lesbian, post-queer cultural studies is engaged in a process of reinventing the wheel. Old debates around inter- and intra-sexual difference are being recast in the slippery language of postmodernism. Ironically, some early lesbian work offered an exemplary interdisciplinary practice which 'queered' master narratives and, by examining 'regimes of the normal', deconstructed hetero-normativity. In addition, lesbian feminist discourse has never ascribed to lifestyle minoritarian values in the way that perhaps gay men's discourse has. In fact it always challenged that model as one which privatized and individualized lesbian and gay experience and masked the operations of gender and other forms of inequality.

Mary McIntosh's essay 'Queer Theory and the War of the Sexes' asks whether queer thinking, rooted in resistance rather than identity, can transcend the binary divisions between women and men in the gay movement.[6] Analysing the separate development of lesbian and gay male history, she argues that both have accepted gender stereotypes of the other which have limited their analyses and that 'each of them could have learnt a great deal from one another':

> Lesbian theory ought . . . to have learnt . . . from gay male theory . . . something of the importance of the sexual and of sexual transgression in the making of the lesbian . . . On the other side, queer theory should not forget that the heterosexuality in terms of which we are defined as other is a highly gendered one, so that our otherness and the forms of meanings of our dissidence are highly gendered. (1993, p. 47)

She concludes that queer theory and politics are important for lesbians and feminists. While it doesn't replace feminism as a humanist and liberatory project with its structural theories of inequality, queer theory provides a critique of the heterosexual assumptions of some feminist work and feminism injects an awareness of gender into queer thought. Indeed, it is the tension between gender and sexuality as they relate to other significant differences that the best lesbian scholarship brings into focus and why in my view it has a continuing salience independently of 'queer'.

Queer futures?

Colleen Lamos, in an essay that exemplifies the new work being produced under the sign 'queer', discusses the teasing conjunction of the lesbian and the postmodern. She begins with the observation that there is something queer about postmodernism, highlighting its association with a camp aesthetic, and concludes in millennial vein:

> The postmodern lesbian is not another lesbian but the end of lesbianism as we know it – as a distinct, minority sexual orientation. Lesbianism was born in the panic of sexual/gender definition at the turn of the twentieth century. As we approach our own *fin-de-siècle* that panic has not subsided; rather what Sedgwick terms 'the crisis of homo/heterosexual definition' has reached a boiling point in which it is no longer theoretically feasible nor politically practical to demarcate lesbianism as a unique identity. (1994, p. 99)

This represents an exemplary statement of the queer decentring of lesbian feminism. Lamos confidently predicts the demise of the lesbian as an oppositional political identity. The postmodern lesbian is not an ontological category but, *pace* Butler, a deconstruction of ontology. The sign 'lesbian' does not designate a cupola, a 'to be', but rather figures a subversive discursive practice. Shildrick in this volume gives an elegant statement of this view, arguing that the role of lesbian theorists is to challenge the constitution of sexuality itself, to queer the master discourse. I'm both attracted and not entirely convinced by this argument. I agree that it is the emphasis on discursive interventions which has enabled lesbian theorists to appropriate cultural and critical discourses and (re)write the cultural body so prolifically in recent times. Yet this work takes place in the context of growing conservatism in the institutional politics of the academy and the political climate of society more generally. Here, difference is a product of market economics, of the competition for, and cuts in, funding in higher education, where 'choice' looks increasingly limited to those who can pay. As Gabriele Griffin and I argued in the introduction, the situation is something of a postmodern paradox. Lesbian studies has ironically benefited from the climate of opportunism that has characterized academia since the mid-1980s, especially when it produces the sexy theory that publishers are so keen to get their hands on.

How then should lesbian academics respond? While we can't be complacent – that is, simply celebrate the proliferation of difference – neither do we need to be quite as pessimistic as some of the contributors to this volume. Arlene Stein's view of contemporary lesbian subjects could be usefully applied to contemporary lesbian cultural studies in their commitment to 'a multiplicity of projects, some of them feminist-oriented, others more queer-identified, many of them incorporating elements of both critiques . . . they see themselves and their lesbianism as located in a complex world marked by racial, class and sexual divisions' (1992, p. 52). On balance, I think it is too early to bury the lesbian; as Mark Twain said, 'the report of my death is an exaggeration'.[7] Indeed, the signs are that, for the time being at any rate, lesbian cultural studies is thriving.

Notes

1. As this volume contains chapters on lesbian interventions in the fields of literature, film and sociology, I shall concentrate on lesbian cultural representations in the areas of popular culture more generally and on the development of a distinctive lesbian cultural theory.
2. In selecting texts for discussion I have concentrated on those which are easily available in anthologies. This means that I have relied heavily on *The Lesbian and Gay Studies Reader*, edited by Abelove *et al.* Although this may have the effect of further reifying a few already canonized texts, the requirement to survey influential material that is also accessible makes this difficult to avoid.
3. As Stein comments: 'the new "co-sexual" queer culture could not compensate for real, persistent structural differences in style, ideology, and access to resources among men

and women. This recurring problem suggested that while the new queer politics represented an assertion of sexual difference which could not be assimilated into feminism, neither could gender be completely subsumed under sexuality' (1992, p. 50).

4. Although Coole's essay does not set out to address lesbian studies, I quote it because I believe it has interesting implications for the future direction of the subject.
5. In this respect ethnographic approaches are an important way of focusing the over-determinations of subjectivity and *lived* difference.
6. McIntosh was of course one of the progenitors of what became lesbian and gay studies; her groundbreaking essay on 'The Homosexual Role' (1968) provided a social constructionist account of the invention of the homosexual identity well before Foucault came on the scene here and in the USA.
7. In a cable from Europe to the Associated Press. Quoted in *The Penguin Dictionary of Quotations* (Harmondsworth: Penguin, 1960).

References

Abbot, S. and Love, B. (1972) *Sappho Was a Right-On Woman: A Liberated View of Lesbianism*. New York: Stein and Day.

Abelove, H., Barale, M.A. and Halperin, D.M. (eds) (1993) *The Lesbian and Gay Studies Reader*. London: Routledge.

Anzaldúa, Gloria (1987) *Borderlands/La Frontera*. San Francisco: Spinsters/Aunt Lute.

Ardill, S. and O'Sullivan, S. (1989) 'Sex in the Summer of '88.' *Feminist Review*. 31 (Spring): 126–34.

Atkinson, T-G. (1974) *Amazon Odyssey*. New York: Links.

Bad Object Choices (eds) (1991) *How Do I Look?: Queer Film and Video*. Seattle: Bay Press.

Boffin, T. and Fraser, J. (eds) (1991) *Stolen Glances: Lesbians Take Photographs*. London: Pandora.

Bourdieu, P. (1984) *Distinction: A Social Critique of the Judgement of Taste*, trans. Richard Nice. London: Routledge and Kegan Paul.

Butler, J. (1990) *Gender Trouble: Feminism and the Subversion of Identity*. London: Routledge.

Butler, J. (1993) 'Imitation and Gender Insubordination.' In Abelove *et al.* (1993).

Case, S.-E. (1993) 'Toward a Butch-Femme Aesthetic.' In Abelove *et al.* (1993).

Clark, D. (1993) 'Commodity Lesbianism.' In Abelove *et al.* (1993).

Coole, D. (1996) 'Is Class a Difference that Makes a Difference?' *Radical Philosophy*. 77 (May/June): 17–25.

Creed, B. (1995) 'Lesbian Bodies: Tribades, Tomboys and Tarts.' In Grosz and Probyn (1995).

Cruikshank, M. (1982) *Lesbian Studies: Present and Future*. New York: The Feminist Press.

de Lauretis, T. (1991) 'Queer Theory: Lesbian and Gay Sexualities: An Introduction.' *differences: A Journal of Feminist Cultural Studies*. 3/2: iii–xvii.

Dhairyam, S. (1994) 'Racing the Lesbian, Dodging White Critics.' In Doan (1994).

Dixon, J. (1988) 'Separatism.' In B. Cant (ed.) *Radical Records: Thirty Years of Lesbian and Gay History*. London: Routledge.

Doan, L. (ed.) (1994) *The Lesbian Postmodern*. New York: Columbia University Press.

Foucault, M. (1979) *The History of Sexuality, Vol. I: An Introduction*. London: Allen Lane.

Frank, L. (ed.) (1993) *Madonnarama*. Pittsburgh, PA: Cleis Press.

Frye, D. (1993) 'Some Reflections on Separatism and Power.' In Abelove *et al.* (1993).

Fuss, D. (1989) *Essentially Speaking: Feminism, Nature and Difference.* London: Routledge.

Fuss, D. (ed.) (1991) *Inside/Out: Lesbian Theories, Gay Theories.* London: Routledge.

Gibbs, L. (ed.) (1994) *Daring to Dissent: Lesbian Culture from Margin to Mainstream.* London: Cassell.

Golding, S. (1991) 'James Dean: The Almost-Perfect Lesbian Hermaphrodite.' In Boffin and Fraser (1991).

Griffin, G. (ed.) (1993) *Outwrite: Lesbianism and Popular Culture.* London: Pluto Press.

Grosz, E. and Probyn, E. (eds) (1995) *Sexy Bodies: The Strange Carnalities of Feminism.* London: Routledge.

Hamer, D. and Budge, B. (eds) (1994) *The Good, the Bad and the Gorgeous: Popular Culture's Romance with Lesbianism.* London: Pandora.

Jay, K. and Young, A. (1978) *Lavender Culture.* New York: Jove.

Johnston, J. (1973) *Lesbian Nation: The Feminist Solution.* New York: Simon and Schuster.

Lamos, C. (1994) 'The Postmodern Lesbian Position: *On Our Backs*.' In Doan (1994).

McIntosh, M. (1968) 'The Homosexual Role.' *Social Problems.* 16/2: 182–92.

McIntosh, M. (1993) 'Queer Theory and the War of the Sexes.' In J. Bristow and A.R. Wilson (eds) *Activating Theory: Lesbian, Gay and Bisexual Politics.* London: Lawrence and Wishart.

Merck, M. (1993) *Perversions: Deviant Readings.* London: Virago.

Moraga, C. and Anzaldúa, G. (eds) (1981) *This Bridge Called My Back: Writings by Radical Women of Color.* Watertown, MA: Persephone Press.

Munt, S. (ed.) (1992) *New Lesbian Criticism: Literary and Cultural Readings.* Hemel Hempstead: Harvester Wheatsheaf.

Nestle, J. (1987) *A Restricted Country: Essays and Short Stories.* London: Sheba.

Penn, D. (1995) 'Queer: Theorizing Politics and History.' *Radical History Review.* 62: 24–42.

Rich, A. (1993) 'Compulsory Heterosexuality and Lesbian Existence.' In Abelove *et al.* (1993).

Rubin, G. (1993) (first published 1984) 'Thinking Sex: Notes for a Radical Theory of the Politics of Sexuality.' In Abelove *et al.* (1993).

Schwichtenberg, C. (ed.) (1993) *The Madonna Connection: Representational Politics, Subcultural Identities.* Boulder, CO; Oxford: Westview Press.

Smyth, C. (1992) *Lesbians Talk Queer Notions.* London: Scarlet Press.

Snitow, A., Stansell, C. and Thompson, S. (eds) (1983) *Powers of Desire: The Politics of Sexuality.* New York: New Feminist Library/Monthly Review Press.

Stein, A. (1992) 'Sisters and Queers: The Decentering of Lesbian Feminism.' *Socialist Review*, 'Queer Innovations.' 22/1 (January–March): 33–55.

Stein, A. (ed.) (1993) *Sisters, Sexperts, Queers: Beyond the Lesbian Nation.* New York and Harmondsworth: Penguin.

Vance, C. (ed.) (1984) *Pleasure and Danger: Exploring Female Sexuality.* Boston, MA: Routledge.

Weston, K. (1993) 'Do Clothes Make the Woman?: Gender, Performance Theory, and Lesbian Eroticism.' *Genders.* 17 (Autumn): 1–20.

Williams, R. (1958) *Conviction.* Norman MacKenzie (ed.). London: MacGibbon and Key.

Wilton, T. (1995) *Lesbian Studies: Setting an Agenda.* London: Routledge.

Wittig, M. (1986) *Les Guérillères.* Boston: Beacon Press.

Wittig, M. (1992) *The Straight Mind and Other Essays.* Hemel Hempstead: Harvester Wheatsheaf.

Wittig, M. (1993) 'One Is Not Born a Woman.' In Abelove *et al.* (1993).

2

Negotiating the Narrow Straits of Education

Yvon Appleby

A lesbian friend who is a school teacher and who is also involved in educational research remarked: 'Well, it will only take you three lines to write about lesbian interventions in education, won't it?' Her simple and expressive comment (although it loses some of the 'clenched teeth' quality upon the page) touches upon several of the issues I wish to explore in this chapter. In the first instance, and quite directly, her comment is a statement of the frustration she feels about the lack of lesbian interventions in the field of education. Any interventions which may have occurred can, in her estimation, be represented within a very small (almost physically non-existent) space. In her case this is particularly significant as she has been involved in raising lesbian issues for some considerable time in her practice as a teacher and within her own educational research. Indirectly her remark illustrates the complex nature of discussing and assessing lesbian issues within this field – a field where sexuality (assumed to be heterosexual) is itself increasingly a 'public' issue (Kelly, 1992) and as such is being incorporated into the rhetoric of 'family values' promoted within the British educational system.[1]

Her remark raises questions about how to assess the existence and/or 'success' of lesbian interventions when education itself remains one of the areas where lesbianism and lesbian subjectivity are still actively suppressed and systematically 'hidden'. Given this active suppression and the general 'invisibility' of lesbian experience/knowledge within education, should any interventions be measured by the light that is shed upon lesbian experience in education (which is often 'invisible'), by the 'voice' given to lesbian subjects in education (who are frequently 'silenced') or by the level of theoretical inclusion (where lesbian knowledges are 'eclipsed' by heterosexist theoretical assumptions) within educational discourses and practices? Before tackling these questions about the nature, content and impact of lesbian interventions within education I would like to outline briefly the parameters of this field, indicating the position and current promotion of heterosexuality within it.

The field of education: tilling the ground and sowing the seeds of heterosexuality

Many lesbians are teachers and educators, and as such are involved in pedagogical issues and debates surrounding lesbian knowledges and theories across different disciplines (see, for example, contributions in Garber, 1994; Griffin, 1993; Cruikshank, 1982), or from within lesbian studies (Wilton, 1995). These teaching endeavours are distinct from the inclusion of lesbianism within the field of education. Education, like many other fields of enquiry, is diverse, incorporating numerous disciplines, theoretical approaches and methodological debates within its overall focus and processes of enquiry. Education also covers a wide field including preschool education, compulsory schooling, special educational needs, post-sixteen and adult/continuing education, in addition to aspects of vocational and professional training. It is impossible within this space to discuss lesbian interventions across all these specific but related areas of education. However, there are several significant general factors which shape lesbian experiences in education: namely, the overall impact of the conservative, conserving and reproductive nature of education (including vocational and professional training) and its direct relationship to the state through the legislative processes, and the organization and administration of schooling and education (Apple, 1993; Giroux, 1991; Sharpe, 1980).

By indicating the impact of these factors I am aware of creating an artificial separation between the transmission and application of lesbian knowledges within specific fields. Although on the one hand this is limiting, as there are obviously many aspects of crossover, there are specific contextual differences which need to be acknowledged between disciplines and within specific fields of enquiry. The relationship between location and context, intervention and modification is usefully discussed by Jennifer Gore (1993, p. 5) in relation to feminist pedagogy. She distinguishes between what she calls 'the pedagogy argued for' and 'the pedagogy of the argument', which she identifies as contextually situated feminist responses. Gore maintains that although there are common understandings and purposes within feminist pedagogy (towards what is generally understood as liberatory empowerment – even though there are critical feminist responses to this 'end'[2]), the process of empowerment is itself shaped by its location either within schools of education or women's studies departments. Gore illustrates that there are specific disciplinary discourses and knowledge claims which we engage, resist and seek to modify. These boundaries in themselves act to shape the nature and praxis of our engagement.

Within the discipline the reproductive and conservative nature of education has been exposed by critical educationalists (Mac an Ghaill, 1994, 1988; Willis, 1977; Freire, 1972), by feminist writers (Purvis, 1991; Spender, 1989; Davies, 1983; Spender and Sarah, 1980) and by some who identify themselves as both (Lather, 1994, 1991). Together they provide a challenge to the unquestioned assumptions of normative gender roles, race and class expectations contained within the educational system and within educational practice (Lees, 1993; Mirza, 1992; Scraton, 1992; Weiner, 1991; Griffin, 1989; Holly, 1989; Whyte *et al.*, 1985). Feminist responses to the task of exposing and challenging the conservation and re/production of gender inequalities (including also race and class) have been varied (see Weiner, 1994) with only some feminist work connecting gender to heterosexuality. Carol Jones and Pat Mahony's collection *Learning Our Lines: Sexuality and Social Control in Education* is a good example of the latter. They describe clearly the connection between the state, education and the reproduction of gendered heterosexuality:

> This is the state's control of sexuality through education. In particular what is at issue is the promotion of a model of heterosexuality in which masculinity (central to which is sexual violence) and femininity (as it is stereotypically understood) go unchallenged. The effect of this is the increased social control of all women and girls. (1989, p. xiii)

The more liberal feminist calls for simple gender 'equality', which does not make this connection, does not disrupt the conservative and heterosexually conserving function of education – either textually or in practice. However, it is not quite this clear cut, as Carol Jones and Pat Mahony also point out (p. xii). Their discussion highlights the need to adopt strategies in response to changes in the state's mechanisms of control within education. They cite the attack upon 'equality of opportunities' as evidence that neither education nor heterosexuality are monolithic institutions. The interrelationship between them, and our responses to them, are also neither stationary nor static.

The renewed and refocused imposition of the hegemony of heterosexuality within education can be seen in the increased profile of sexuality as a 'public' issue (Kelly, 1992) and one which as such has received heightened political attention (Epstein, 1994a; Cooper, 1989; Jones and Mahony, 1989). This interest in, and regulation of, sexuality has been particularly apparent within the area of sex education which, as lesbian and feminist writers have shown (Thompson, 1994; Kelly, 1992; Melia, 1989), has been used to promote normative heterosexuality through the rhetoric of 'family values' – values which are 'traditionally' white, able-bodied and always heterosexual. More recently new forms of radical conservatism have sought to recreate educational mechanisms for the reimposition of the hegemony of heterosexuality. This shows clearly the relationship between educational conservation and reproduction, the ideology of conservatism and the state. Madeleine Arnot and Len Barton (1992) make the connection between recent political ideological changes within education and the influence of what they call the supporters of a radical form of conservatism who have, they argue, a 'commitment to sustaining the social order through family, "nation" and a new morality' (p. xii). Family, nation and morality, used in this context, are both highly regulatory in terms of gender, race and sexuality and are exclusively heterosexual.

Education represents, then, an arena where immense social and political pressure has been, and is increasingly being, exerted in relation to the state's regulation and control of sexuality. The resurgence and reconnection of 'morality' to 'family' (both promoted uncritically as 'natural' and 'good') has reinforced the stronghold of conservatism and conservative thinking within education, producing increasingly narrow straits for lesbians to negotiate within this field.

Lesbian subjects: subjugated knowledge?

In spite of these limitations and constraints, lesbian subjects and the 'subject' of lesbianism do exist, marginally, in the practices and discourses of education. There are lesbians involved in education as practitioners, recipients and researchers who have themselves challenged what Debbie Epstein and Richard Johnson (1994) call the 'heterosexual presumption' within education by signalling their presence. In order to do this lesbians, and their heterosexual allies, have to make 'visible' lesbian experiences and knowledges. Without this action of disclosure/exposure lesbian identity remains largely unacknowledged and hidden within the enforced assumption of heterosexuality. Through personal disclosure lesbian teachers have given 'voice' to their experiences, making their frequently negative experiences textually 'visible' (Sullivan, 1993; Gill, 1989; Squirrell, 1989). Some have striven for 'visibility' and 'voice' within teaching unions (Spraggs, 1994). Others have run the risk of individual exposure by working upon the implementation of school policies (Andrews, 1990; Gill, 1989; Epstein, 1994b) including strategies and alliances used to teach the 'issue' of lesbian and gay sexuality in schools (Patrick and Sanders, 1994; Sanders and Burke, 1994).

Creating a presence, by being seen and heard as lesbians, does not always or necessarily result in positive change or even accurately reflect lesbian experience (Luke, 1994). It does illustrate the conditions of heterosexist oppression in education by explicating the everyday rules through which it operates (Smith, 1988). Lesbian (and gay) presence can promote positive change and increased representation within schools (Harris, 1990) and within teaching unions (School's Out newsletter, 1996;[3] Cant, 1988);

however, there are also drawbacks to 'visibility'. In her description of the Positive Images campaign in Haringey, Davina Cooper (1989) shows how being 'seen' (by the inclusion of lesbian images) created a political and educational backlash in the face of fears about promotion/proselytizing engendered by Section 28.[4] Debbie Epstein (1994b) and others (Wilton, 1995) also point out that the prohibitory intention behind Section 28 did not have only negative consequences; it also galvanized a 'visible' lesbian and gay response. Thus vigorous resistance coexists alongside the inestimable self-censorship and fear created and sustained by this legislation.

The backlash in response to lesbian/gay 'visible' interventions also occurred within other educational systems, particularly in parts of the USA, and came from right-wing and conservative pressure groups (see McLaren, 1995, p. 107 for the demise of the Rainbow Curriculum created by New York City's Board of Education). Evidence of backlash has also been reported within more liberal institutions (Norris, 1991). Lesbian presence, which is reproduced as marginal, is not in itself sufficient to overturn the conserving mechanisms of a heterosexist educational system. Nevertheless, when lesbian and gay communities are numerically more significant there is the possibility of a greater local impact producing localized educational interventions. Particular areas in the USA (notably San Francisco and other parts of California) have lesbian and gay programmes, lesbian and gay educational officers and even lesbian and gay scholarships (Woog, 1995). The context of these positive interventions needs to be acknowledged and compared with the educational work with drop-outs which is carried out in less privileged urban environments (for example, the Harvey Milk school in New York, in Woog, 1995). These local, and localized, initiatives, however, while showing the potential and possibilities for lesbian and gay interventions, have a limited effect upon what Peter McLaren (1995, p. 108) describes as the more general condition of sexual apartheid which (American) society and therefore education is premised upon.

The balance between understanding and representing lesbian agency and its relationship with the oppressive structure of a heterosexist education system is problematic. The positioning of lesbian experience and knowledge in this context as only marginal/'invisible'/subjugated can act to obscure other interventions which do occur. Lesbians and their allies in education have had to take on the task of challenging lesbian 'invisibility' by naming and speaking of lesbian experiences of heterosexist oppression. This has been important in challenging the totality of lesbian (and gay) erasure within a heterosexist education system. However, in the attempt to illustrate and illuminate this experience, often by speaking to the masters in their own words, lesbian interventions which do occur through invisibility and silence are not represented. When 'visibility' and 'voice' potentially attract violent or negative sanctions for lesbians in education

(Kitzinger, 1989; Trenchard and Warren, 1984), frequently controlling and shaping responses through an omnipresent fear of heterosexual reprisal (Sparkes, 1994; Sullivan, 1993), it can only limit rather than define our presence or describe our impact.

These were some of the issues which I attempted to address in my recent doctoral study of the experiences of lesbians in education. In order to avoid reinscribing lesbians as simply victims (see Bhavnani, 1988) or survivors, I examined the question of lesbian agency in the heterosexist structure of the educational system. The research, which explored feminist methodology in researching lesbian subjects (see Appleby, 1997), was a small-scale in-depth qualitative study of the experiences of lesbian mothers with school-age children, post-sixteen/mature lesbian students and lesbian teachers. Two of the twenty-one participants publicly acknowledged their lesbian identity in their educational environment. The majority of the participants used strategies of 'invisibility' and 'silence'. These were used, in various ways, not just as protection against potential harassment and discrimination but also as a form of resistance.

Prior to any discussion of the direct experiences of education I talked with each participant about her lesbian identity. Despite some individual variations, what emerged very strongly in most of their accounts was a perception of themselves as strong, self-defined women in relation to their lesbian identity. Nearly all the participants expressed a very high self-regard for these two aspects of their identity, although less than a third said that they were feminists, with at least the same number expressing some hostility to what they thought of as feminism (see Stuart, 1990). This sense of positive difference (Appleby, 1996), based upon a self-understanding of being strong and independent as women, was expressed simultaneously with a sense of lesbian vulnerability within their different educational settings. It is significant that all of the participants identified themselves as white. Any sense of self-understanding of difference in identifying as a lesbian will be individually experienced through other identities such as race, age or disability (Mason-John and Khambatta, 1993; Neild and Pearson, 1992; Hearn, 1988). Lesbian identity, including a sense of difference, may be experienced as negative and may be in tension with other aspects of identity (Akanke, 1994). The participants in my study described how their vulnerability was connected to external perceptions of their lesbian identity. The strength/vulnerability interrelationship was important in understanding the participants' experiences of education both as 'visible' women and as 'invisible' lesbians. It also shows how many of the participants strategically chose to remain 'invisible' as lesbians so that their self-identity as strong women could be harnessed effectively within their teaching (see also Stein, 1988). This was particularly noticeable in several of the teachers' accounts where resistance and individual interventions were carried out quietly and subversively.

Jeanette (pseudonym), who works as a secondary school supply teacher, shows aspects of both vulnerability and strength in her account. She explains that she felt vulnerable at school because she did not fit the heterosexual feminine gender stereotype expected of female teachers:

> I used to wear a jacket you see, because I felt protected. I don't wear one now. And they couldn't cope with that, the kids. And they were always saying 'Miss, what's a transsexual?' You know, so as to get you going and embarrass you. So I got used to that one. And at one school I was in a boy kept sitting there and saying 'lesbian, lesbian' you know, behind his hand. And then they sent around a questionnaire trying to decide whether I was a man or a woman. And I was just furious, you know?

And yet Jeanette, having faced such lesbian baiting because of her non-conforming appearance (Vasquez, 1992), also described how she wanted to intervene to challenge the pupils' assumptions about (heterosexual) conformity, in the hope of teaching them about difference:

> I'm a free agent and yet I can tell the kids 'You don't need to conform' you know. I mean I can just say that. I don't need to say 'Oh well go and be a dyke' but if I can say 'Well not everyone conforms, you don't need to conform, you have to do what's right for you' and that sort of thing. So that's a positive thing . . . and actually making them aware. . . . And, um, if you can get them to be a bit more objective about how things are it gives them more chance to change things for themselves.

Pat, who is a secondary school drama teacher, also exhibits a similar juxtaposition of strength and vulnerability in her experiences as a teacher. She explained how her non-conforming appearance, which also marked her as different, attracted criticism and hostility. Isobel Gill, who provides an early account[5] of being a lesbian teacher, remarks that 'in a vulnerable position anything can be picked on. And wearing skirts won't help. Being assertive in the classroom, refusing to be flirted with, challenging any sexist or heterosexist comment' (1989, p. 110). This mirrors Pat's account, nearly a decade later, of how her deviation from pupils' gendered (and therefore sexualized) assumptions made her vulnerable at school:

> I did get a lot of hassle and harassment and seriously nasty stuff. Well, them shouting 'lesbian' at me as I walked down the corridor. . . . It wasn't just that they used to have a go about me physically, about the way that I dress. They used to insult me because I didn't shave my legs. I mean I wasn't brandishing, but like if I wore a skirt and it happened to be colourful, it was like total ridicule.

In spite of this harassment and vulnerability, Pat also intervened to make the space for them to question gender and sexual conformity – the workings of heterosexism. She described one of her drama lessons where she felt this had occurred.

> Like, one boy role-playing being bisexual and doing it really. He chose to do that. It was an exercise where they could choose to be any character that they wanted and then the others would ask questions to that character. You know, a hot-seating exercise. And he chose to be a bisexual character and he was totally real about it. It was sensational. You know. Some of them will do 'Oh I'm a transvestite and I've got three willies' [high pitched silly voice]. But it wasn't like that, he was totally real about it. And they asked him, the kids asked him things like 'Did he have a girlfriend?' and 'Oh have you got a boyfriend?' [silly voice]. And he said 'Not at the moment although I am bisexual' or something like that.
>
> YA: Wow.
>
> Pat: Mmm. He was just totally ordinary about it. And I think someone said 'Oh what does that mean?' [silly voice], trying to be stupid. And he said 'Well I sleep with both men and women.' He was totally real about it. I mean I'm not saying that that child will necessarily choose to be bisexual. But I thought it was really good that he could do it in a, um, respectful way.

What both Pat and Jeanette's descriptions of their experiences as lesbian teachers in a heterosexually organized education system show is that there are other significant aspects of intervention which are more difficult to see and which lie outside of interventions made through 'visibility' and 'voice'. Importantly, the type of intervention which they both describe is located within their resistance to the promotion of *heterosexism* within education and not simply in response to *homophobia* (see Kitzinger, 1996). This was a common theme across most of the participants' accounts. Whether as students, mothers or teachers, most of the participants resisted, often unseen and subversively, the heteropatriarchal construction of their gender as normatively feminine and their sexual identity as unquestioningly heterosexual.

Theorizing lesbian subjects in education

A formidable void exists between the increase of lesbian (and gay) knowledges within the academy generally and the integration of these knowledges within the field of education specifically. Debbie Epstein, in the introduction to *Challenging Lesbian and Gay Inequalities in Education*, notes what she describes as the almost frenzied interest in sexuality both in the academy and in the media, commenting that 'Suddenly, in the late 1980s and early 1990s, an area which has been the preserve of a few brave (usually feminist or gay male) souls has become everybody's key interest' (1994a, p. 1). However, she observes that 'the growing interest within the academy in sexuality in general and lesbian and gay studies in particular, seems to have bypassed the world of education' (p. 1). Tamsin Wilton identifies a similar concern with 'academic bridging' and 'theoretical fit' in her description of the academic positioning of lesbian studies (which for her does include education). She argues that lesbian studies does not fit pre-existing academic bases because 'women's studies is dogged by heterosexism, gay studies by sexism' (1995, p. 18). What Wilton identifies is that the type of theoretical explanation of lesbian identity and the relationship of this to the gendered organization of heterosexuality creates differently located explanations of the 'lesbian' and of her position in society. She describes the difficulty for lesbian studies created by this impasse:

> Caught at the dynamic confluence of feminist and queer theory but inadequately incorporated within either; exposed as the demonised chimera of the patriarchal imagination but inadequately protected by poststructuralism from the sticks, stones and prisons of heteropatriarchal materiality. (p. 49)

The theoretical tension described here is, I believe, at the heart of Debbie Epstein's observation above. Differing theoretical explanations of lesbian identity give rise to different explanations of existing material conditions of oppression and therefore provide different possibilities and explanations for lesbian agency. Education is an institution, and one which is central to the conservation and ideological reproduction of heterosexuality. Lesbian theories which do not reflect the institutional constraints and mechanisms which operate through both sexual identity and its relation to gendered identity are limited (Jeffreys, 1994). Queer theorist Eve Sedgwick's discussion of the epistemology of the closet illustrates such a limitation. On the one hand Sedgwick's problematizing of gay self-disclosure, in which she argues that the 'reign of the telling secret was scarcely overturned with Stonewall' (1993, p. 45), is helpful in understanding the complex and diverse pressures in education of being out (what I refer to individually and collectively as 'visibility' and 'voice'). However, her argument that 'in the theatrical display of an already institutionalized ignorance no transformative potential is to be looked for' (p. 52) represents a closure in terms of lesbian agency and potential resistance. Lesbians in education engage daily with already institutionalized heterosexist ignorance.

Queer theorist Diana Fuss provides what could be a potentially useful analysis for looking at the relationship of lesbians to a heterosexist educational system. Fuss rejects a simple inside/outside dichotomy as she argues that this disguises 'the fact that most of us are both inside and outside at the same time' (1991, p. 5). In view of the difficulties surrounding 'visibility' and 'voice', this would appear to offer a multi-layer approach. However, her alternative is not easy to relate to education. Fuss argues: 'What we need is a theory of sexual borders that will help us to come to terms with, and to organize around, the new cultural and sexual arrangements occasioned, by the movements and transmutations of pleasure in the social field' (p. 5). The disregard for the existing institutional constraints (the old cultural and sexual arrangements) within this recommendation makes it difficult to relate to education, as it ignores the conditions which already operate and which are continually being reproduced. Moreover, the optimism for the potential of new cultural and sexual arrangements based upon pleasure is difficult to envisage in the field of education. The media witch-hunt of lesbian head teacher Jane Brown is a clear indication that existing sexual borders (between heterosexuality and lesbianism) are being clearly defined and continually reinforced within the practice of education.

In her attempt to develop an autonomous theory of sexuality, Gayle Rubin moves from her previous position of seeing an explicit connection between sex and gender (and describing heterosexuality as compulsory) to one that rejects a link between them. Suggesting that some (radical) feminist discourses on sexuality are a form of demonology, Rubin argues, 'In contrast to my perspective in "The Traffic in Women", I am now arguing that it is essential to separate gender and sexuality analytically to reflect more accurately their separate social existence' (1993, p. 33). Her radical solution is to argue that lesbians share what she describes as the same 'sociological features' and therefore suffer the same consequences and 'social penalties' as gay men, sadomasochists, transvestites and prostitutes (p. 33). Rubin appears to be arguing that those who identify themselves, or are identified by others, as existing outside of normative heterosexuality are 'equal' to each other as 'outsiders'. This ignores the power differential implicit within other aspects of these also gendered identities. Education reproduces heterosexuality, which is premised upon unequal gendered power relations. Carol Jones and Pat Mahony argue that within heterosexuality 'masculinity and femininity are unequal' and that 'backed by the threat of violence the institution of heterosexuality is organized according to a power imbalance' (1989, p. xiv). Mairtin Mac an Ghaill's (1994) study of young black gay students also reveals a complex interplay between the participants' gendered, sexual and ethnic identities which would not be automatically transferable, or necessarily held in common, with other young gay men.

The lesbian participants in my study, on the whole, made a strong connection between gender and sexual identity (although experienced in different ways depending upon situation and location), which was reflected in their resistances to the institutionalized forms and local mechanisms of heterosexism in education. The theoretical analysis which provides a clear understanding of heterosexism within education and allows for the possibility of resistance is Adrienne Rich's concept of 'compulsory heterosexuality'. Although apparently dated (someone remarked how 'old fashioned' my use of this analysis was) and not without gaps and omissions (Appleby, 1992), it nevertheless provides for an analytical connection between heterosexist institutional structures and lesbian subject agency which can be applied to education. Rich illustrates the pervasive force which lies behind the reproduction/promotion of heterosexuality as compulsory: 'We are confronting not a simple maintenance of equality and property possession, but a pervasive cluster of forces, ranging from physical brutality to control of consciousness' (1986, p. 39). It is helpful to view the conservation and reproduction of heterosexuality as compulsory within education in these terms. Heterosexuality is not taught or presented as an equal 'choice' (Appleby, 1995) but, as I have argued, has been promoted within the field of education where sexuality is highly regulated and reproduced as heterosexual within an increasingly moral framework.

Conclusion

In considering my friend's negative remark regarding the paucity of lesbian interventions, I have considered the question of what constitutes a lesbian intervention in education. I have looked at the relationship between lesbian experience of education and lesbian knowledge/theory, particularly in terms of the existence of 'visibility' and 'voice'. This presence in itself may be seen to constitute an intervention. My study of lesbian experience in education demonstrated a high degree of individual resistance to heterosexism, particularly to heterosexual gender assumptions about femininity. In some instances interventions were made to disrupt heterosexual assumptions for others in educational environments. The interventions were not 'visibly' lesbian in themselves but responded to the participants' own understanding of themselves as strong self-determined women engaging with a heterosexist education system. It was through the connection of gender and sexual identity (experienced within a strength/vulnerability relationship) that resistance and survival occurred.

Lesbian interventions in the field of education are complex. It is difficult to estimate and measure their relationship to this heterosexist institution. This complexity, added to the heterosexually conserving function of education, may go some way to explain my friend's assumption that the incorporation of lesbian issues in any lesbian interventions may be summed up in three lines. Heterosexual theories of education which do not address sexual identity in relation to oppression, and lesbian theories which do not address institutionalized gendered power relations within education may well exacerbate the situation. The fact that increased theoretical interest in sexuality in the academy has not impacted upon the field of education confirms this. Lesbian and feminist work which has analysed these connections provides clear models which may help to develop our understanding of our lesbian experiences in education. These models enable us to recognize and name our interventions in, and our resistance to, a heteropatriarchal education system.

Notes

1. While the field of education is international in the sense of commonly held philosophies and beliefs (Paulo Freire's *Pedagogy of the Oppressed* (1972) and bell hooks's *Teaching to Transgress: Education as the Practice of Freedom* (1994), for example, can be applied across many different educational systems), the relationship of the field to the academy is more closely tied to specific educational systems.
2. Increasingly, feminist writers have challenged some of the more hidden aspects of power which reside within notions of empowerment (for example, Gore, 1992; Ellsworth, 1992). Others have questioned the potentially disempowering nature of 'voice' and 'visibility' for those who have marginalized identities including that of being a lesbian (for example, Luke, 1994).
3. School's Out, a lesbian and gay organization working for lesbian and gay equality in education, reported in their May 1996 newsletter that the NUT's 1996 Annual Conference had agreed to pass the School's Out Lesbian and Gay Equality motion almost unanimously. This motion will encourage the NUT to represent lesbian and gay education workers' rights and to pursue wider lesbian and gay educational issues. School's Out can be contacted at BM School's Out, London, WC1N 3XX.
4. Section 28 of the Local Government Act 1988 states:
   (1) A local authority shall not
      a) intentionally promote homosexuality or publish material with the intention of promoting homosexuality;
      b) promote the teaching in any maintained school of the acceptability of homosexuality as a pretended family relationship;
   (2) Nothing in subsection (1) above shall be taken to prohibit the doing of anything for the purpose of treating or preventing the spread of disease.
   (3) In any proceeding in connection with the application with this section a court shall draw such inferences as to the intention of the local authority as may reasonably be drawn from the evidence before it. (Colvin and Hawksley, 1989).
5. Isobel Gill first published an article in 1986 in *Teaching London Kids* which she called 'Miss Is a Lesbian'. Her chapter 'Trying Not Just to Survive: A Lesbian Teacher in a Boys' School' in Holly (1989) reproduces part of this earlier paper.

References

Akanke (1994) 'Black in the Closet.' In D. Epstein (ed.) *Challenging Lesbian and Gay Inequalities in Education.* Buckingham: Open University Press.

Andrews, J. (1990) 'Don't Pass Us By: Keeping Lesbian and Gay Issues on the Agenda.' *Gender and Education.* 2/3: 351–5.

Apple, M. (1993) *Democratic Education in a Conservative Age.* London: Routledge.

Appleby, Y. (1992) 'Disability and Compulsory Heterosexuality.' *Feminism and Psychology.* 2/3: 502–5.

Appleby, Y. (1995) 'Heterosexuality: Compulsion, Choice or a Strong Pair of Arms?' *Feminism and Psychology.* 5/1: 136–9.

Appleby, Y. (1996) '"Decidedly Different": Lesbian Women and Education.' *International Studies in Sociology of Education.* 6/1: 67–86.

Appleby, Y. (1997) '"How Was It for You?": Talking about Intimate Exchanges in Feminist Research.' In M. Ang-Lygate, H. Millsom and C. Corrin (eds) *Desperately Seeking Sisterhood: Still Challenging and Building.* London: Taylor and Francis, pp. 138–50.

Arnot, M. and Barton, L. (eds) (1992) *Voicing Concerns: Sociological Perspectives on Contemporary Education Reforms.* Wallingford, Oxfordshire: Triangle Books.

Bhavnani, K. (1988) 'Empowerment and Social Research: Some Comments.' *Texts.* 8/1–2: 41–50.

Cant, B. (1988) 'Normal Channels.' In B. Cant and S. Hemmings (eds) *Radical Records: Thirty Years of Lesbian and Gay History.* London: Routledge.

Colvin, M. and Hawksley, J. (1989) *Section 28: A Practical Guide to the Law and Its Implications.* London: Liberty.

Cooper, D. (1989) 'Positive Images in Haringey: A Struggle for Identity.' In Jones and Mahony (1989).

Cruikshank, M. (ed.) (1982) *Lesbian Studies: Present and Future.* New York: The Feminist Press.

Davies, L. (1983) 'Gender, Resistance and Power.' In S. Walker and L. Barton (eds) *Gender, Class and Education.* Lewes, Sussex: Falmer Press.

Ellsworth, E. (1992) 'Why Doesn't This Feel Empowering? Working through the Repressive Myths of Critical Pedagogy.' In C. Luke and J. Gore (eds) *Feminisms and Critical Pedagogy.* London: Routledge.

Epstein, D. (1994a) 'Introduction: Lesbian and Gay Equality in Education – Problems and Possibilities.' In D. Epstein (ed.) *Challenging Lesbian and Gay Inequalities in Education.* Buckingham: Open University Press.

Epstein, D. (1994b) 'Lesbian and Gay Equality within a Whole School Policy.' In D. Epstein (ed.) *Challenging Lesbian and Gay Inequalities in Education.* Buckingham: Open University Press.

Epstein, D. and Johnson, R. (1994) 'On the Straight and the Narrow: The Heterosexual Presumption, Homophobias and Schools.' In D. Epstein (ed.) *Challenging Lesbian and Gay Inequalities in Education.* Buckingham: Open University Press.

Freire, P. (1972) *Pedagogy of the Oppressed.* Harmondsworth: Penguin.

Fuss, D. (ed.) (1991) *Inside/Out: Lesbian Theories, Gay Theories.* London: Routledge.

Garber, L. (ed.) (1994) *Tilting the Tower: Lesbians Teaching Queer Subjects.* London: Routledge.

Gill, I. (1989) 'Trying Not Just to Survive: A Lesbian Teacher in a Boys' School.' In L. Holly (ed.) *Girls and Sexuality: Teaching and Learning.* Buckingham: Open University Press.

Giroux, H. (1991) 'Democracy and the Discourse of Cultural Difference: Towards a Politics of Border Pedagogy.' *British Journal of Sociology of Education.* 12/4: 501–19.

Gore, J. (1992) 'What We Can Do for You! What Can "We" Do for "You"?:

Struggling over Empowerment in Critical and Feminist Pedagogies.' In C. Luke and J. Gore (eds) *Feminisms and Critical Pedagogies*. London: Routledge.

Gore, J. (1993) *The Struggle for Pedagogies: Critical and Feminist Discourses as Regimes of Truth*. London: Routledge.

Griffin, C. (1989) (reprinted) *Typical Girls?: Young Women from School to the Job Market*. London: Routledge.

Griffin, G. (ed.) (1993) *Outwrite: Lesbianism and Popular Culture*. London: Pluto Press.

Harris, S. (1990) *Lesbian and Gay Issues in the English Classroom*. Buckingham: Open University Press.

Hearn, K. (1988) 'Oi! What about Us?' In B. Cant and S. Hemmings (eds) *Radical Records: Thirty Years of Lesbian and Gay History*. London: Routledge.

Holly, L. (1989) 'Introduction: The Sexual Agenda of Schools.' In L. Holly (ed.) *Girls and Sexuality: Teaching and Learning*. Buckingham: Open University Press.

hooks, b. (1994) *Teaching to Transgress: Education as the Practice of Freedom*. London: Routledge.

Jeffreys, S. (1994) 'The Queer Disappearance of Lesbians: Sexuality in the Academy.' *Women's Studies International Forum*. 17/5: 459–72.

Jones, C. and Mahony, P. (eds) (1989) *Learning Our Lines: Sexuality and Social Control in Education*. London: The Women's Press.

Kelly, L. (1992) 'Not in Front of the Children: Responding to Right-Wing Agendas on Sexuality and Education.' In M. Arnot and L. Barton (eds) *Voicing Concerns: Sociological Perspectives on Contemporary Education Reforms*. Wallingford, Oxfordshire: Triangle Books.

Kitzinger, C. (1989) 'Coming Out Once Again.' *Guardian*, 6 September.

Kitzinger, C. (1996) 'Heteropatriarchal Language: The Case Against "Homophobia".' In L. Mohin (ed.) *An Intimacy of Equals*. London: Onlywomen Press.

Lather, P. (1991) *Getting Smart: Feminist Research and Pedagogy with/in the Postmodern*. London: Routledge.

Lather, P. (1994) 'The Absent Presence: Patriarchy, Capitalism and the Nature of Teacher Work.' In L. Stone (ed.) *The Education Feminism Reader*. London: Routledge.

Lees, S. (1993) *Sugar and Spice: Sexuality and Adolescent Girls*. London: Penguin Books.

Luke, C. (1994) 'Women in the Academy: The Politics of Speech and Silence.' *British Journal of Sociology of Education*. 15/2: 211–30.

Mac an Ghaill, M. (1988) *Young, Gifted and Black: Student–Teacher Relations in the Schooling of Black Youth*. Buckingham: Open University Press.

Mac an Ghaill, M. (1994) '(In)visibility: Sexuality, Race and Masculinity in the School Context.' In D. Epstein (ed.) *Challenging Lesbian and Gay Inequalities in Education*. Buckingham: Open University Press.

McLaren, P. (1995) 'Moral Panic, Schooling and Gay Identity: Critical Pedagogy and the Politics of Resistance.' In G. Unks (ed.) *The Gay Teen: Educational Practice and Theory for Lesbian, Gay and Bisexual Adolescents*. London: Routledge.

Mason-John, V. and Khambatta, A. (1993) *Lesbians Talk: Making Black Waves*. London: Scarlet Press.

Melia, J. (1989) 'Sex Education in Schools: Keeping to the "Norm".' In C. Jones and P. Mahony (eds) *Learning Our Lines: Sexuality and Social Control in Education*. London: The Women's Press.

Mirza, H. (1992) *Young, Female and Black*. London: Routledge.

Neild, S. and R. Pearson (1992) *Women Like Us*. London: The Women's Press.

Norris, W. (1991) 'Liberal Attitudes and Homophobic Acts: The Paradoxes of Homosexual Experience in a Liberal Institution.' *Journal of Homosexuality*. 22/3–4: 81–120.

Patrick, P. and Sanders, S. (1994) 'Lesbian and Gay Issues in the Curriculum.' In D. Epstein (ed.) *Challenging Lesbian and Gay Inequalities in Education.* Buckingham: Open University Press.

Purvis, J. (1991) *A History of Women's Education in England.* Buckingham: Open University Press.

Rich, A. (1986) 'Compulsory Heterosexuality and Lesbian Existence.' In *Blood, Bread and Poetry.* London: Virago.

Rubin, G. (1993) 'Thinking Sex: Notes for a Radical Theory of the Politics of Sexuality.' In H. Abelove, M. Barale and D. Halperin (eds) *The Lesbian and Gay Studies Reader.* London: Routledge.

Sanders, S. and Burke, H. (1994) 'Are You a Lesbian Miss?' In D. Epstein (ed.) *Challenging Lesbian and Gay Inequalities in Education.* Buckingham: Open University Press.

Scraton, S. (1992) *Shaping Up to Womanhood: Gender and Girls' Physical Education.* Buckingham: Open University Press.

Sedgwick, E. (1993) 'Epistemology of the Closet.' In H. Abelove, M. Barale and D. Halperin (eds) *The Lesbian and Gay Studies Reader.* London: Routledge.

Sharpe, R. (1980) *Knowledge, Ideology and the Practice of Schooling.* London: Routledge and Kegan Paul.

Smith, D. (1988) *The Everyday World as Problematic: A Feminist Sociology.* Buckingham: Open University Press.

Sparkes, A. (1994) 'Self, Silence and Invisibility as a Beginning Teacher: A Life History of Lesbian Experience.' *British Journal of Sociology of Education.* 15/1: 93–119.

Spender, D. (1989) *Invisible Women: The Schooling Scandal.* London: The Women's Press.

Spender, D. and Sarah, E. (eds) (1980) *Learning to Lose: Sexism and Education.* London: The Women's Press.

Spraggs, G. (1994) 'Coming Out in the National Union of Teachers.' In D. Epstein (ed.) *Challenging Lesbian and Gay Inequalities in Education.* Buckingham: Open University Press.

Squirrell, G. (1989) 'Teachers and Issues of Sexual Orientation.' *Gender and Education.* 1/1: 17–34.

Stein, A. (1988) 'What's a Lesbian Teacher to Do?' In S. Hope-Parmeter and I. Reti (eds) *The Lesbian in Front of the Classroom: Writings by Lesbian Teachers.* Santa Cruz: Herbooks.

Stuart, A. (1990) 'Feminism: Dead or Alive?' In J. Rutherford (ed.) *Identity, Community, Culture, Difference.* London: Lawrence and Wishart.

Sullivan, C. (1993) 'Oppression: The Experiences of a Lesbian Teacher in an Inner City Comprehensive School in the United Kingdom.' *Gender and Education.* 5/1: 93–101.

Thompson, R. (1994) 'Moral Rhetoric and Public Health Pragmatism: The Recent Politics of Sex Education.' *Feminist Review.* 48: 40–60.

Trenchard, L. and Warren, H. (1984) *Something to Tell You.* London: London Gay Teenage Group.

Vasquez, C. (1992) 'Appearances.' In W. Blumenfeld (ed.) *Homophobia: How We All Pay the Price.* Boston: Beacon Press.

Weiner, G. (ed.) (1991) (reprinted) *Just a Bunch of Girls.* Buckingham: Open University Press.

Weiner, G. (1994) *Feminisms in Education: An Introduction.* Buckingham: Open University Press.

Whyte, J., Deem, R., Kant, L. and Cruikshank, M. (1985) *Girl Friendly Schooling.* London: Routledge.

Willis, P. (1977) *Learning to Labour: How Working Class Kids Get Working Class Jobs.* Farnborough: Saxon House.

Wilton, T. (1995) *Lesbian Studies: Setting an Agenda.* London: Routledge.

Woog, D. (1995) *School's Out: The Impact of Gay and Lesbian Issues on America's Schools.* Boston: Alyson Publications.

3

Lesbian Law, Lesbian Legal Theory

Rosemary Auchmuty

Lesbians have a love/hate relationship with the law. On the one hand, the legal processes, if not the laws themselves, have clearly been significant areas of oppression for lesbians. On the other, women have been criticized for ascribing too much power to law – for expecting law reform to transform our lives (Smart, 1989) – and in so far as this is true, lesbians have sometimes been as naive as other women. 'The master's tools will never dismantle the master's house', wrote Audre Lorde (1984, p. 112). Yet many lesbian feminists have resolutely refused to look at a patriarchal institution like law to tackle patriarchal oppression, preferring instead to work *outside* the law in direct action (for example, burning down sex shops) or by providing services for victims of rape or domestic violence. Some, however, have made a conscious decision to engage with the law: in the 1970s and 1980s a generation of lesbian feminist graduates moved into criminological research focusing on women's issues, while others chose to study law and become solicitors, barristers and legal advice workers with a clearly articulated mission first to understand and then to change the system. This was a time when lesbian and gay rights featured on the agendas of some local authorities (Cooper, 1994); the Greater London Council, for example, provided funds for organizations such as LESPOP (the Lesbians and Policing Project) and LAGER (Lesbian and Gay Employment Rights).

Feminism, sexuality and violence

The link between lesbian scholarship and feminist criminology lies in the radical feminist analysis of women's oppression developed in the UK and the USA during these decades. Radical feminism put equality and male violence on the feminist agenda. The first four demands of the Women's Liberation Movement – equal pay, equal education and job opportunities, 24-hour childcare, and abortion and contraception on demand – reflected the socialist-feminist concerns of its founders, and also their heterosexuality. Radical feminists, however, identified the role of male violence and 'compulsory heterosexuality' (Rich, 1981) in maintaining men's power over women (rhodes and McNeill, 1985). Feminist research, theorizing and campaigns were accompanied, not coincidentally, by a shift in sexual practice for many women who now chose to live as lesbians (Leeds Revolutionary Feminist Group, 1981). It was therefore not accidental that many lesbian/radical feminists produced (and are still producing) so much work around violence against women in its many forms: domestic violence, wifeslaughter, prostitution, pornography and the sexual abuse of children (see Radford and Russell, 1992; Kelly, 1988a–c, 1989a,b, 1990; Cameron and Frazer, 1987; Kappeler, 1986; Jeffreys, 1985; Tong, 1984; Radford, 1982). This research found its way on to sociology, women's studies and finally law reading lists. Many of its authors now have tenured university jobs, and their work is widely read by academic and practising lawyers.

Other feminists have also concerned themselves with sexual abuse and violence. Significant contributions by, for example, Mary McIntosh and Elizabeth Wilson are distinguishable from the radical feminist work in that they take a much more cautious approach to legal intervention (McIntosh, 1988), if not (as in the case of pornography) repudiating it altogether (Rodgerson and Wilson, 1991). Radford and Kelly, however, see a positive role for law: 'Legal change is one route to creating social change, within which inequality is both recognized by, and challenged through, law' (1995, p. 197). Their goal is nothing less than the 'creation of feminist law', the transformation of a legal system based exclusively on men's lives and perceptions into one which includes 'new laws which are grounded in the experiences, material situations and cultural contexts of women's and children's lives' (pp. 186, 188). It is this goal which has led them to propose a new defence of manslaughter, 'Self-Preservation', as a better way forward in homicide cases where the female defendants have suffered long-term domestic violence, rather than the extension of 'Provocation' (in their view, an 'inherently male defence', p. 192) or resorting to 'Diminished Responsibility', which places women at the mercy of medical experts who pathologize their behaviour. Radford and Kelly's work remains grounded in radical feminism, in a recognition of the 'interconnectedness of theory, activism and methodology, politics, policy and research in feminist practice' (p. 186).

The lesbian in law

Much has been written about the legal disabilities of lesbians in other places and at other times, but in modern Britain, at least until recently, it has been effectively a non-issue. This is because lesbians have suffered very little *direct* discrimination in English law. Annabel Faraday's account

'Lesbian Outlaws', published in the radical feminist journal *Trouble and Strife*, surveyed Parliament's (unsuccessful) attempts to legislate against lesbian sexual activity, highlighting the tension between one group's desire to criminalize lesbianism and another's wish to ignore it so as not to bring it to the attention of women. In the UK, in 1921, the latter argument won. 'Such acts of official silencing demonstrate the extent to which lesbian existence threatened patriarchal dictates embodied in the law', Faraday concluded (1988, p. 16). Only in the armed forces does lesbianism remain illegal, leading to dismissal under the Armed Forces Act 1971.

The law's attitude to lesbians is in stark contrast to its attitude to gay men, whose consenting sexual acts (criminalized under the Criminal Law Amendment Act 1885) were only legalized in 1967 under the Sexual Offences Act, and whose age of consent, recently reduced to eighteen from twenty-one, still remains higher than that for heterosexual males and females, which is sixteen. There is no age of consent for lesbian sex in England. It also contrasts with the situation of lesbians in other parts of the world. Ruthann Robson's *Lesbian (Out)Law* surveys the forms of lesbian sexual expression which are criminalized in half the jurisdictions in the USA. In a literary *tour de force* she subjects five long quotations from a sexually explicit novel by Judith McDaniel, *Just Say Yes* (Firebrand Books, 1990), to an exhaustive legal analysis which reveals 'how our sexual practices violate – and fail to violate – the various laws in various states in idiosyncratic ways' (1992, p. 50).

Nevertheless, although lesbians are largely ignored by the criminal law, which generally proceeds on the assumption that women are sexually passive, 'when a woman's lesbianism is before the court as part of the general evidence another agenda operates', Helena Kennedy QC tells us. '[S]ome lesbians challenge the idea of passivity so strongly that the law is used symbolically for public condemnation' (1992, p. 156). She goes on to describe how a lesbian will be punished more severely than a heterosexual woman or man for similar offences, and how a wife's lesbianism may provide a defence of provocation, with consequent reduction of sentence, for the husband who kills her.

In civil law, too, the fact of being a lesbian is very likely to affect a woman's treatment. Lesbians have, for example, no legal protection against discrimination in employment; the Sex Discrimination Act 1975 does not cover sexuality (Beer *et al.*, 1983). Lesbian couples cannot marry, and from this inability to form a legal union flow further disadvantages in property, immigration, nationality, pension and tax rights (Crane, 1982; Cohen *et al.*, 1978). But the context which, in this country, has provided greatest scope for legal discussions of the lesbian is the custody dispute. Here, once again, academic concern was sparked by feminist initiative.

Lesbians in the courts

The Lesbian Custody Project was started in 1982 by Rights of Women (ROW) 'to campaign and research around the difficulties lesbian mothers face in retaining custody of their children' (Rights of Women Custody Group, 1986). In 1984 it published a report on lesbian mothers and child custody, *Lesbian Mothers on Trial*, based on the experiences of thirty-two lesbian mothers who sought custody of their children. With the addition of a hundred pages of practical advice, this was later expanded into the *Lesbian Mothers' Legal Handbook* (1986). ROW continues to advise and campaign on behalf of lesbian mothers, and a new edition of the handbook is in preparation.

Before the 1980s, lesbian custody cases were rarely reported in the Law Reports, in keeping with the general assumption that women's issues did not involve significant points of law and that lesbianism was best left under legal wraps. In a survey of the case law, ROW demonstrated how the 'welfare principle' – the idea that the welfare of the child should be the paramount concern in custody cases – gave judges an almost unfettered discretion to decide custody on the basis of the mother's sexual orientation. Such words as 'proclivities', 'deviant', 'abnormal', 'not right' and 'unnatural' besprinkled their judgements, which relied heavily on the 'expert' testimony of psychiatrists brought in to inform the court of how children brought up in lesbian households would be 'blemished', 'scarred permanently' or 'subject to social embarrassment and hurt' (ROW, 1986, p. 121). Given power by the assumption that 'homosexuality is some sort of mental disease', psychiatrists called by each side presented conflicting views to the court, allowing 'the judge to choose and rely upon a view close to his own view of the matter' (p. 122).

The court's guiding principles that young children should be left with their mothers and/or that the status quo should be maintained in living arrangements were superseded in cases where the children lived with a mother who was a lesbian, even where doubts were raised about the father's care (p. 116). The judges were adamant that children were better off in 'normal' households of heterosexual males and females than with a lesbian mother. ROW concluded its survey with a reminder of recent research demonstrating the extent of sexual abuse of children by heterosexual men within families (p. 124).

Lesbian custody in the legal literature

Lesbian custody was first considered by an English law journal in 1976 when an anonymous correspondent contributed a brief article called 'A Case of Heads He Wins – Tails She Loses?' to *Family Law*. It began with deceptive objectivity – 'An interesting contested custody case came before the Family Division . . .' – but quickly took on an unexpectedly partisan tone. Considering the evidence of two psychiatrists called by the father that the five-year-old boy would have 'difficulty in growing up unblemished by his abnormal situation', the writer pointed out that not only was there no published evidence concerning the effects of being brought up in lesbian households on children,

> but equally there is no evidence to suppose that children so brought up will be damaged. It is very difficult to ascertain exactly what constitutes 'damage' and it could be argued that the vast majority of heterosexual couples 'damage' their children in some way for the simple fact is that we are human and not infallible. (*Anon.*, 1976, p. 230)

The writer goes on to accuse the psychiatrists and the judge of 'pure, simple, bias' for removing the child from his mother's care when no ill-treatment or neglect had been found. 'Many women in a similar position to this mother have had their hopes crushed', the article concludes. (Most *Family Law* readers must have been surprised to learn that there *were* many mothers in this position.) 'Perhaps in twenty years the situation will be different . . . [But for] this lesbian couple it will be too late. They have to live childless with their memories – and their tears' (p. 231).

The tone of this article is far removed from the usual dispassionate law journal treatment. Whoever the writer was, she must have had the sympathies of the *Family Law* editorial team. Certainly family law has always had its feminist wing. Most accounts of women in family law from the 1980s include a discussion of lesbian custody cases (O'Donovan, 1993; Brophy and Smart, 1985; Maidment, 1985, 1984; Smart, 1984). Of these, however, Smart alone sees implications for heterosexuality: in *The Ties that Bind* she draws her readers' attention to the judge who, in giving custody of a little girl to her lesbian mother, made it clear that he had done so only because the alternative was to place her in care, and that had a 'normal' household been available, he would have taken the child away from her:

> This kind of ideological support for the biological nuclear family would be undermined if the law took into account the contribution made by others to the rearing of children, and if the privileges currently given to the heterosexual couple were withdrawn. (1984, p. 122)

In the late 1980s and 1990s, the reporting of cases involving lesbian mothers became more common and so did the likelihood of a decision favourable to the mother. This can only have been due to the greater amount of awareness and knowledge of the subject within the legal community. An article in *Family Law* (Tasker and Golombok, 1991) – 'Children Raised by Lesbian Mothers: The Empirical Evidence' –

considered three arguments currently advanced against lesbian mothers: that the children's mental well-being would be adversely affected, that they would feel less secure in their gender roles than children raised in heterosexual households, and that they would be stigmatized. The authors concluded that all three arguments remained unsubstantiated, or were contradicted, by the published evidence (p. 184).

Canadian scholar Susan B. Boyd's article in the *Modern Law Review*, 'What Is a "Normal" Family?', carried the attack to a wider legal audience. Quoting Lord Justice Glidewell's remark in C v. C [1991] 1 FLR 223, 'It is axiomatic that the ideal environment for the upbringing of a child is the home of loving, caring and sensible parents, her father and her mother', she observes: 'The use of the phrase "it is axiomatic" renders this assumption a "truth" about which there is no need to explain or justify, despite the fact that this "truth" is challenged factually by the increasing diversity of familial forms . . .' (1992, p. 272). Further, Boyd notes that where (some) judges are careful these days to bear in mind that the customs and ideas of particular religious or ethnic groups, though different from those of the white Christian majority, may be equally valid, they do not feel constrained to show the same consideration to the customs or ideas of people of different sexuality. In C v. C, she notes, Lord Justice Balcombe did not feel he should

> put aside his personal beliefs, or what he perceived to be the dominant beliefs of 'society'. The ways in which such an approach inevitably privileges the entrenched morals of a class-based exclusionary society built upon sexist, racist and homophobic 'morals' are not even considered in such a statement. (p. 273)

Next Boyd tackles the 'stigma' argument – the idea (which surfaced after the notion of lesbianism as a perversion or sin lost its legal force) that the children of lesbian households will be teased or ostracized by their peers. 'This argument allows one discriminatory act (homophobia in the community) to condone another (depriving lesbians and homosexual men of custody)' (p. 274). No judge today, she reminds us, would deny custody to parents in a mixed-race relationship simply because the child might suffer racist taunts in the schoolyard. Indeed, Boyd suggests that it is better for children to face up to the reality of prejudice and discrimination, since openness presents a challenge to that very prejudice and makes for greater health and happiness than growing up with a shameful secret.

What is at issue in lesbian custody cases, Boyd concludes, is not so much the mother's sexual *identity* as the possibility of an *alternative familial model*. In this respect, black families and gay and lesbian families share a common experience of marginalization and disqualification. In the 'normal' white heterosexual family, men exercise institutional power and women play a subordinate role. In the lesbian household, the controlling hand of the male is absent. This point is omitted from liberal versions of the lesbian custody debate, which tend to turn on the conviction that a woman's sexuality is not and should not be a relevant factor in her claim for custody of her children. In truth, her sexuality *is* relevant, simply because a lesbian household presents a familial model which threatens male power.

Of course, as Boyd goes on to explain, to suggest that lesbian parenting might not be just as good but actually *better than* heterosexual parenting – for example, in tending to produce children who are 'more open-minded and tolerant of differences' – would be 'risky' in court (p. 274). Faced with a judiciary constituted as ours is – overwhelmingly white, male, Oxbridge-educated and out of touch, especially in the higher courts – Boyd can only recommend that judges acquaint themselves with social science research which problematizes heterosexual families (p. 278).

By setting up the heterosexual couple as the 'norm' and the 'ideal', courts are able to pre-set the parameters of the debate in such a way that lesbian mothers must present themselves as being as 'near the norm' as possible. As American lesbian lawyer Nancy D. Polikoff puts it:

> While no formula will guarantee victory in courtroom custody disputes involving lesbian mothers or gay fathers, one thing is clear: the more we appear to be part of the mainstream with middle-class values, middle-of-the-road political beliefs, repressed sexuality, and sex-role stereotyped behaviour, the more likely we are to keep custody of our children. (1986, p. 229)

Polikoff is clear about the consequences for lesbians of pandering to judicial prejudice: 'When we construct courtroom scenarios that deny our differences from heterosexual society, we quickly forget that our strength and our promise are rooted in those very differences' (p. 234). Why, she asks, should we welcome research which shows that there is no discernible difference between the children of heterosexual and lesbian mothers? '[A]s a lesbian, a feminist, and a mother with a vision of an entirely different way of raising our children, . . . I am not pleased to discover that my lesbian sisters pose no threat to the perpetuation of patriarchal childrearing' (p. 230). Polikoff suggests that lesbian lawyers must, while supporting their clients' radical visions, make it clear that they are all, lawyers and clients, actors in a drama directed by others. Moreover, lesbian lawyers need to keep hold of their own radical vision, without which, she believes, we may lose our sense of 'pride and of the positive value in homosexuality' (p. 231).

Finally, Polikoff argues that to protect lesbian mothers, legislative change is needed:

> The strength and value to all lesbians of some lesbians choosing to have children is that we mothers are pushed out into the world, that

> we challenge at home and in public the transmission of patriarchal values, and that we offer the opportunity to explore the significance of equal power between two mothers. (p. 234)

Such attempts to work towards 'equal power' in our relationships – one of the attractions of lesbianism for many feminists – cannot properly be sustained, in her view, without *equal rights* as parents. At this point, Polikoff's radical feminism, pragmatically applied as it always must be by those working within patriarchal structures, merges into a different discourse, that of rights.

Lesbians and rights

The 'rights' discourse in relation to sexuality came to prominence in the 1980s. A number of landmarks chart its rise (Cooper, 1994). One was the ideological shift which prompted (some) western governments to adopt policies aimed at reducing discrimination. Lesbian and gay rights appeared on national and local agendas for the first time. Another was the AIDS epidemic which, while it directly affected lesbians less than any other group, drew many into solidarity with gay men. Working with terminally ill people brought home to many lesbians the extent of the law's failure to accord gays and lesbians the rights of married couples in matters ranging from housing tenure and pension benefits to the making of medical decisions and funeral arrangements for their partners.

In the UK a third factor, in part a backlash against these two, was Clause 28 of the Local Government Bill, which prohibited the 'promotion' of homosexuality by local authorities and the teaching in a maintained school that homosexuality 'as a pretended family relationship' is acceptable. In opposition to the proposed clause, lesbians and gays mounted a concerted campaign, supported by many heterosexuals. By the time Clause 28 had become Section 28 of the Local Government Act 1988, the lesbian political agenda had largely been subsumed into a struggle for a composite 'lesbian and gay rights'. Out of the Clause 28 campaign came Stonewall, founded in 1989 to lobby for equality for lesbians and gays. Though headed by a lesbian, Angela Mason, its agenda is largely shaped by masculine concerns such as the gay (male) age of consent. Issues like lesbian custody come a long way down Stonewall's list of priorities (Palmer, 1995).

The rights discourse does not sit comfortably within the English legal system. As law teachers love to tell their students, there *are* no rights in English law – only remedies, and not always those. Unlike the USA and other jurisdictions, we have no Bill of Rights. Membership of the European Union has provided Britons with new forms of action but the European Convention on Human Rights has not been incorporated into domestic law in this country, although the UK is a signatory. Without a history of constitutional protection, we also lack the disillusionment and pessimism which many activists feel in countries which are so 'protected'. This helps to account for the enthusiasm and trust in the potential of legal reform expressed by so many campaigning for lesbian and gay rights in the UK today.

Lesbians and the state

The contemporary lesbian and gay rights movement has produced quite a body of legal literature (Galloway, 1983), some of which has impacted upon the legal disciplines. Invaluable in terms of *informing* people of the ways in which the law affects our lives, it often moves beyond highlighting areas of discrimination to offer practical advice for dealing with it, propose reform and suggest strategies for achieving it. In 1989, for example, the *Harvard Law Review* produced an issue devoted to developments in 'Sexual Orientation and the Law' (Anon., 1989). On the face of it purely descriptive, the 163-page account revealed by its citation of contextual material (for example, Rich, 1981) and its tone a liberal, reformist stance. Similarly, a review of Kees Waaldijk and Andrew Clapham's (1993) edited volume *Homosexuality: A European Community Issue* points out that 'this collection exists, quite simply, to serve the purpose of promoting law reform at a European level'. But, as the reviewer noted, whether law reform was the best way to tackle the problem of discrimination against lesbians and gays, and whether European intervention would be effective, were questions not even asked, let alone answered (Bamforth, 1995, pp. 114, 118).

Quite different is the specifically *lesbian* approach of Davina Cooper and Didi Herman to the relationship of lesbian and gay rights to the state. Both write as participants as well as researchers and both, as feminists, discuss the methodological issues their dual role raises. In *Sexing the City: Lesbian and Gay Politics within the Activist State*, Cooper (1994) records the rise and fall of local government initiatives for lesbian and gay equality in the UK in the 1980s. The local authorities she discusses were motivated by a conception of 'gays and lesbians' as a fixed, self-defining and non-threatening group who, like an ethnic or religious minority group, deserved acceptance, equal treatment and, if necessary, protection. Such a definition had particular appeal for gay men, anxious to divest themselves of the imagery of sin, perversion and predatoriness which had long characterized discussions of homosexuality. Involving no criticism of heterosexuality as an institution which helped to maintain patriarchal power, it was strategically more likely to win acceptance within a liberal, multicultural society. Similar representations were made by prominent gay (male) activists like Ian McKellen and Chris Smith MP in the campaign against Clause 28. They argued that gays were born, not made, so presented no danger to heterosexuals; homosexuality, in short, could not be promoted.

In *Rights of Passage: Struggles for Lesbian and Gay Legal Equality*, Didi Herman (1994) reveals how the same ideology dominated the movement for lesbian and gay rights in Canada.

Both authors describe how this benign view of homosexuality met with considerable resistance. In the UK, many parents reacted furiously to Haringey's 'Positive Images' campaign, culminating in a hysterical outcry at the discovery of *Jenny Lives with Eric and Martin* in local libraries. Indeed, Section 28 was passed precisely *because* the idea of the fundamental harmlessness of homosexuality was not swallowed by the government, which recognized instead the revolutionary potential of gay rights. In Canada, too, the New Christian Right depicted homosexuality as a practice, not an essence, one which reproduced itself by luring vulnerable children away from 'God's design'. Their opposition to lesbian and gay rights, which they perceived as *privileges*, was 'rooted in their design to strengthen, model, and reproduce patriarchal gender relations' (Herman, 1994, p. 84), making it a mirror-image of the lesbian feminist analysis.

As both Cooper and Herman indicate, some lesbian activists were content to go along with the 'unthreatening minority group' representation of themselves, even if they did not agree with it, as a trade-off for the rewards that rights might bring. Others persisted in trying to include a feminist analysis of power on the gay agenda. 'Heterosexuality, as a social construction, benefits men at the expense of women', wrote Harriet Wistrich in an article on Clause 28 in *Trouble and Strife*: 'We should not just be saying, "please, it's not fair, validate my lifestyle too", but lesbianism is a choice we want to promote as a positive alternative to heterosexuality: an institution which oppresses women' (Alderson and Wistrich, 1988, p. 8). By and large, however, the feminist analysis remains conspicuously absent from the lesbian and gay rights discourse. Cooper and Herman regret this; for both of them, oppression on grounds of sexuality cannot be separated from gender, nor from lesbians' other identities as, for example, Jewish, black or able-bodied. Both stress the limitations of state intervention, yet remain cautiously optimistic about using it in the pursuit of sexual liberation. Symbolic achievements, they show, are often more significant than actual legal 'victories'. They welcome the shifting of discussions of sexuality from the private to the public sphere, but point out that it leaves unaddressed 'one of the primary sites of the construction and enforcement of heterosexuality – home and family relations' (Herman, 1994, p. 44). Thus, when lesbian and gay couples claim family rights, they overlook the feminist critique of the family, not to speak of the claims of the uncoupled. But these, Herman hopes, may be the goals of future campaigns.

Davina Cooper (1995) further develops her ideas in *Power in Struggle: Feminism, Sexuality and the State*. As its subtitle indicates, this book is a feminist exploration of the relationship between sexuality and the state, and one of her case studies, the right's attempts to confine access under the Human Fertilization and Embryology Act 1990 to married women, is of particular relevance to lesbians and the law. Cooper is a feminist who avoids grand theories yet maintains a political vision; she balances the picture of lesbians struggling against a hostile 'state' with a recognition of the limits of state power, balanced in turn by the limitations placed on lesbian freedom by factors *outside* the state. She shows, for example, how the effectiveness of Section 13(5) – 'A woman shall not be provided with treatment services unless account has been taken of the welfare of any child who may be born as a result of the treatment, . . . including the need of that child for a father' – was restricted by the impossibility of controlling private donor insemination arrangements, and how the debate gave recognition to the hitherto oxymoronic expression 'lesbian mother'. On the other hand, the existence of Section 13(5) validated the anti-lesbian stance and actions of many people, including those working in clinics, making it difficult for lesbians to receive information and help.

Lesbians in the law school

Visiting the law department of an 'old' British university recently, I was intrigued to be told that undergraduate students were having to discuss lesbian issues in no fewer than *three* separate modules that week. Does this signify our integration? It is a fact that courses now exist in sexuality and law and women and law on many LLB degrees, and that other subjects like family law and property law may include some recognition of lesbian experience. It is a fact, too, that there are significant numbers of lesbian law teachers in British universities today, some in quite senior positions. We are part of the increased representation of women in law schools over the past twenty years and are to be found in all areas of the law (Leighton *et al.*, 1995, pp. 9, 11).

But we have a long way to go. 'We build legal careers around our lesbianism, and we erect legal careers around our lesbian closets' (Robson, 1992, p. 177). Even now, 'women' and 'sexuality' – until recently not accepted teaching or research areas in law schools – tend to be regarded as ancillary to one's *real* legal discipline (property, crime, or whatever). This increases the invisibility of lesbian law teachers whose lesbianism is still defined as a private matter by many academic lawyers. Still, the fact that law teachers whose research interests lie in the directions of women and sexuality are actually being recruited *and for that reason* – especially if they have a number of publications to their name – suggests that we have market forces (student demand) and, paradoxically, the Research Assessment Exercise to thank. Some lesbian law teachers have been role models for their students and some have been active in defence of lesbian interests by, for instance, ensuring that sexuality appears on university equal opportunities policies.

But, of course, 'including' lesbians on the staff and in law syllabuses and even 'recognizing' their particular oppressions are not, in the end, enough. Feminism came late to the law school, and we still do not speak of 'feminist law' (let alone *lesbian* law) as we speak of, for example, feminist history or literature. But feminist legal theory is a new and burgeoning field in the UK in which the lesbian experience might be expected to make a significant impact.

Lesbians and feminist legal theory

In 'Feminist Jurisprudence: Grounding the Theories', American law professor Patrician A. Cain outlines the development of feminist thinking about law, noting the virtual absence of any consideration of lesbian experience. First, feminist activists strove for *equality with men*, for equal rights and equal treatment. They wrote from an 'unquestioned heterosexual perspective' – except when they considered lesbian custody (1991, p. 265). In the second stage, feminists began to write about ways in which law needed to take account of the *differences* between women and men – for example, the fact that women became pregnant. But here again, Cain comments, 'while the focus on difference remained limited to biological differences between women and men, lesbian experience had no special insights to offer' (p. 265). Once the exploration of difference went beyond biology, other theories emerged. Robin West (1991) argued that law is a 'masculine' construction, lacking the 'feminine' values of 'connection' and 'caring'. Catharine MacKinnon (1987) explained difference in terms of power. Men and women are treated differently in law because men are dominant and women subordinate. Law reinforces and perpetuates existing inequality.

Cain is critical of both theories for failing to take account of lesbian experience. West's 'feminine' values are based on women's experience of heterosexual penetration and motherhood, not, for example, on the 'connection' experienced by lesbian lovers. MacKinnon argues that even lesbians, whom she defines as 'women having sex with women, not with men' (a definition Cain finds insulting), cannot escape the dominance/subordination model of heterosexuality:

> women's sexuality remains constructed under conditions of male supremacy; women remain socially defined as women in relation to men; the definition of women as men's inferiors remains sexual if not heterosexual, whether men are present at the time or not. (1989, pp. 141–2)

Cain's response is that MacKinnon has wilfully refused to listen to women who claim experience of non-subordination through living as lesbians (1991, p. 267).

In the third stage of feminist legal theory, postmodernism, the idea of 'one essential commonality among all women' is rejected because it fails to encompass 'the full complexity of female experience' (p. 267), which is affected by factors beyond sex and gender including race, class, age, physical ability and sexuality. Cain would not reject women's commonalities – 'When we identify what we have in common, we begin to build bridges and connections' – but she urges legal theorists not to ignore the differences – 'because any connection that fails to recognize differences is not a connection to the *whole* of the other self' (p. 269).

For Cain, being a lesbian is *not* just like being a heterosexual woman except for the sex of your lover. Being a lesbian involves risks and dangers unknown to heterosexuals, vigilance, defensiveness, lies and secrecy. Cain urges heterosexual women to try to imagine what it must be like to live like this. 'I sometimes wonder whether heterosexual women really understand the role that heterosexuality plays in the maintenance of patriarchy', she muses. 'Indeed, I sometimes wonder whether lesbians understand' (p. 270). But alongside the negative differences exist positive ones. Contrary to MacKinnon's view, we 'who live our private lives removed from the intimate presence of men do indeed experience time free from male domination. When we leave the male-dominated public sphere, we come home to a woman-identified private sphere.' Cain is not suggesting that lesbians exist outside the institution of patriarchy or that lesbian withdrawal from its private expression challenges its existence in the world outside, merely that lesbians 'experience significant periods of nonsubordination, during which we, as women, are free to develop a sense of self that is our own and not a mere construct of the patriarchy' (p. 273). Out of this lesbian experience, Cain argues, it may be possible to build a legal theory genuinely based on connection, caring and non-subordination, a *woman-centred* strategy and solution for women.

Ruthann Robson has attempted to do just that – to develop a lesbian theory of law. In *Lesbian (Out)Law* she argues that, although lesbians need to use the law to ensure our own survival, we must avoid 'domestication' or the internalization of legal norms which determine how we see ourselves, instead keeping sight of our own categories and priorities (1992, p. 70). In American discrimination cases, for example, courts seek an 'immutable identifiable characteristic' (p. 82) as the basis for discrimination. Why should we try to fit lesbianism into this definition when the reality for many of us is that our sexuality has not been immutable and we do not regard it as such?

Robson, like Cain, is critical of feminist legal theory because it tends to relate women to a male standard in pursuit of legal equality or to elide 'lesbian and gay oppression'. In both cases, she says, specifically lesbian experience is ignored. This is hardly a fair description of feminist approaches to law and, keen as she is to dissociate herself, Robson often adopts a recognizably feminist position. For example, she has difficulty supporting campaigns for the acceptance of lesbians and gays in the military, not because the discrimination is in any way justifiable, nor because 'lesbianism mandates pacifism', but because 'the allegiance to nation demanded by the military is ultimately inconsistent with lesbian survival [and] . . . lesbianism, as love for women, is inconsistent with a belief that some women should be killed because of conflicts between nations' (p. 97). To those seeking legal recognition of lesbian partnerships on a marriage model, she says: 'our quest for lesbian survival is not furthered by embracing the law's rule of marriage. Our legal energy is better directed at abolishing marriage as a state institution and *spouse* as a legal category' (p. 127). Radical feminists would not disagree!

Robson's contribution to legal theory has been widely recognized, but more, perhaps, for its symbolic value than its persuasiveness. Undoubtedly she has put lesbian experience on the agenda of feminist legal theory, from which it has been notably absent (Rush, 1995). (The usual approach, exemplified by Regina Graycar and Jenny Morgan in their book of over 400 pages, *The Hidden Gender of Law* (1990), is only to mention lesbians in the context of custody disputes.) But Robson's work has been roundly criticized for its presentation of 'lesbian' as a category that (a) needs no definition (Phelan, 1995, p. 199) and (b) represents a homogeneous group without other 'social identities' and 'ideological commitments' (Herman, 1995, pp. 181–2). Didi Herman points out that lesbians can, at times, feel more in common with those who share their race, class or politics than with other lesbians: 'Lesbian identity, in itself, does not give rise to a shared "theory" about the world or how to change it, despite some shared experience' (p. 183). Shane Phelan notes that, in urging us to centre 'lesbian interests' in our legal theory, even supposing we can identify what lesbian interests *are*, Robson seems to be saying that our 'desires are the command of the law' (p. 199). This merely privileges 'lesbian' desires above everyone else's.

While Robson is clear about the power of law to shape our social identities, she implies that once deconstructed we will find (as Didi Herman puts is) 'some kind of "natural lesbian" that both produces and *needs* her own theory' (1995, p. 183). Robson falls into the trap of giving too much power to law, even as she argues for the removal of its (domesticating) influence in our lives. And in focusing on lesbianism as an essential category, Robson ignores the relationship of sexuality to gender, a connection of central importance to feminists. As another critic has put it, 'Women are oppressed in many ways, and sexuality is only one of them' (Arriola, 1994, p. 133).

Elvia Arriola attempts a practical solution to the problem of centring lesbian experience within one area of law and legal theory. She proposes a 'holistic/irrelevancy' model for determining discrimination cases, which would recognize that a person's identity depends on a number of factors including sex, race, ethnicity, class, age *and* sexuality (p. 139). Though she writes of the American context, her model would not be out of place in the UK where the Sex Discrimination Act 1975 does a lamentably poor job of tackling women's subordination in the workplace and cannot deal at all with the interplay of multiple factors such as sex and race or sex and sexuality.

It is not insignificant that Arriola's very scholarly essay appears in the *Berkeley Women's Law Journal*, set up in 1985 to publish work about 'unrepresented women'. Every issue carries the rationale: 'The founders recognized that failing to address the differences among women implicitly allowed white, heterosexual, middle-class, able-bodied women to represent *all* women.' British law journals lag behind those of North America and Australasia in giving lesbians a voice.

All three critics discussed here, Arriola, Phelan and Herman, see the necessity for lesbian input into legal theory but reject 'lesbian legal theory' as a false direction. What we need, they seem to say, is a legal theory which not only incorporates lesbian experience but puts lesbians *with all their differences* at the centre of the analysis – because, as Herman writes rather cynically, 'if we do not do this, no one else is likely to' (1995, p. 189). But it must be a *feminist* theory – that is, one which not only rejects a universal or 'normal' heterosexuality but identifies the key role of heterosexuality in women's oppression – and which distinguishes lesbian and gay interests.

A chapter that appears in the same volume as Herman's and Phelan's essays demonstrates all too clearly what happens to women's issues when an identity of lesbian and gay interests is assumed. Anya Palmer, the (female) deputy director of Stonewall, writes:

> For lesbians and gay men in Britain, 1994 could go down in history as the year Parliament reaffirmed our status as second-class citizens by refusing to enact an equal age of consent; the year Parliament reaffirmed a system of sexual apartheid. (Palmer, 1995, p. 32)

By linking lesbians and gay men in this way, Palmer implies that *both* are subject to the 'sexual apartheid' she describes. But the age of consent referred to here has nothing to do with lesbians. Far from being discriminated against, in this respect lesbians have been *privileged* over men and heterosexuals of both sexes in having no legal regulation of the age of consent to lesbian sex.

When a notion of the common oppression of lesbians and gay men on the basis of sexuality is adopted, it is all too easy for men's concerns to be prioritized and women's separate oppression to be overlooked. Subsuming 'lesbian' into 'gay' parallels the old assimilation of 'woman' into 'man', and has the same consequence: *we disappear*. The danger has been warned against by feminists in other disciplines (Auchmuty *et al.*, 1992). The dominance of the rights discourse is particularly worrying in law, where male power is so strongly institutionalized and women's voices so often unheard (Smart, 1989). The more recent aligning of the transgendered rights movement with lesbians and gays is equally problematic for us, since transsexuals occupy a diametrically opposed theoretical position to lesbian feminists: they (literally) shape themselves to society's gender norms, while we resist them. Of the two, lesbians present a greater challenge to society, for we try to change its sex-role expectations, while transsexuals change *themselves* to conform to them (Nataf, 1996, pp. 37–43).

Conclusion

In our struggles to locate lesbian experience within feminist legal theory we have come full circle from the revolutionary feminists of the 1970s who saw lesbianism – the refusal to engage in heterosexual relations with men – as a weapon against male power, and the political lesbians, who *chose* lesbianism in an effort to live out their vision of an egalitarian society free of institutionalized male power. As both essentialist and postmodern lesbians attempt to construct legal theories based on lesbian experience, such a distinguished revolutionary feminist and political lesbian as Sheila Jeffreys is currently working on 'Prostitution as a Human Rights Issue' (Jeffreys, 1995), bringing her feminist politics within the rights discourse. The challenge for lesbians is, as Ruthann Robson puts it, to use the law to further *our* goals and *our* visions, without being used by it (Robson, 1992, p. 13). But in order to do so, we must *have* a clear vision; and for many of us – including myself – that vision must be a feminist one.

References

Alderson, L. and Wistrich, H. (1988) 'Clause 29 [*sic*]: Radical Feminist Perspectives.' *Trouble and Strife*. 13: 3–8.

Anon. (1976) 'A Case of Heads He Wins – Tails She Loses?' *Family Law*. 6: 230.

Anon. (1989) 'Developments – Sexual Orientation and the Law.' *Harvard Law Review*. 102: 1508–1671.

Arriola, E.R. (1994) 'Gendered Inequality: Lesbians, Gays, and Feminist Legal Theory.' *Berkeley Women's Law Journal*. 9: 103–43.

Auchmuty, R., Jeffreys, S. and Miller, E. (1992) 'Lesbian History and Gay Studies: Keeping a Feminist Perspective.' *Women's History Review*. 1/1: 89–108.

Bamforth, N. (1995) 'Sexuality and Law in the New Europe.' *Modern Law Review*. 58: 109–20.

Beer, C., Jeffery, R. and Munyard, T. (1983) *Gay Workers and the Law*. London: National Council for Civil Liberties, 2nd edn.

Boyd, S.B. (1992) 'What is a "Normal" Family? *C v C (A Minor) (Custody:*

Appeal).' Modern Law Review. 55: 269–78.

Brophy, J. (1985) 'Child Care and the Growth of Power: The Status of Mothers in Child Custody Disputes.' In Brophy and Smart (1985), pp. 97–116.

Brophy, J. and Smart, C. (eds) (1985) *Women-in-Law: Explorations in Law, Family and Sexuality*. London: Routledge and Kegan Paul.

Cain, P.A. (1991) 'Feminist Jurisprudence: Grounding the Theories.' In K.T. Bartlett and R. Kennedy (eds) *Feminist Legal Theory: Readings in Law and Gender*. Boulder, CO: Westview Press, pp. 263–80.

Cameron, D. and Frazer, E. (1987) *The Lust to Kill: A Feminist Investigation of Murder*. Cambridge: Polity Press.

Cohen, S., Green, S., Merryfinch, L., Jones, G., Slade, J. and Walker, M. (1978) *The Law and Sexuality: How to Cope with the Law if You're Not 100% Conventionally Heterosexual*. Manchester: Grass Roots Books.

Cooper, D. (1994) *Sexing the City: Lesbian and Gay Politics within the Activist State*. London: Rivers Oram Press.

Cooper, D. (1995) *Power in Struggle: Feminism, Sexuality and the State*. Buckingham: Open University Pres.

Crane, P. (1982) *Gays and the Law*. London: Pluto Pres.

Faraday, A. (1988) 'Lesbian Outlaws: Past Attempts to Legislate Against Lesbians.' *Trouble and Strife*. 13: 9–16.

Galloway, B. (ed.) (1983) *Prejudice and Pride: Discrimination against Gay People in Modern Britain*. London: Routledge and Kegan Paul.

Graycar, R. and Morgan, J. (1990) *The Hidden Gender of Law*. Sydney: Federation Press.

Herman, D. (1994) *Rights of Passage: Struggles for Lesbian and Gay Legal Equality*. Toronto: University of Toronto Press.

Herman, D. (1995) 'A Jurisprudence of One's Own? Ruthann Robson's Lesbian Legal Theory.' In A. Wilson (ed.) *A Simple Matter of Justice?: Theorizing Lesbian and Gay Politics*. London: Cassell, pp. 176–92.

Jeffreys, S. (1985) 'Prostitution.' In rhodes and McNeill (1985), pp. 59–70.

Jeffreys, S. (1995) 'Prostitution as a Human Rights Issue.' Paper given to the MA Women's Studies course, University of Westminster, July.

Kappeler, S. (1986) *The Pornography of Representation*. Cambridge: Polity Press.

Kelly, L. (1988a) 'What's in a Name?: Defining Child Sexual Abuse.' *Feminist Review*. 28: 65–73.

Kelly L. (1988b) 'The US Ordinances: Censorship or Radical Law Reform?' In G. Chester and J. Dickey (eds) *Feminism and Censorship: The Current Debate*. Bridgeport, Dorset: Prism Press, pp. 52–61.

Kelly, L. (1988c) *Surviving Sexual Violence*. Cambridge: Polity Press.

Kelly, L. (1989a) 'Bitter Ironies: The Professionalisation of Child Sexual Abuse.' *Trouble and Strife*. 16: 14–21.

Kelly, L. (1989b) 'Our Issues, Our Analysis: Two Decades of Work on Sexual Violence.' In C. Jones and P. Mahony (eds) *Learning Our Lines: Sexuality and Social Control in Education*. London: The Women's Press, pp. 129–56.

Kelly, L. (1990a) 'Journeying in Reverse: Possibilities and Problems in Feminist Research on Sexual Violence.' In L. Gelsthorpe and A. Morris (eds) *Feminist Perspectives in Criminology*. Milton Keynes: Open University Press, pp. 107–14.

Kelly, L. (1990b) 'Abuse in the Making: The Production and Use of Pornography.' *Trouble and Strife*. 19: 32–7.

Kennedy, H. (1992) *Eve Was Framed: Women and British Justice*. London: Vintage.

Leeds Revolutionary Feminist Group (1981) 'Political Lesbianism: The Case Against Heterosexuality.' In *Love Your Enemy? The Debate between Heterosexual Feminism and Political Lesbianism*. London: Onlywomen Press.

Leighton, P., Mortimer, T. and Whatley, N. (1995) *Today's Law Teachers: Lawyers or Academics?* London: Cavendish.

Lorde, A. (1984) *Sister Outsider: Essays and Speeches*. Freedom, CA: The Crossing Pres.
McIntosh, M. (1988) 'Introduction to an Issue: Family Secrets as Public Drama.' *Feminist Review*. 28: 6–15.
MacKinnon, C. (1987) *Feminism Unmodified: Discourses on Life and Law*. London: Harvard University Press.
MacKinnon, C. (1989) *Toward a Feminist Theory of the State*. London: Harvard University Press.
Maggiore, D.J. (ed.) (1992) *Lesbians and Child Custody: A Casebook*. New York and London: Garland Publishing.
Maidment, S. (1984) *Child Custody and Divorce*. Beckenham, Kent: Croom Helm.
Maidment, S. (1985) 'Women and Childcare: The Paradox of Divorce.' In S. Edwards (ed.) *Gender, Sex and the Law*. Beckenham, Kent: Croom Helm, pp. 28–49.
Nataf, Z.I. (1996) *Lesbians Talk Transgender*. London: Scarlet Press.
O'Donovan, K. (1993) *Family Law Matters*. London: Pluto Press.
Palmer, A. (1995) 'Lesbian and Gay Rights Campaigning: A Report from the Coalface.' In A.R. Wilson (ed.) *A Simple Matter of Justice?: Theorizing Lesbian and Gay Politics*. London: Cassell, pp. 32–50.
Phelan, S. (1995) 'The Space of Justice: Lesbians and Democratic Politics.' In A.R Wilson (ed.) *A Simple Matter of Justice?: Theorizing Lesbian and Gay Politics*. London: Cassell, pp. 192–220.
Polikoff, N.D. (1986) 'Lesbian Mothers, Lesbian Families: Legal Obstacles, Legal Challenges.' In Maggiore (1992), pp. 229–37.
Radford, J. (1982) 'Marriage Licence or Licence to Kill? Womanslaughter in the Criminal Law.' *Feminist Review*. 11: 88–96.
Radford, J. and Kelly, L. (1995) 'Self Preservation: Feminist Activism and Feminist Jurisprudence.' In M. Maynard and J. Purvis (eds) *(Hetero)sexual Politics*. London: Taylor and Francis, pp. 186–99.
Radford, J. and Russell, D.E.H. (eds) (1992) *Femicide: The Politics of Woman Killing*. Buckingham: Open University Press.
rhodes, d. and McNeill, S. (eds) (1985) *Women Against Violence Against Women*. London: Onlywomen Press.
Rich, A. (1981) *Compulsory Heterosexuality and Lesbian Existence*. (pamphlet). London: Onlywomen Press. Also in A. Rich (1986) *Blood, Bread and Poetry: Selected Prose 1979–1985*. London: Virago, pp. 23–75.
Rights of Women (1984) *Lesbian Mothers on Trial: A Report on Lesbian Mothers and Child Custody*. London: Rights of Women.
Rights of Women Custody Group (1986) *Lesbian Mothers' Legal Handbook*. London: The Women's Press.
Robson, R. (1992) *Lesbian (Out)Law: Survival under the Rule of Law*. Ithaca, NY: Firebrand Books.
Rodgerson, G. and Wilson, E. (eds) (1991) *Pornography and Feminism: The Case Against Censorship, by Feminists Against Censorship*. London: Lawrence and Wishart.
Rush, S.E. (1995) 'Sexual Orientation: A Plea for Inclusion.' *Berkeley Women's Law Journal*. 10: 69–78.
Smart, C. (1984) *The Ties that Bind: Law, Marriage and the Reproduction of Patriarchal Relations*. London: Routledge and Kegan Paul.
Smart, C. (1989) *Feminism and the Power of Law*. London: Routledge.
Tasker, F.L. and Golombok, S. (1991) 'Children Raised by Lesbian Mothers: The Empirical Evidence.' *Family Law*. 21: 184–7.
Tong, R. (1984) *Women, Sex, and the Law*. New York: Rowman and Allanheld.
Waaldijk, K. and Clapham, A. (eds) (1993) *Homosexuality: A European Community Issue – Essays on Lesbian and Gay Rights in European Law and Policy*. Dordrecht: Martinus Nijhoff.
West, R. (1991) 'Jurisprudence and Gender.' In K. Bartlett and R. Kennedy (eds) *Feminist Legal Theory: Readings in Law and Gender*. Boulder, CO: Westview Press, pp. 201–34.

4

Born Queer? Lesbians Interrogate Biology

Lynda Birke

> We know that our sexual orientation, like our tastes in music and our memory of our last vacation, is engraved in some morphological or chemical substrate in the brain.
>
> Heterosexual intercourse [is] so simple, one hardly needs a brain to do it.
>
> (both quotations from Simon LeVay, *The Sexual Brain*, 1993, pp. 47 and 108)

'Born queer': an evocative phrase. Undoubtedly, many people do feel that they were 'born with' the sexuality that they now express: for them, the feelings that they identify in adulthood as, say, lesbian, were remembered so early in life that it can only feel inborn. Perhaps, then, that feeling of being born queer reflects some difference in an underlying biology – perhaps a genetic difference, or some subtle alteration in the brain. That, at least, is the thinking behind several recent attempts to delineate a biological link to homosexuality.

Scientists have long sought a biological indicator of gayness, something which bodily marks us off from the others. In these days of queer politics, and an insistence on sexuality and gender as performance, I sometimes find it hard to remember how lesbians used to have abnormal bodies. Not literally, I hasten to add, but in medical discourse, which flourished in earlier decades with the scientific search for some stigmata of 'the' lesbian body.

While scientists no longer overtly seek the characteristics of the 'lesbian body' the focus of scientific enquiry has now switched to the brain and to genes. Perhaps the differentness of lesbians or gay men can be located hidden away in the folds of the brain? In 1991, for example, Simon LeVay published the results of experiments which were reported in the press as demonstrating the existence of a 'sex centre' in the brain. Gay men, he suggested, had a sex centre that looked very like that of straight women. More recently, we have witnessed claims for a 'gay gene' – a gene allegedly found in gay men that they inherited from their mothers (Hamer and Copeland, 1994). Biology, it would seem, is indeed what makes us gay or straight.

Being a biologist, as well as a feminist and a lesbian, I cannot take such claims lying down, so to speak. I have to take them seriously; by that I mean that I take them seriously enough to criticize them. I do not believe that there is any substantive evidence to support the claims. Over the years, I have therefore spent much time and energy refuting the allegations that any social categories (of gender, race or sexuality) are fixed by biology. Like many other feminist biologists, I have assembled ammunition against biological determinism (Fausto-Sterling, 1992; Hubbard, 1990; Birke, 1986); among other things, this entails emphasizing the complexity and cultural variability of desire. This political strategy has been necessary in order to oppose crass claims about the naturalness of male dominance, lesbians-who-want-to-be-men, and so on. But it has not been without problems, as I shall argue. Among other things, there are many among our communities who do feel – like Cherrie Moraga in 'The Voices of the Fallers' (Moraga, 1983) – that they were 'born queer'. How does that fit with my refusal of biological stories?

Here, now, I am asked to write about the field of biology and lesbianism: what, the editors asked, has lesbian politics contributed to the 'straight' practice of my discipline, to biology and biological ideas – if anything? My first thought was that there was enough to say about biological theories of lesbianism; so, the first part of the chapter looks critically at some of these. But there was little indeed that I might say positively about the straight study of biology and how it might have been modified by lesbianism and/or feminism. However, my second thoughts reminded me of the growing literature on embodiment. Although much of this comes from philosophy and the social sciences, it has begun – at last – to recognize the significance of the 'biological' body in becoming who we are. In the second part of this chapter, then, I want to link these debates about embodiment to lesbian studies – preferably without recourse to 'the' lesbian body of 1940s medical journals.

Creating the invert

It's tricky being a lesbian biologist; the discursive diet of biology is one in which reproduction is the highest aim of organisms. Spreading the genes around in (hetero)sexual intercourse is what everyone seeks to do in biological texts: the 'selfish gene' is quintessentially a straight one. This makes homosexuality rather awkward – for what are we doing on the earth if we are not spreading our genes? Leaving aside the fact that there are many gay parents in the world, the problem has led to speculations about how gay-ness could arise, biologically; if it fails to spread genes, then why has it not simply disappeared? The answer, apparently, may lie in our willingness to help siblings raise *their* young.)

As a young girl, I learned that those secret longings for older girls were thought to be abnormal, just as was my desire *not* to reproduce. I learned, too, that those desires were associated with the dreaded L-word, signifying a person who had an abnormal body and looked like a man. That I encountered this stereotype is not surprising: even if I never saw her on the streets, she certainly existed in the minds of medical men. Journal articles of the 1950s and 1960s claimed to have found 'wide shoulders, narrow hips, irregular menses, and protruding clitoris' among lesbians (see examples in Birke, 1980). Perhaps it is just as well that I did not read medical articles as a child.

This stereotype was assumed never to have had children; yet, when the medical reports did go so far as to mention a control group, the controls might well turn out to be straight (usually married) women with kids. If lesbians did emerge from these studies as different from straight women, it would not be too great a surprise.

The 'mannish lesbian', with a masculine physique, is a well-established stereotype, much described in the sexology books of the late nineteenth century. The 'true invert' was mannish and 'born that way', like Stephen Gordon in Radclyffe Hall's *The Well of Loneliness*. The corollary of this image is the argument that the cause of lesbianism lies in some mishap of development that tips the balance towards masculinity. Accordingly, Karl Ulrichs, in the 1890s, suggested that homosexuality might arise if the brain failed to develop into proper 'male' or 'female' forms. There is, he suggested, an intermediate stage, representing a 'third sex' – the invert.

Belief in 'the invert' could not, of course, have developed until 'the homosexual' had become defined as a specific type of person, as Foucault has emphasized. As different kinds of sexualities, attached to different kinds of persons, emerged in the nineteenth century, so there followed explanations for how such diversity of persons arose. And just as differences between women and men became increasingly codified and defined in terms of underlying biology throughout that century (Jordanova, 1991), so too did the body of 'the' lesbian become a biological problem to be explained.

The development, during the nineteenth century, of the theory of evolution made the existence of these special beings a greater problem still. Darwin's insistence on sexual selection as a force in evolutionary change helped to prioritize (hetero)sexual reproduction in the discourse of science. If females are a scarce resource, the modern version of this story goes, then males compete for females. As a result, there is selection over time for those males who are better at attracting female attention – perhaps by having a bigger, brighter tail or showier plumage. (An amusing – if somewhat biologically inaccurate – cartoon shows two peahens looking unimpressed at the peacock's display of his big, bright tail: 'Cut the crap', they chorus, 'show us your willy.')

So, by the turn of the twentieth century, science had produced an account of *why* heterosexuality was so dominant, rooted in the age-old conflation of heterosexual behaviour with procreation. It had also indirectly produced accounts of how heterosexuality was the norm, as tales abounded of the biological causes of the abnormality of 'deviant' sexualities. As the twentieth century progressed, scientists began to discover the sex steroids – the hormones popularly (and somewhat erroneously) referred to as male and female hormones (for history, see Oudshoorn, 1994). Once these hormones were discovered, and labelled by gender (that is, named as 'male' or 'female'), then the hunt was on for abnormalities of such hormones in homosexuals. During the 1940s, a number of papers emerged suggesting that gay men had too little, and lesbians too much, of the 'male hormones' (such as testosterone). If so, then corrective hormone treatment might make them normal – or so the reasoning went. It did nothing of the sort.

After that failure, the next milestone (or millstone) on the path towards a biological theory of gender and/or sexuality was the development of the organizational theory of brain development. According to this, the brain was permanently 'organized' in gendered directions by the action of hormones during early foetal development. Sloshing the brain around in male hormones led to the brain becoming male; in their absence, the brain becomes female (for critiques of this theory, see Van den Wijngaard, 1995; Birke, 1989). The sexism implied by the theory is reminiscent of Freud's characterization of woman as lack; in this case, it is lack of the appropriate hormones that were supposed to lead to female development. To become a *real* male (that is, heterosexual), the foetus needed to have just the right dose of macho testosterone, at just the right time. Not enough, and you end up as a gay male, or worse, female.

An important characteristic of this century of seeking the underlying biology is that it is only the effeminate male or the mannish female who counts in the biological stakes. Butch gay men, or femme lesbians, aren't usually categorized as homosexual in scientific accounts. Even when scientists claimed to have created 'homosexual rats', through hormonal manipulations, it was only those male rats who were *being* mounted who counted. The male stud rats who did the mounting were, of course, respectably heterosexual.

The latest story in the hormonal saga is Simon LeVay's claim that he has identified a nucleus in the brain (called, for short, the INAH3) that differs between gay and straight men. Unfortunately, he tells us, he was unable to find any lesbian brains, so his comparison was between gay/straight men, and women, presumed straight. The supposition here derives from the rat studies: LeVay believes that there are male rats who are homosexual and who therefore have 'female' brains, as a result of experimental exposure to lower-than-normal levels of male hormones while they were young. This, he supposes, affects the development of the putative 'sex centre', deep in the part of the brain called the hypothalamus. From here, he hypothesizes that early exposure of the human brain to hormones might have an effect on adult sexuality. Thus began his search for a bit of the brain that looks different by gender and/or sexual orientation (for an excellent critique of this and similar studies, see Fausto-Sterling, 1992).

On the whole, much of this search for a biological substrate has focused on gay men and how they might have become feminized; a focus on lesbians is (thankfully) rarer. At one level, it seems irrelevant to the lives of many lesbians; I simply do not care how I 'got to be this way'. Perhaps I was a tomboy in my mother's womb. Many gay activists and feminists would insist that our sexuality is socially constructed, and complexly produced. Biological explanations seem irrelevant and grossly simplistic. Yet there are two reasons why we cannot simply dismiss biologism. The first is that some of the recent claims for a biological base have come from scientists who are themselves gay. While not always explicitly stated, part of the motivation to look to biology for explanations relates to the growing power, in the USA, of religious fundamentalism. Religious rhetoric insists that homosexuality is chosen, and a sin. If chosen, then we can repent and behave ourselves (preferably by pursuing the other sex). Unnervingly, some of this stuff repeats exactly the kind of critique of the biological arguments that feminist biologists have long made, focusing for example on the methodological problems with the research. An appeal to a biological cause, then, serves a political purpose for lesbian and gay communities: if homosexuality is inborn, then we can seek civil rights because we are born that way.

The second reason for caution is that biological explanations often lead to attempts at 'cures': the sorry history of medicine's involvement in gay people's lives is testimony to such intervention, from hormone and electric shock 'treatments' to removal of part of the brain. And no doubt the religious right can alter their doctrine, from sin to sickness: absolution with pills.

'Biological' accounts of homosexuality are not new, just as there have long been stories of the biological inevitability of patriarchy and of women's place by the kitchen sink. In that sense, LeVay's experiments have a long, if dishonourable, tradition in the search for hormonal effects on the brain. But the claims that scientists have found a gene 'for' homosexuality are breaking new ground. Genetics has now taken over from the hormonal studies of recent decades. In the last twenty years, there has been an unprecedented growth in genetic research, fuelled in part by what some scientists have euphorically called the search for the 'Holy Grail' of biology; by this they mean the multimillion dollar project to map all human genes – the Human Genome Project. An aspect of this project is the search for specific genes that are connected to specific diseases. There is no doubt that some genetic diseases cause terrible suffering and early death – cystic fibrosis and thalassaemia, for example. But, as many critics have warned, there is a potential danger of moving toward a slippery slope: where do we draw the line? If we abort foetuses with genes for nasty diseases (the only answer at present to detecting such genes) then what next? Do we start selecting for babies with particular characteristics? Such as not having the gay gene?

Such eugenic anxieties aside, modern biology is heavily dominated by molecular genetics. In turn, the discourse of genetics itself feeds the belief that our complex human characteristics are merely a product of a genetic blueprint. Hence, the literature is littered with claims of genes 'for' not only homosexuality, but 'for' schizophrenia, 'for' conformity, 'for' learning disabilities, and so on. This language is deeply problematic – partly on epistemological grounds[1] and partly because it reinforces the notion that there are specific kinds of individual. The *damatis personae* multiply in the genetic lexicon. Not only do we now have the homosexual as a specific entity but genetics also helps to define 'the' learning disabled, 'the' biologically determined criminal, and many more. The stage is thus set for individuals to bear the blame for their 'condition'; we thus need look no longer at, say, the problems with an underfunded education service to explain learning difficulties (Hubbard and Wald, 1993).

Science is supposed to be about the pursuit of truth, about discovering the ways of nature. Sometimes, scientific experiment leads to surprising discoveries; at other times, it seems merely to prove what most people already know. One example of the latter in my files is a paper reporting the amazing discovery that there is increased blood flow to a woman's vagina as she orgasms. Stating the obvious, one might have thought, though no doubt the scientists got a grant to study the phenomenon. And that is precisely the point about studies of 'biological bases' of homosexuality. Such studies – given homophobia and the underlying assumption of the primacy of reproduction – are likely to be taken seriously within the scientific community. What that means is that, among other things, such studies are likely to get grants and to be published. Anne Fausto-Sterling (1992) has pointed out how the prestigious American journal *Science* ran the article submitted by LeVay, even though the data were dubious. As she emphasized, a paper on some other topic would probably never have got past the peer review process. Not only that, but the journal failed to run many of the critical reviews or letters that were subsequently submitted. And after *Science* came all the media coverage that ensured the notion of 'gay brains' became widely known.

Boundaries and contagion?

In 'Epistemology of the Closet', Eve Kosofsky Sedgwick (1993) points out the paradox of cultural insistence on defending the boundaries of heterosexuality against potentially contagious homosexuality, while simultaneously demanding belief in 'the' homosexual. For our culture cannot have it both ways. If homosexuality is dangerous enough to worry so many heterosexuals, if there is the possibility of same-sex desire lurking in the heart of every god-fearing married couple, then it cannot be built into the body of a special kind of person.

It occurs to me that, despite my suggestion of similarity between the claims about hormones/brains and those about genes for homosexuality, there are also differences. Both, certainly, are rooted in discourses of procreation. Yet there are differences, I suggest, within the similarity – specifically, in the way that each of these theories might endanger the god-fearing. If a scientist tells me that my brain is permanently etched by hormones sloshing around long before I was born, then I am, presumably, unlikely to endanger anyone (except perhaps in the guise of predatory or vampiric lesbian). But genes are another matter: as socio-biologists so often remind us, genes are for spreading around. In that sense, they can become a threat to the stability of heterosexuality. What happens to that sacred institution if we who have these aberrant genes start following our biological imperative? It is no wonder that there is so often an outcry when lesbian parenting is discussed. Genes are suspiciously contagious.

It seems to me quite ironic that, while biological theories (allegedly) may serve to deflect homophobic concerns from the notion of contagion, the genetic story also reinvents contagion. It does so through the narrative of 'spreading genes around': to be reproductively successful, an individual needs to ensure that plenty of his or her genes are passed on to the next generation. The best bet for doing this is to do as many other creatures, and reproduce asexually (for example, by budding off a new individual). The new individual is genetically the same as the old one, so ensuring that all the genes are passed on. But some species, including humans, rely on the dangerous procedures of sexual reproduction, which involves the tricky business of getting your genes mixed up with, and diluted by, someone else's. And who knows? Even the most apparently heterosexual person might find that they have gay offspring; no doubt the other parent supplied the suspicious gene.

The scientific stories are, like all of science, part of the wider culture. Michèle Aina Barale points out that

> Heterosexuality . . . seeks to create lesbians whose desires are as apprehensible as its own . . . the lesbian body itself is made the site for such self-depiction. . . . By according lesbians the Butch's assumed 'male' body or the Femme's supposed 'female' body, the Otherness of same-sex desire is rendered knowable. (1991, p. 237)

The narratives of science do just that: whether they depict the 'lesbian rat', the sexual antics of chimpanzees or the brains of humans, scientific tales recreate homosexual desire as a reflection of heterosexual desire, but a desire in which something is amiss. It does so by reinforcing the myth that some lesbians are masculinized, inhabiting a 'male' body. Barale analyses the ways in which lesbian bodies are represented in cover illustrations for various editions of *The Well of Loneliness*; in these, she suggests, can be found covert references to the myth of clitoral enlargement among 'mannish' lesbians. Only thus can lesbian activities be understood.

Yet it is precisely that (alleged) similarity of lesbian desire to heterosexual that makes it dangerous. Where danger lurks, however, the knight on white charger gallops in; in writing stories of brains that lack, or hormones that don't quite make it, science saves the day. Thus, not only is homosexuality an abnormality of brain or hormone, it also fails by the standards of reproduction. 'One vagina plus another vagina still equals zero', averred Reuben (1970) in *Everything You Always Wanted to Know about Sex*; two women together cannot spread their genes around, unless they enlist the help of a (suitably phallic) syringe.

Feminist questions?

From that rather sorry history, I would like to be able to move on to something more positive, perhaps an identification of ways in which the content and practice of biological studies have changed in response to either feminism or lesbian politics. But the page would be blank. Lesbians, like women generally, are notable largely for their (apparent) absence as practitioners of science.[2]

In so far as feminism has impacted on biology, it has done so mainly in the work of feminists working in biology who put forward detailed critiques and sketched out ways in which biology might be done differently (for example, essays in Birke and Hubbard, 1995; Fausto-Sterling, 1992). Feminist ideas have thus influenced the way that researchers see primate societies, as Donna Haraway (1991) has noted; from tales of dominant males accompanied by harems that dominated the field in the 1940s, feminist influences have ensured that we can now read about the role of females as the focus of social groups.

Whether because of feminist influences or not, there are also now more accounts that acknowledge the possibility of homosexual behaviour in non-human animals. The bonobo, or pygmy chimpanzee, for instance, is said to engage in 'lesbian' encounters. To be fair, there have been reports of homosexual behaviour among animals for some time, but these have tended to remain in the background.

The dominant paradigm of biology, however, remains that of reproduction. So, even lesbian behaviour among (say) seagulls must be explained in terms of reproductive success (helping relatives). If chimpanzees escape partly from the reproductive straitjacket in the way they are described, then I suspect this has something to do with their closeness to humans. Increasingly, the other apes are becoming drawn into a widening circle of beings who are accorded sentiency. In that sense, they are moved into different categories from non-primate animals. Is that why the narratives of science have begun to allow them deviant sexualities – because other animals are described in terms that imply reproduction machines?

In other areas of biology, the work of feminists has generally sought to challenge biological determinism – including claims that lesbians are created by some biological mishap. In part, our challenge has relied mostly on critiques that emphasize the important role of social and cultural factors; thus we might for instance discuss the cultural variability of lesbian sexuality and the enormous differences among us in the ways that we express it (for example, Fausto-Sterling, 1992; Birke, 1980).

Feminist work on science has had to deal with the existence of biological determinism. Yet this literature, which has developed considerably since the early 1980s, is, I believe, rather less heterosexual than many other areas of women's studies. Marilyn Frye, writing about her experiences of teaching and researching as a lesbian in women's studies, notes that 'The predominance of heterosexual perspectives, values, commitments, thought, and vision is usually so complete and ubiquitous that it cannot be perceived, for lack of contrast' (1982, p. 194). With that I must agree; that too is my experience of much of women's studies. But in some ways, the growing feminist concern with science seems less so (not least because some of the tiny band of feminist theorists working on science are lesbians themselves).

The scientific narratives are both familiar and predictable. Yet just as predictable must be the response of critical biologists; we are doomed always to challenge the scientific claims from within. We must note that there is evidence against the claims – they are bad science, for example. This move, while necessary as a form of challenge within the discourses of science, is an example of what Sandra Harding (1986) calls 'feminist empiricism': it is based on an empiricist assumption that 'better science' can be done. We can often point to deficiencies in the studies that might lead to reasonable doubt. One example is LeVay's study, in which he obtained data from only forty-one brains, and could not be sure of the sexual histories involved (Fausto-Sterling, 1992). The empiricist response comes in handy when talking to scientists (not for them such dataless notions as Butler's concept of gender performativity!). But, as Harding emphasizes, feminist empiricism implicitly assumes that we *can* do a 'better' science, as though science can be done in a way that is value-free. The trouble with that assumption is that none of us quite believes it. Feminist biologists regard science as always in culture, and so always embedded in socio-cultural values.[3]

In line with that set of beliefs, another side of feminist work in biology has sought to develop alternative approaches to research, to write different narratives, in Haraway's (1991) evocative phrase. This might, for example, entail emphasizing ways in which foetal development (of humans or animals) is a complex product of many interacting factors: that is, how we develop and become what we are or look like emerges out of many factors, 'biological', cultural and environmental. It is meaningless to try to pick them apart. It is just as meaningless to see 'the biological' as some kind of bedrock, ultimately separable from everything else. By this I mean that there is a tendency in some feminist writing to speak of 'the biological' as though it is foundational, the basis on which gender is written. We cannot, therefore, do much about it, while we concentrate on the details of social constructionism. But this implied view should be challenged; on the contrary, our 'biological' bodies and how they work are intimately products of culture: one transforms the other (Birke and Vines, 1987).

The insistence on complexity and transformability, rather than assuming that everything has simple one-to-one causes, is important in order to move away from biological determinism. Even in animals it is possible to demonstrate that 'biological' factors such as hormones do not act in isolation. Thus, from the observation that there are differences in the frequency of some behaviours between female and male in some populations of animals (males might mount more than females, for instance, or engage in more play – on average), researchers have looked for something inside the *individual* animals that might lead to population differences. Usually, they look at hormones as possible causes of 'sex differences'. That is, from a statement about a population average, we move to what is happening inside individual bodies. But, even in the humble laboratory rat, hormones do not act in isolation. If the researcher gives a hormone injection to a rat pup during an experiment, the other rat behaves differently towards it: so how can we even begin to separate out the effects? How much is due to the hormone and how much to the hormone's effect on mum? And what about the brothers and sisters?

Telling different stories is one way that feminist biologists have influenced the practice of biology. To be sure, it has done little to push the juggernaut of biological determinism off course. What it does do, though, is to create a space for alternative stories. In that space is a plurality of possibilities rather than a simple boy-meets-girl tale, and biology is only part of these complex possibilities rather than an underlying imperative.

Part of the alternative narrative must be a rejection of the assumption that sexuality is either inborn or 'chosen' – an opposition much favoured by the religious right in the USA. They argue against the 'born queer' line precisely on the basis that if we have 'chosen' to be queer, then we can jolly well unchoose it and stop sinning. Choice is a funny word though: it seems, in their rhetoric, to conjure up images of consumer choice at the supermarket. It might be fun to think of buying a lesbian at Safeway along with the washing powder, but the element of choice is not quite like that. To me, 'choice' might have entered my decisions early in life, but I don't think I 'choose' to be anything now; I can imagine that that could just as well feel as though I was born lesbian.

So, telling different stories must be part of our practice; we need, I would argue, to reject tales of inborn (hence, biological) versus 'choice' (hence, cultural). The 'biological' tales in turn rely on a particular narrative of procreation – itself a cultural product. In these narratives, 'nature' is not so much red in tooth and claw as forever pregnant.

The queer challenge

It is, I think, from outside science that the main challenges to biological determinism arise. Notions of 'queer' emphasize, for example, how boundaries can never be fixed and can be transgressed: they emphasize, indeed, the cultural production of plural possibilities of sexual expression. Moreover, they refute the easy elision between gender and sexuality that runs through the pages of medical textbooks: lesbian equals masculine, gay man equals feminine. In line with these developments, writers such as Judith Butler insist on moving away from earlier notions of lesbian identity (who or what is a lesbian?) and ask us to consider gender and sexuality as performance (Butler, 1990).

It is in thinking about lesbian sexuality as performance that we can see the contrast between the 'mannish lesbian' inhabiting the strange pages of the medical journals and the lesbians in our communities. The lesbian represented in those pages has desires that are believed to be 'male'; indeed, she *is*, in some senses, male in so far as she is said to have over-masculinized hormones/brain/genes. The notion that she could be consciously taking on this role does not enter medical discourse. Moreover, this representation of the lesbian does not allow her any sexuality as performance except in the sense of an inevitable acting out of her genetic or hormonally induced desires. The notion of 'butch in the street and femme between the sheets' becomes impossible in the medical lexicon.

Yet it is precisely in the alleged 'mannishness' of butch roles that we can find a challenge to notions of biological innateness. Sue-Ellen Case notes the reclamation of butch/femme play from what she calls the feminist closet (a point also made by Joan Nestle, 1987). That play of seduction, of performance, is wilful – and so unlikely to be an inevitability wired into the genes. In her advocacy of a 'butch-femme aesthetic' Case argues, for example, that

> In recuperating the space of seduction, the butch-femme couple can, through their own agency, move through a field of symbols . . . playfully inhabiting the camp space of irony and wit, free from biological determinism, elitist essentialism, and the heterosexist cleavage of sexual difference. (1993, p. 305)

At present, playful border crossings, camp irony and spaces of seduction do indeed challenge the rigid borders of biological categories: as far as mainstream biological thinking is concerned, sexuality equals reproduction. Everything outside that does not count (including, of course, non-procreative sexual practices between heterosexual partners). It is within lesbian/gay/queer communities that these challenges are most obvious. Yet, within many of those same communities, there is also a risk of a reclamation of biological determinism. For it is precisely around the possibility of transgender/ transsexualism that medical – hence biological – interventions become increasingly possible. Transsexualism often means hormone treatments; sometimes it means surgical transformation. Here, the biological seems to fix into flesh precisely through its potential to effect bodily change.

Medical discourse is slow to change. It may be a long time before it catches up with the possibility of playful border crossings - and perhaps it never will. But it *does,* already, have a language for its own expression of border crossing, in the guise of transsexual surgeries. Marjorie Garber has described how the medical interventions and language of transsexualism form part of the efforts to fix sex and gender; yet, paradoxically, such efforts 'serve only to reveal . . . the instability and insubstantiality of each of those categories' (1993, p. 321). She goes on to conclude that 'transsexualism demonstrates that essentialism *is* social construction'.

At a theoretical level, of course we need – as Garber suggests – to deconstruct the binary of constructionism versus essentialism (but see Fuss, 1989). Yet in doing so there is a danger that we move so far into cultural constructions that we lose sight of the ways in which biomedicine has the power to exert *material* effects on our lives. In her analysis of the scientific work involved in discovering the sex hormones, Nelly Oudshoorn (1994) notes how powerful have been the discourses of biomedicine in shaping our understandings of gendered bodies and hormones. But the science is more than just narrative, she points out: it has also had the power to produce hormonal drugs which can have profound effects on our lives – for good and ill. Instability of categories may indeed be revealed by medical attempts further to fix gender. But they also reveal the persistent power of modern medicine both to exert control over our bodily lives and also to (re-)create the categories by which sexuality and gender are discursively constructed.

Biological thought can certainly be analysed in terms of its narratives; that insight is, perhaps, one of the more important interventions into science made by lesbians and feminists. But lesbians must never lose sight of one important point: there are material consequences of biomedical narratives which go beyond the theoretical destabilization of categories. These are narratives which can seriously damage our health.

Notes

1. That is, what genes, in the form of DNA, actually do is that they contain the information that enables the cell in which they reside to make proteins. Proteins, in turn, can serve as the building blocks of cells and tissues, or they might be enzymes (which help to speed up various chemical reactions). That is fine as far as it goes. But it is a huge leap of faith to move from the chemical instructions for protein manufacture to complex human socio-cultural behaviour(s).
2. Which is not to say that lesbians *are* absent – after all, I am myself a scientist! There are, moreover, several networks of lesbians in science (see Hynes, 1982).
3. This is not to say that all values or accounts of the world are equally valid. Feminist biologists generally do not go that far. Some accounts are better because they are more socially representative or inclusive – what Harding calls 'strong objectivity'. I would argue, then, that feminist accounts are better than androcentric ones precisely because feminists do seek to acknowledge the knower and his or her social location.

References

Abelove, H., Barale, M.A. and Halperin, D.M. (eds) (1993) *The Lesbian and Gay Studies Reader.* London: Routledge.

Barale, M.A. (1991) 'Below the Belt: (Un)covering *The Well of Loneliness.*' In D. Fuss (1991).

Birke, L. (1980) 'From Zero to Infinity: Scientific Views of Lesbians.' In Brighton Women and Science Group (eds) *Alice through the Microscope: The Power of Science over Women's Lives.* London: Virago.

Birke, L. (1986) *Women, Feminism and Biology: The Feminist Challenge.* Brighton: Harvester.

Birke, L. (1989) 'How Do Gender Differences in Behavior Develop? A Reanalysis of the Role of Early Experience.' In P.P.G. Bateson and P.H. Klopfer (eds) *Perspectives in Ethology, 8: Whither Ethology?* New York: Plenum Press.

Birke, L. and Hubbard, R. (eds) (1995) *Reinventing Biology: Respect for Life and the Creation of Knowledge.* Bloomington, IN: Indiana University Press.

Birke, L. and Vines, G. (1987) 'Beyond Nature vs. Nurture: Process and Biology in the Development of Gender.' *Women's Studies International Forum.* 10/5: 555–70.

Butler, J. (1990) *Gender Trouble: Feminism and the Subversion of Identity*. London: Routledge.

Case, S.-E. (1993) 'Toward a Butch-Femme Aesthetic.' In Abelove *et al.* (1993).

Fausto-Sterling, A. (1992) *Myths of Gender: Biological Theories about Women and Men*. New York: Basic Books.

Frye, M. (1982) 'A Lesbian Perspective on Women's Studies.' In M. Cruikshank (ed.) *Lesbian Studies: Present and Future*. New York: The Feminist Press.

Fuss, D. (1989) *Essentially Speaking: Feminism, Nature and Difference*. London: Routledge.

Fuss, D. (ed.) (1991) *Inside/Out: Lesbian Theories, Gay Theories*. London: Routledge.

Garber, M. (1993) 'Spare Parts: The Surgical Construction of Gender.' In Abelove *et al.* (1993).

Hamer, D. and Copeland, P. (1994) *The Science of Desire: The Search for the Gay Gene and the Biology of Behavior*. New York: Simon and Schuster.

Haraway, D. (1989) *Primate Visions*. London: Routledge.

Haraway, D. (1991) *Simians, Cyborgs and Women*. London: Free Association Press.

Harding, S. (1986) *The Science Question in Feminism*. Milton Keynes: Open University Press.

Hubbard, R. (1990) *The Politics of Women's Biology*. New Brunswick and London: Rutgers University Press.

Hubbard, R. and Wald, E. (1993) *Exploding the Gene Myth*. Boston: Beacon Press.

Hynes, H.P. (1982) 'Towards a Laboratory of One's Own: Lesbians in Science.' In M. Cruikshank (ed.) *Lesbian Studies: Present and Future*. New York: The Feminist Press.

Jordanova, L. (1991) *Sexual Visions*. Brighton: Harvester.

LeVay, S. (1993) *The Sexual Brain*. Cambridge, MA: Massachusetts Institute of Technology.

Moraga, C. (1983) *Loving in the War Years*. Boston: South End Press.

Nestle, J. (1987) *A Restricted Country: Essays and Short Stories*. London: Sheba.

Oudshoorn, N. (1994) *Beyond the Natural Body*. London: Routledge.

Reuben, D. (1970) *Everything You Always Wanted to Know about Sex – But Were Afraid to Ask*. London and New York: W.H. Allen.

Sedgwick, E. Kosovsky (1993) 'Epistemology of the Closet.' In Abelove *et al.* (1993).

Van den Wijngaard, M. (1995) 'The Liberation of the Female Rodent.' In L. Birke and R. Hubbard (1995).

5

Now You See Her, Now You Don't: The Lesbian in Theatre Studies

Jill Davis

In this chapter I shall identify key moments of lesbian intervention into the critical practice of theatre studies, but it is important to say here that the discipline is more than the mere practice of critical reading and discourse. Its specificity as a discipline lies in the nature of its interaction with its object of study, the theatre; many theatre studies departments see themselves as a part of the cultural process of producing theatre, both through their own theatre-making and as part of the training system of professional theatre-makers. The creative practice of theatre and performance and the interrelationship of theory and practice are therefore crucial concerns of the discipline. It follows that the academy as a place of teaching and learning is as important as the academy as a place of academic discourse: what 'comes out' of the theatre studies departments is both writing about theatre and people who will make theatre. In this chapter I will therefore also highlight moments when the practice of lesbian theatre has constituted an intervention into the discipline, and how these interventions, both theoretical and theatrical, have offered the potential for theatre practice in the academy, or for theatre studies as a discipline to (re)conceptualize itself, particularly around the relation of theory to practice.

Lesbians and theatre – the first date

Lesbians began to make upfront lesbian theatre in the UK in the late 1970s. In that first 'coming out' phase – roughly the mid-1970s to mid-1980s – lesbian theatre, writings about lesbian 'identity' and theatre studies were all marked by a concern with 'positive images'. Lesbian theatre and lesbian writing were telling the 'truth' about who lesbians were, a truth which had been 'hidden from history', but could now be told by lesbians (for) themselves.[1]

Theatre studies as a discipline was already engaged with the issue of those historically excluded from representation, through a focus on the alternative political theatre which developed in Britain from the late 1960s. Part of the aim of this theatre was the recovery of working-class identity from its misrepresentation in dominant cultural forms (Gooch, 1984; McGrath, 1981). It was this model of the ethical purpose of theatrical representations which was inherited by the second wave of alternative theatre, the 'communities of identity' theatre (which included gay and lesbian theatres), formed as feminist, anti-racist and gay liberationist activism impacted on left politics and ideas of theatre.

The key issue of this theatre, and thus the focus of theatre studies as a discipline at this time, was *representation*: representation both in the theatrical sense – how to stage critiques of the misrepresentations of the dominant (white, male, bourgeois, heterosexual) culture and how to replace this with an authentic self-representation – and in the political sense, namely, how theatre might contribute to agitation for the right to political representation.

Theatre studies as a discipline became engaged for the first time with 'theory' (rather than theatre history or dramatic criticism) as a consequence of its interaction with alternative theatre, and its necessary engagement with Marxist theory. A deconstructive dramatic criticism of dominant forms was derived from political theory, and aesthetic practice could be theorized in terms of achievement of politically appropriate forms of representation.

But theatre studies also derived from its engagement with political theatre a legitimating concept of itself as necessary to the process of theatre production, rather than as simply imitative and secondary. The most exciting theatre of the time was one in which practice was fuelled by theory, the province of the academy; indeed, it was in some sense the product of the academy (its workers were mostly graduates – that is, drama graduates, rather than graduates of the drama schools), and with its thoroughly theorized aesthetic of minimal means it was a theatre which could be made in the academy to the same standards as outside it.

Positive images and lesbian feminism

At first lesbian theatre, and writings about it within the academy, did not constitute a major intervention into the discipline; rather, it was one of a series of political theatres for which theatre studies had an existing theoretical framework.[2] Lesbian theatre at this time did not appear to demand theorization. 'The lesbian' seemed an unproblematic category; lesbian theatre simple in purpose and aesthetic. But critical scrutiny gradually revealed that these first lesbian plays did not just present 'authentic' images of lesbians, they were also engaged in constructing a 'new lesbian', an ideal lesbian identity, and as such represented an intervention into lesbian theorization.

In *Any Woman Can* (Jill Posener, 1975), the first lesbian play presented by Gay Sweatshop, Britain's oldest gay and lesbian theatre company, the central character visits the Gateways, the legendary lesbian club, and is picked up by another character referred to only as 'Older Woman':

Ginny: Suddenly you realise you've spent your life getting away from that. That wasn't a woman: that was a male impersonator and that's not what I want. I want a woman who wants to be a woman. (Davis, 1987, p. 21)

The 'new lesbian' is 'a woman who wants to be a woman'. This is a clear attempt to occlude an earlier lesbian identity, the 'invert' of early twentieth-century psycho-sexology, the butch of lesbian cultural history (significantly here represented by 'Older Woman'), and to contest it by an inversion of that 'inversion'. Gay Sweatshop's second lesbian show, *Care and Control* (Wandor, 1980, pp. 63–113), about lesbian custody battles, dramatized the common interests of lesbians and heterosexual women. (Significantly the play was created after a major debate within the company over the marginalization of the women by the dominance of gay men/gay men's issues.)

The political content of these plays rests on an underlying theoretical proposition about what a 'lesbian' is, a proposition which comes from a lesbian need to contest a history of negatives, and chimes with contemporary feminist theory. Lesbians are 'women' (where 'woman' remains an unproblematic term), and have no truck with masculinity, either in the form of an alliance with gay men or in accepting the masculine lesbian. The butch as the product of a 'wrong' – because male – idea must be abolished.

The theoretical counterpart to these theatrical representations was to be found in feminist political theory as it was inflected, from around the early 1980s, by lesbian interventions. Adrienne Rich's essay 'Compulsory Heterosexuality and Lesbian Existence' is the best-known version of this radical feminist position, with its proposition that the term 'lesbian' describes 'woman-identification' in all its forms, not simply 'the fact that a woman has had or consciously desired genital sexual experience with another woman' (1981, p. 20). Rich's radical critique of heterosexuality as unnatural and violently enforced upon women throughout history proposed lesbian as another – that is 'the' – name for the essential feminine experience and the essential history of women. Thus the lesbian achieves a double triumph: a theoretical abolition of the ghost of the mannish lesbian and the appropriation of feminism in the name of the lesbian.[3]

The impact of radical feminist ideas on theatre studies may be regarded as the first specifically lesbian intervention into the discipline. They provided the material ground – the representation of the 'lesbian continuum', 'woman-identification', 'sisterhood' – for experimental lesbian/feminist theatre-making in the academy, explorations which then developed beyond these limits, as lesbian feminist graduates formed their own theatre companies, to influence the lesbian/feminist theatre scene.

Radical feminism's concern with 'herstory' provided the conceptual ground for lesbian academic writing, as essays explored/created a tradition of neglected or unrecognized lesbian theatre work (Davis, 1991; Whitelaw, 1990; Holledge, 1981), or deconstructed the representational violence done to women in the classic texts of theatre (Davis, 1992). Such ideas spread fairly rapidly from being the province, even ghetto, of lesbian/feminist theatre academics and feminist theatre courses to become an approach to the reading and writing of theatre history and criticism which at the very least had to be recognized and negotiated across the discipline.

Theorizing the feminine

One of the contradictions – perhaps even the strategic manoeuvres – of radical feminist thought was its denial of itself as theory. Radical feminist thinking presented itself, in writing which valued transparency and accessibility, as the revelation of suppressed truths and histories. It was the product of an activist feminism whose purpose was to urge and enable change. 'Theory' was resented as elitist and exclusive, inimical to a movement in which identity and (self-)identification – as a woman, as a lesbian – were the 'qualifications' for inclusion. But no sooner had lesbian and radical feminist academic activism introduced lesbian knowledge into women's studies in the academy than the theoretical problematization began.

Two key theoretical problems are posed by radical feminist propositions about 'the lesbian'. First, the lesbian is subsumed into 'woman', a category which elides differences between women in favour of an identity seemingly reducible to/identical with a biological essence. Second, radical feminism repudiates a lesbian difference based on sexuality, as evidenced in the Rich quotation above. Although historically it was protest at this second point which came first in lesbian culture, it was the former issue which initially preoccupied academic discourse and which I shall therefore consider at this point.

At first glance the work of the francophone theorists of the feminine, Luce Irigaray and Hélène Cixous, may seem to be an intense theoretical elaboration of a position not dissimilar to that of anglophone radical feminism. Certainly the capture of feminist literary studies (and later film and theatre studies) in the academy by their work may be attributed to their provision of a theoretical framework in which 'the feminine' is asserted as an absolute difference (and thus a legitimate object of study), but which avoids the reduction of 'the feminine' to biological essence. What this work and the founding assumptions of radical feminism share are the emphases on a repressive patriarchy, on the coercion of women into compulsory heterosexuality, on the exclusion of women from speech/representation, on the authenticity of the body as marking women's history and on the desire to release women into a denied wholeness. In both, the feminine is centrally connected to the homoerotic. But what makes Irigaray's and Cixous's work different is that it is not based on empirical or materialist argument, it does not situate the feminine as identical with the female sexed body and it is not work of political activism (both Cixous and Irigaray avoid the terms 'feminist' and 'feminism'). Their work is grounded rather in a philosophical and psychoanalytic tradition, and their questions about sexual difference are ontological rather than pragmatic.

The work of both Irigaray and Cixous proceeds from Freudian and Lacanian psychoanalytic theory and the Oedipal narrative of sexual difference. In that narrative the founding human moment occurs with the repression of the mother and the recognition of the power of (the Name or Law of) the father. Women are positioned as lacking (the penis or phallus), as lack personified. Fear of becoming that lack, through castration, polices the small boy into the masculine subject position, while the small girl is relegated to the object position, a status derived from her eventual fate as the desired object of the powerful male and as the mother of his children.

The theoretical intensification of women's inferiority which psychoanalysis provides explains why feminism, and especially lesbian feminism, initially rejected it. But the contribution of Irigaray, as a practising psychoanalyst, and Cixous, as a writer and literary critic, has been to take on psychoanalysis and critique it using its own methods and formulations. Irigaray's (1985) particular contribution has been to demonstrate that there are, in fact, no women in Freudian/Lacanian psychoanalytic theory, only men. It is not a theory of sexual difference, rather an assertion that there is only one sex. Deconstructing Lévi-Strauss, Irigaray posits that 'women' are merely 'the goods' which are exchanged to facilitate a social relationship which is always and only between men. Her project is to theorize the psychic development of women into psychoanalytic theory: theorizing the relation of girl to mother as a narrative in which the mother is something more than the lost, related and despised object for the girl, and something other than the self-lacking maternal body for herself.

The particular relevance of Cixous's and Irigaray's work for academic disciplines concerned with writing, performance or the visual image is their central concern, *à la* Lacan, with language and/as the symbolic. 'Language is the residue and alternative accomplishment of dissatisfied desire, the variegated cultural production of a sublimation that never really satisfies' (Butler, 1990b, p. 43). What is sublimated (under the threat of castration) is the prohibited incestuous desire for the mother.

Symbolization – language – is thus always already masculine, and heterosexual. Irigaray and Cixous accept that women are thus excluded from representing themselves through language and both are concerned with identifying the ways in which women may or do signal their being, and may come to represent themselves. For both Irigaray and Cixous the body, as that which precedes the symbolic, is that which women are attempting to 'speak'. Irigaray talks of the development of a 'morpho-logic that is appropriate to [women's] bodies' (Irigaray, 1993, p. 59); Cixous asserts that 'women are body' and urges that 'women must write through their bodies' (1981, pp. 257, 256). Both pay attention to gesture and movement, voice/vocalization (rather than language) and the multiplicity rather than singularity of the feminine.

Although taken up by/as feminist theory, and certainly constituting the dominant feminist theoretical discourse in literary and image studies in the academy from the mid-1980s, these theorizations of the difference of the feminine circulate around, depend upon even, an erotic relation between women. Indeed, at points in the work of both it seems as if this is the very meaning of the difference. The *jouissance*, the overflowing bodily pleasure of/in the feminine 'coming to writing' in Cixous's (1991b) work, as well as the 'lips speak[ing] together' and the 'goods get[ting] together' of Irigaray's (1985) essays, speak of the pleasures and subversiveness of the homo- as well as the auto-erotic. The feminine homoerotic is that which (alone) can both point to a place and a desire outside the masculine 'hommosexual' [*sic*] economy and evidence the abolition of the 'phallic mother' in favour of the un-repression of the maternal/feminine body. Cixous's play *Portrait of Dora* dramatizes that through Dora's passionate connection to the maternal body and her erotic desire for another woman. But the crucial point is that what Dora speaks cannot be heard . . . Once again the lesbian (a term almost never used in this work) turns out to be the crucial figure in feminist theory, only to be, as in Rich, collapsed into the feminine, the impossible and the utopian.[4]

The work of the francophone theorists, complete with its central trope of homoerotic *jouissance*, has affected theatre studies as much as any other discipline in the academy. Offering an escape from the oversimplicity of the first phase of feminist and lesbian studies of theatre, it represented a critical approach which seemed content to identify and celebrate 'women in . . .' while risking a banal 'political correctness' when dealing with male texts. The psychoanalytically grounded work of Irigaray and Cixous (encapsulated in Cixous's claim that '[i]t is always necessary for a woman to die in order for the play to begin' (1984, p. 546)) enables far more complex and interesting analyses of the workings of masculine 'representation' and the absence or fantasy of 'women' therein, as men address men in a 'homosexual' exchange. It also makes possible a critical analysis of women's theatre work which identifies the traces of the feminine in the writing/performance rather than assuming it to follow automatically from the sex or 'identity' of the theatre-maker.[5] A crucial point, since Cixous allows that it is at least theoretically possible for a feminine writing to come from a male writer. What is to be looked for, in writing or performance, what constitutes the feminine, according to Cixous's theorization in her short and influential polemic on theatre 'Aller à la Mer', are the ways in which the apparatus of representation is disrupted. No longer will dead women, obliterated others, begin the (logical and linear) plot; it will mean 'a different Story' (1984, p. 547), since masculine drama will always reprise the Oedipus narrative. The feminine in theatre will be marked by an intensity of 'body-presence' (p. 547) and the voice; its images will come from the return of the feminine unconscious, which will mean the destruction of narrative order, and its relation to audiences will be one of immediacy of connection rather than gazing from a distance.

A major effect of these theoretical propositions, and particularly in the emphasis on the expressive feminine body, on theatre studies in the academy has been to bring women's performance art into the critical gaze (Champagne, 1990; Juno and Vale, 1991) and to provide a way of 'reading' it (Carr, 1993; Forte, 1990). Cixous's vision of a stage where 'Woman is Whole' (1984, p. 548) and in which the body is both the text and the performance (space) seems closer to being made flesh in that work than in most women's theatre writing. Of recent feminist writing in the British theatre, only Caryl Churchill's (1994) *The Skriker,* with its mixing of theatre, dance and opera, supernatural characters and realist narrative, and particularly its use of alliteration and word association as the basis of speech, seems to challenge conventional representation in the ways Cixous would identify as stylistically marking the feminine. Interestingly, however, the only works radically to refigure the mother/daughter narrative, the central concern of this discourse, are – as if to prove that a feminine homoerotics will flow from the return of the repressed mother – by lesbian writers. Holly Hughes's performance piece *World without End* (1990, pp. 3–32) narrates how she learned her mother's 'French', learning erotic desire from and for her mother; whilst Phyllis Nagy's plays *Entering Queens* (1993) and *Butterfly Kiss* (1994) focus in different ways on the problematic but unrepressed mutual desire of lesbian characters and their mothers.

Theories of the feminine and their application to critical practice have also had an effect on theatre practice in the academy, specifically in its interaction with other performance theory. The focus of theatre-making has shifted away from the play to the performance, from the ensemble to the individual performer and from the public/political text to the utterance of the unconscious through the body. And crucially 'theory' has been further enshrined as a necessary component of practice, thus intensifying the theatre studies department's sense of itself as a key player in the production of avant-garde theatre. There is no longer theory and practice, but theory/practice.

Lesbian performance/theory

There is no doubt that French psychoanalytic feminism has constituted a major intervention into feminist theory, affecting a wide range of studies in the academy, including, because of its relation to the homoerotic as a major component of the feminine, the development of lesbian theorization. But even as the lesbian is placed at a theoretical centre she remains locked into a theory of binary sexual difference, unable to articulate a lesbian difference. Just as lesbian desire was repressed in radical feminist theory, so now homoerotic desire is unreadable, unrepresentable, utopian. Eventually, inevitably, a lesbian theory was to develop which insisted on the difference of the lesbian experience, its material and desiring reality, even as it negotiated with the terms of French psychoanalytic feminist theory (for examples see Jagose, 1994; Wittig, 1992; Butler, 1990b; Case, 1989a; De Lauretis, 1994, 1988).

Culturally this began in the mid-1980s in what are now referred to as the 'sex wars', as lesbians who defined themselves through sexual practice fought the desexualizing of the lesbian in radical feminism. These battles – at conferences, in journals and the gay/lesbian press (Ardill and O'Sullivan, 1986) – proved bitter, as 'pro-sex' lesbians celebrated the butch/femme history of lesbian culture (Nestle, 1987), the pleasures of S/M and pornography (Califia, 1988), and lesbian sexuality as radical transgression (Bright, 1990). In the short term in lesbian culture, and in the slightly longer term in lesbian theory, the 'bad girls' won.

Since the late 1980s suits, piercings, singlets, leather, lipstick, rubber, dildos and frocks have been the lesbian cultural and sexual wardrobe. If the body is a text the lesbian body contradicts that cliché of much women's performance art, where the naked female body is the authenticating witness of the personal/confessional text. The lesbian body is a theatrical scene, a playing space, a performer.

Theatre, as performance and as artifice, has been a central image in recent lesbian theory. Indeed the cultural inspiration of some of the key texts has been the lesbian theatre of Split Britches. This American trio in fact includes one heterosexual performer, and the company's work has been concerned with a range of issues, but it is above all a theatre of camp and seductive lesbian performance. It is the butch and femme performances of Peggy Shaw and Lois Weaver which excite attention and which have led to the discursive recovery of the butch/femme couple as the specific figure of lesbian desire (Hart, 1993; Case, 1989a, 1989b; Dolan, 1987; Davy, 1986).

The critical attention attracted by Weaver and Shaw's work in Split Britches (performed at the WOW cafe in New York, which they helped to establish) and as individual performers, has, as Sue-Ellen Case describes,

> composed the dialogue around issues such as how 'lesbian' is visible in performance, how a lesbian address is constituted, the unique nature of a lesbian audience reception, the relation of lesbian performance to community or subculture, the dynamics of lesbian desire within the system of representation, the function of butch-femme role-playing, and the lesbian uses of camp. (1996, p. 11)

The relationship between the academy and Split Britches may be regarded as paradigmatic of the ideal relationship between theatre studies and theatre practice. A discourse which is about lesbian performance has made an important intervention in the wider theorization of lesbian desire. As such it marks a different exchange between theatre studies as a discipline and lesbian knowledge. Here it is theatre studies and lesbian theatre academics, through critical analysis of representation, who make an intervention into lesbian theory. As Split Britches' theatre work has attracted the gaze of lesbian theatre academics and as its performers increasingly interact with the academy (through residencies with students and as performers and speakers at academic conferences), their theatre work has become marked by the consciousness of critical and theoretical discourse. Such interactiveness has intensified theatre studies' sense of itself as a crucible for the exchange of cultural theory and creative practice.

Queer performance

Almost as soon as the lesbian emerged from theoretical submersion in feminism she – he? – found herself disappearing again as an entity in the latest phase of lesbian and gay theory – queer theory. A key theorist of this cultural turn is Judith Butler (Butler, 1990a, 1990b, 1991, 1993), whose work as a philosopher, currently hugely influential across a range of disciplines, uses the multiple problematics in the sentence 'I am a lesbian' – the founding utterance of a lesbian identity – to trouble all notions of genders, sexes and sexualities as fixities, thus troubling the notion of 'identity' itself. What is a 'lesbian'? What constitutes the 'I'? What is it to 'be'? Drawing, *inter alia*, on the work of J.L. Austin, Butler proposes gender as a performance, not an identity, not a continuous mode of being. It is through performing prescribed acts and scenes (and crucially by not performing proscribed other scenes) that a gender is constructed, an 'I' is formed. It is the doing that is 'I', not the I who does the doing.

Butler does not propose that the gender performance is simply voluntary; on the contrary the scripts are already written, only a small degree of improvisation is tolerated, and there are stiff punishments for refusal to perform the right script. What Butler does is provide a theoretical counter to the intensification of binary sexual difference in feminist and psychoanalytic theory, and thus a glimmer of a hope of evading its dismal consequences. The radical implication of Butler's work lies in the claim for gender's fictiveness, its daily made-up-ness, its discontinuities, the difficulty of getting the performance right every time: in short, its proneness to disruption allows for the possibility of other performances, the proliferation of other genders. Butler suggests that in a thinking system which insists on the absoluteness of sexual difference, a transvestite, for example, does not trouble the binary; s/he in fact confirms it. But

> [i]f the reality of gender is constructed by the performance itself, then there is no recourse to an essential and unrealized 'sex' or 'gender' which gender performances ostensibly express. Indeed the transvestite's gender is as fully real as anyone whose performance complies with social expectation. (1990a, p. 278)

If the philosophical notion of performativity is central to the theory of queer, then so too is theatrical performance itself. Butler herself claims that '[t]o oppose the theatrical to the political within contemporary queer politics is . . . an impossibility' (1993, p. 232). Politically, (to) queer is to expose the fictiveness of gender by playing sexual difference to death, parodying it, ridiculing it, performing it to excess. The necessary political tools, then, are the traditional artifices of the theatre: impersonation, costume, make-up, props, scripts and scenes. The theatrical tradition of gays, lesbians and the transgendered – camp, butch/femme, drag and the masquerade – have become (once again) the signature performances of queer (Lucas, 1994).

As queer is taken up beyond its origins among gays and lesbians to become part of the postmodern theoretical and cultural avant-garde, it has a particular resonance for theatre studies. Performance/practice suddenly becomes an important way in which gender can be, is perhaps best, theoretically investigated, since performance is what gender is. Queer shifts the theoretical focus away from ideas of 'representation' towards the nature of theatricality itself, as self-conscious artifice, play, display and spectacle. It brings back into the critical gaze objects and traditions of performance and theatricality which have been marginalized in the more recent emphasis on theatre as ideological practice. Rather than continuing to deconstruct the classical canon, exploring the transgressive in marginal and 'illegitimate' traditions of theatre becomes the interesting project (Meyer, 1994; Ferris, 1993). Queer has also brought the theatre and the academy, practice and theory, closer together, as evidenced in the international 'Queering the Pitch' conference held in Manchester in 1994.

But there is also a danger in queer for theatre studies. The theatrical may be the trope of queer, but the theatre itself is no longer an important cultural space – as venue, as drama. There is queer performance and theatre: the Split Britches/Bloolips 1991 show *Belle Reprieve* (their version of *A Streetcar Named Desire*) is a paradigm of queer, as the cast list demonstrates (Case, 1996, p. 150):

MITCH, a fairy disguised as a man [Paul Shaw]

STELLA, a woman disguised as a woman [Lois Weaver]

STANLEY, a butch lesbian [Peggy Shaw]

BLANCHE, a man in a dress [Bette Bourne][6]

But the true theatre of queer is, necessarily, the street, the bar, the club (Alicia, 1994), the individual performance, the sexual scene. The intervention of queer thus raised a problem for theatre studies about the parameters of the discipline. How legitimate is its claim to separateness if the theatrical is manifesting itself across a range of cultural forms which include not only the related media of television and film but fashion, club culture, image production, etc., areas traditionally within the purview of other disciplines? Does queer, as part of the wider discourse of the postmodern, theoretically dissolve theatre studies as a discipline? A related problem is raised by the proliferation of theoretical and critical studies inspired by the cultural visibility and academic prominence of gay/lesbian/queer theorists. Is theatre studies in the academy in danger of becoming a theoretical discipline of paratheatrical studies as theatre declines and 'theory' is seen as far more sexy?

And for 'the lesbian', is she dissolved under queer? Indeed the question queer theory raises is whether she ever existed as a unified (id)entity. The answer would seem to be that the category 'lesbian', like all other fixed categories of gender and sexuality produced by the idea of a binary sexual difference, was always a fiction; an impossible term to encompass what turned out to be a number of genders and a number of sexualities, indeed a number of bodies (Nataf, 1996).

The 'lesbian' in theatre studies

This chapter has attempted to answer the question of whether theatre studies as an academic discipline has been changed, or modified, by, as the editors put it in their invitation to contribute to this volume, 'lesbian theory and knowledge'. My conclusion has been broadly yes, but with two caveats.

My first hesitation is in speaking for/about a single notion of theatre studies. Certainly it is possible to assert that the department of theatre studies whose critical and creative work remains unaffected by more than fifteen years of feminist/gay and lesbian/gender theory would be odd indeed; but there is no single 'academy', and how far the potentialities offered by the theoretical perspectives I have discussed in this essay have been taken up in practice across the discipline is a matter for a more empirical approach to this topic than I have chosen to take.

My second reservation is a more crucial one. The term 'lesbian' is notoriously (and properly, I think) unstable; so to identify a clear and separate 'lesbian knowledge' is, for me at least, quite impossible. I might have found a way out of that theoretical impasse by selecting for discussion, and elaborating at greater length, only theoretical and critical work which identifies itself as lesbian. Had I done so, I think my conclusion about the effect of 'lesbian' knowledge on theatre studies would have been different: that explicitly lesbian knowledge and lesbian performance theory has been influential in creating a field of lesbian theatre studies, but its influence remains confined to that.

What I have chosen to do instead is focus on theoretical perspectives which have had a major influence across the whole discipline of theatre studies (as they have had on other disciplines in the academy since the early 1980s), perspectives which I identify as coming from a 'lesbian' knowledge or circulating around a 'lesbian' figure, even when the 'lesbian' in that formulation contains identifications as different as 'woman-identified-woman', dyke, homoerotic feminine, butch, femme, bisexual, transgendered, etc. I would argue, furthermore, that they are theoretical perspectives, through which lesbian theorization itself has been enabled. These political and theoretical perspectives (and their authors) do not necessarily identify themselves as in any way 'lesbian' and may be intertwined with feminist theory, gender theory or gay theory. However, my argument is that 'lesbian' knowledge is central to them, and thus they may be seen as Trojan horses entering the 'straight' academy. As they have disgorged their contents over the past twenty years, the concept of gender insolence which is at the heart of the 'lesbian' in all/any of its meanings has left its mark all over many disciplines, not least theatre studies, by its nature the study of a cultural institution which has long had a powerful attraction for the gender dissident.

Notes

1. For examples of lesbian theatre writing of the 1970s and 1980s, see K. McDermott, *Places Please!: The First Anthology of Lesbian Plays* (Santa Cruz, CA: Aunt Lute Book Co., 1985); J. Davis, *Lesbian Plays* and *Lesbian Plays Two* (London: Methuen, 1987 and 1989); P. Osment (ed.), *Gay Sweatshop: Four Plays and a Company* (London: Methuen, 1989). As an example of an early attempt to recover a lesbian literary history, see J. Rule, *Lesbian Images* (New York: Doubleday, 1975). A. Stewart-Park and J. Cassidy (eds), *We're Here: Conversations with Lesbian Women* (London: Quartet Books, 1977) is a good contemporary example of lesbians speaking/coming out.

2. Lesbian theatre was included in academic writing, as in undergraduate courses, as an example of, variously, political theatre, community theatre or, most frequently, feminist theatre. For general accounts of, and contemporary approaches to, political theatre, see S. Craig, *Dreams and Deconstructions* (London: Amber Lane Press, 1980); C. Itzin, *Stages in the Revolution* (London: Methuen, 1980). For the feminist context, and accounts of lesbian theatre, see M. Wandor, *Understudies* (London: Methuen, 1981); S.-E. Case, *Feminism and Theatre* (London: Macmillan, 1988); T.R. Griffiths and M. Llewellyn-Jones (eds), *British and Irish Women Dramatists since 1958 – A Critical Handbook* (London: Open University Press, 1993); L. Goodman, *Contemporary Feminist Theatres – To Each Her Own* (London: Routledge, 1993); J. Devlin, 'Siren Theatre Company: Politics in Performance', in L. Hart and P. Phelan (eds) *Acting Out: Feminist Performances* (Ann Arbor, MI: University of Michigan Press, 1993).
3. For a flavour of the issues and positions of radical lesbian feminism, see the journal *Gossip* published by Onlywomen Press, London, from 1986 to 1988. For examples of the construction of a radical lesbian feminist 'herstory', see L. Faderman, *Surpassing the Love of Men: Romantic Friendship and Love between Women from the Renaissance to the Present* (London: The Women's Press, 1986); S. Jeffreys, *The Spinster and Her Enemies: Feminism and Sexuality 1880–1930* (London: Pandora, 1987); Lesbian History Group, *Not a Passing Phase: Reclaiming Lesbians in History 1840–1985* (London: The Women's Press, 1989).
4. Perhaps this accounts for the fact that feminist critical works on Cixous and Irigaray generally make little of their homoerotics. Interestingly, while Irigaray in particular has become an essential reference point for lesbian as much as feminist theorists it is in fact Cixous's work which celebrates love and eroticism between women (1991a). Irigaray's writing about the lesbian is at the least ambiguous; Annamarie Jagose rightly highlights Irigaray's 'tendency . . . to promote then abandon the notion of a female homosexuality in preference to that "difficult and complex" heterosexuality, that "most mysterious and creative couple"' (1994, p. 26).
5. French psychoanalytic feminism has had such a dynamic effect on feminist theatre criticism and theory that it would be tedious if not impossible to provide an exhaustive list of references. The following volumes contain significant chapters or essays illustrative of the approach: L. Hart (ed.), *Making a Spectacle* (Ann Arbor, MI: University of Michigan Press, 1989); E. Brater (ed.), *Feminine Focus* (New York: Oxford University Press, 1989); J. Redmond (ed.), *Themes in Drama: Women in Theatre* (Cambridge: Cambridge University Press, 1989); G. Austin, *Feminist Theories for Dramatic Criticism* (Ann Arbor, MI: University of Michigan Press, 1990); S.-E. Case (ed.), *Performing Feminisms: Feminist Critical Theory and Theatre* (Baltimore: Johns Hopkins University Press, 1990); L. Hart and P. Phelan (eds), *Acting Out: Feminist Performances* (Ann Arbor, MI: University of Michigan Press, 1993). See also J.L. Savona, 'French Feminism and Theatre' and J. Feral, trans. B. Kerslake, 'Writing and Displacement: Women in Theatre', both in *Modern Drama* 4 (1984).
6. Other recent or current queer work has included several seasons at the ICA London (*Queer Notions* and *Fierce and Queer* in 1993 *inter alia*); the work of Neil Bartlett with Gloria, now based at the Lyric Theatre, Hammersmith, London; Peggy Shaw's (*Two Big Girls*, 1994; *You're Just Like My Father*,

1995 and 1996) and Lois Weaver's (*Faith and Dancing*, 1996) individual performance works; the continuing work of Lindsay Kemp, perhaps the pioneer of queer performance with work spanning twenty years; the in-your-face queer stand-up work of Claire Dowie (*Why Is John Lennon Wearing a Skirt?*, 1991; *Leaking from Every Orifice*, 1994); the transgender performance of Kate Bornstein (*Hidden – A Gender*, 1994).

References

Alicia, N. (1994) 'Sex on Stage: Performance in Lesbian Clubs.' *GLINT: Gays and Lesbians in Theatre*. II/2: 2–3.

Ardill, S. and O'Sullivan, S. (1986) 'Upsetting an Applecart: Difference, Desire and Lesbian Sadomasochism.' *Feminist Review*. 23: 31–57.

Bright, S. (1990) *Susie Sexpert's Lesbian Sex World*. San Francisco: Cleis Press.

Butler, J. (1990a) 'Performative Acts and Gender Constitution: An Essay in Phenomenology and Feminist Theory.' In Case (1990).

Butler, J. (1990b) *Gender Trouble: Feminism and the Subversion of Identity*. New York: Routledge.

Butler, J. (1991) 'Imitation and Gender Insubordination.' In D. Fuss (ed.) *Inside/Out: Lesbian Theories, Gay Theories*. London: Routledge.

Butler, J. (1993) *Bodies that Matter*. New York: Routledge.

Califia, P. (1988) *Macho Sluts*. Boston: Alyson Publications.

Carr, C. (1993) 'Unspeakable Practices, Unnatural Acts' and '"Telling the Awfullest Truth": An Interview with Karen Finley.' Both in L. Hart and P. Phelan (eds) *Acting Out: Feminist Performances*. Ann Arbor, MI: University of Michigan Press.

Case, S.-E. (1989a) 'Towards a Butch-Femme Aesthetic.' In L. Hart (ed.) *Making a Spectacle*. Ann Arbor, MI: University of Michigan Press.

Case, S.-E. (1989b) 'From Split Britches to Split Subject.' In E. Brater (ed.) *Feminine Focus*. New York: Oxford University Press.

Case, S.-E. (ed.) (1990) *Performing Feminisms: Feminist Critical Theory and Theatre*. Baltimore, MD: Johns Hopkins University Press.

Case, S.-E. (ed.) (1996) *Split Britches*. London: Routledge.

Champagne, L. (ed.) (1990) *Out from Under: Texts by Women Performance Artists*. New York: Theatre Communications Group Inc.

Churchill, C. (1994) *The Skriker*. London: Nick Hern Books.

Cixous, H. (1979) *Portrait of Dora*, trans. A. Barrows. In *Benmussa Directs*. London: John Calder.

Cixous, H. (1981) 'The Laugh of the Medusa.' In *Signs*, reprinted in E. Marks and I. de Courtivron (eds) *New French Feminisms*. Hemel Hempstead: Harvester Press (French original 1976).

Cixous, H. (1984) 'Aller à la mer', trans. B. Kerslake. *Modern Drama*. 27: 546–8.

Cixous, H. (1991a) *The Book of Promethea*, trans. B. Wing. Lincoln, NB: University of Nebraska Press (French original 1983).

Cixous, H. (1991b) *'Coming to Writing' and Other Essays*, trans. S. Cornell, A. Liddle and S. Sellers. Cambridge, MA: Harvard University Press.

Davis, J. (1987) (ed.) *Lesbian Plays*. London: Methuen.

Davis, J. (ed.) (1989) *Lesbian Plays Two*. London: Methuen.

Davis, J. (1991) '"This Be Different": The Lesbian Drama of Mrs Havelock Ellis.' *Women – A Cultural Review*. 2/2: 134–8.

Davis, J. (1992) 'The New Woman and the New Life.' In V. Gardner and S. Rutherford (eds) *The New Woman and Her Sisters: Feminism and Theatre 1850–1914*. London: Harvester Wheatsheaf.

Davy, K. (1986) 'Constructing the Spectator: Reception, Context and Address in Lesbian Performance.' *Performing Arts Journal*. 10/2: 43–52.

de Lauretis, T. (1988) 'Sexual Indifference and Lesbian Representation.' *Theatre Journal* 40/2, reprinted in Case (1990).

de Lauretis, T. (1994) *The Practice of Love: Lesbian Sexuality and Perverse Desire*. Bloomington, IN: Indiana University Press.

Dolan, J. (1987) 'The Dynamics of Desire: Sexuality and Gender in Pornography and Performance.' *Theatre Journal*. 39/2: 156–74.

Ferris, L. (ed.) (1993) *Crossing the Stage: Controversies on Cross-Dressing*. London: Routledge.

Forte, J. (1990) 'Women's Performance Art: Feminism and Post-Modernism.' In Case (1990).

Gardner, V. and Rutherford, S. (eds) (1992) *The New Woman and Her Sisters: Feminism and Theatre 1850–1914*. London: Harvester Wheatsheaf.

Gooch, S. (1984) *All Together Now: An Alternative View of Theatre and the Community*. London: Methuen.

Hart, L. (1993) 'Identity and Seduction: Lesbians in the Mainstream.' In L. Hart and P. Phelan (eds) *Acting Out: Feminist Performances*. Ann Arbor, MI: University of Michigan Press.

Holledge, J. (1981) *Innocent Flowers: Women in the Edwardian Theatre*. London: Virago.

Hughes, H. (1990) *World without End*. In Champagne (1990), pp. 3–32.

Irigaray, L. (1985) *Ce sexe qui n'est pas un*, trans. C. Porter and C. Burke as *This Sex Which Is Not One*. Ithaca, NY: Cornell University Press (French original 1977).

Irigaray, L. (1993) *Je, tu, nous: Towards a Culture of Difference*, trans. A. Martin, New York: Routledge (French original 1990).

Jagose, A. (1994) *Lesbian Utopics*. New York: Routledge.

Juno, A. and Vale, V. (1991) *Angry Women*. San Francisco: Re/Search Publications.

Lucas, I. (1994) *Impertinent Decorum*. London: Cassell.

McGrath, J. (1981) *A Good Night Out*. London: Methuen.

Meyer, M. (ed.) (1994) *The Politics and Poetics of Camp*. London: Routledge.

Nagy, P. (1993) *Entering Queens* (unpublished).

Nagy, P. (1994) *Butterfly Kiss*. London: Nick Hern Books.

Nataf, Z. (1996) *Lesbians Talk Transgender*. London: Scarlet Press.

Nestle, J. (1987) *A Restricted Country*. New York: Sheba.

Rich, A. (1981) 'Compulsory Heterosexuality and Lesbian Existence.' *Signs* 5/4, reprinted London: Onlywomen Press.

Wandor, M. (ed.) (1980) *Strike While the Iron Is Hot*. London: Journeyman Press.

Whitelaw, L. (1990) *The Life and Rebellious Times of Cicely Hamilton*. London: The Women's Press.

Wittig, M. (1992) *The Straight Mind and Other Essays*. Hemel Hempstead: Harvester Wheatsheaf.

6

She Must Be Theorizing Things: Fifteen Years of Lesbian Film Criticism, 1981–96

Julia Erhart

Cinema studies now seems more or less congenial to lesbian work, perhaps because of its own historical struggle for institutional recognition. I say 'more or less' to emphasize that experiences will vary depending on institutional location and disciplinary issues. Although progressive departments may include the occasional course on lesbian film, faculty in more conservative programmes still have trouble teaching women's films – let alone explicitly lesbian ones. While lesbians are recognized in some cinema studies domains – on panels and at caucuses at the annual 'Society for Cinema Studies' conference, for example – the lack of representation in other areas, such as academic employment, demonstrates how much remains to be achieved.

The purpose of this chapter is to provide a historical and thematic overview of the lesbian film criticism that has emerged since the momentous publication of the 'Lesbian and Film' section of *Jump Cut* that appeared in 1981, collectively edited by Edith Becker, Michelle Citron, Julia Lesage and Ruby Rich. While lesbianism was a topic in film writing prior to 1981 (Tyler, 1972), the special section was the first place where lesbians materialized as a critical collective, articulating and furthering lesbian scholarly concerns beyond the 'images of' criticism associated with Parker Tyler and later with Vito Russo (1981). And, in spite of some important distinctions – most notably a stronger connection to radical lesbian feminism and an absence of the word 'queer' – the special section was for the most part remarkably prescient. Among the matters of interest to the editors were the oversights of feminist film theory, the value of subtexting or reading against the grain, and the homophobia that animates 'progressive' film-making – in other words issues that remain central to lesbian film criticism.

In what follows, I will consider how lesbian work has shifted or qualified the field of film studies since (and including) the appearance of the 1981 *Jump Cut* special section, asking how lesbians have furthered the discipline, advanced the findings of other scholars and appropriated approaches that others have departed from. This chapter focuses on three areas pertinent to lesbian film criticism: historical and contemporary reclamation, deconstruction and spectatorship. While the historical developments in feminism and queer theory since the early 1980s have been important to the growth of lesbian cinema studies, chronology is not sufficient to explain a host of seminal differences that divide critics today (such as the issue of text-based versus viewer-oriented criticism). For this reason, the essay is not arranged to reflect the seamless development of the field but to highlight the different approaches that lesbians have chosen.

Lesbian scholarship has principally benefited from and advanced the research of two schools of theory. From British cultural studies and reception criticism as practised in the USA, lesbians have borrowed and furthered the notion of a socially located, interpretive community of viewers for whom film-watching is a contested, open-ended and context-dependent process. Cultural critics such as Janice Radway, Stuart Hall and Jacqueline Bobo have argued that meaning, rather than residing within discrete texts, is found in the negotiation between texts and viewers. I will have more to say about lesbian film studies' debt to cultural studies when I discuss the matter of genre and reception. Second, from feminist revisions of Althusserian psychoanalytic film theory by Laura Mulvey, Claire Johnston and Mary Ann Doane, lesbians have appropriated the critique of the genderedness of looking, pleasure and identification, using the language of feminist film theory to propose alternative spectatorial relations. I will return to the subject of this second legacy when I consider the issues of deconstruction and spectatorship.

Looking (for) lesbians

If there is a single factor that unites lesbians working in all areas of film study, it is the problem of the paucity of lesbians both onscreen and in production. Initially a result of more than twenty-five years of institutional censorship that forbade even the vaguest references to 'sex perversion', let alone depictions of it, the problem is one that lesbian scholars now seek to rectify.[1] Broadly speaking, the relative scarcity of recognizably lesbian characters on the screens of classical Hollywood, independent and European cinemas – not to mention Mexican, Taiwanese, Cuban or Israeli cinemas – has continued unabated since the repeal of the censorship code. In spite of the hiccup that is heard once a year at lesbian and gay film festivals, independent theatres still infrequently show films with lesbian characters, and chain theatres almost never do.

The situation for lesbians on the other side of the camera is almost as gloomy. Historically, there have never been 'enough' lesbians making films, either in the first world or elsewhere. Although the small trickle of features that have appeared in the mid-1990s has led some to be optimistic, lesbian film-makers, particularly *out* lesbian film-makers, continue to work independently. And regardless of how high one's regard for independent cinema is, its working conditions tend to translate into compromised salaries, streamlined production budgets and inferior terms of distribution.

The problem of paucity has been compounded since the late 1980s by what has in some other ways seemed like a blessing, namely the practice of collaboration between lesbian studies and gay men's studies. While lesbians have certainly profited from the heightened visibility and consolidated institutional power derived from 'queer studies', the convergence hasn't always been beneficial. The problem, as others have noted, is that too often collaboration has resulted in the erasure of the lesbian side of things; too often 'queer studies' has meant 'gay male' studies, or worse, white gay male studies.[2] Presumed to have a foot in both 'women's cinema' and 'gay cinema', lesbian film scholarship has frequently found itself with no leg to stand on. To take a recent example: when a colleague added a week on queer cinema to his class on contemporary Hollywood cinema, the film that he chose to present was Tom Kalin's *Swoon*. Because *Swoon* deals with issues of sexuality and identity, and since the class already featured a section on women's cinema, a third component on lesbian cinema was deemed unnecessary, in spite of the absence of lesbians from both the queer and the women's cinema sections. When lesbian cinema and gay cinema are collapsed together, the lesbian component collapses too.

Happily, the situation in the print world does not reflect such paucity. High-profile academic film journals such as *Wide Angle*, *Quarterly Review of Film and Video* and *Screen* have historically been quite friendly to lesbian research, featuring special issues on the topic of queer cinema. Others such as *Camera Obscura*, *Cineaste*, *Cinema Journal* and *Jump Cut* continue to welcome lesbian work, publishing lesbian-related articles on a fairly frequent basis, as have queer and feminist university presses. The years 1994 and 1995 were bumper years for lesbian and queer scholars, witnessing no fewer than eight new edited collections giving significant space to lesbians and film, including three anthologies that focused exclusively on lesbian concerns.[3] And to speak of only scholarly journals and university press books is to exclude more popular writing where significant advances have also been made.[4]

In different and complementary ways, each of these publication venues has continued to prioritize lesbian visibility. But while many lesbians would concur that visibility is empirically determined, something that an increase in body count cannot hurt, many have argued that it is not *solely* empirically determined. For these theorists, it is not enough simply to add more representations; what's necessary is to alter the conditions of vision, to learn new ways of seeing, and of being seen.

Lesbian cinema studies is dominated by three approaches: an interest in the reclamatory, a deconstructive practice and a concern with spectatorship. In the following, I shall therefore consider the reclamation of lesbians in places where initially we thought there weren't any: in the Code films, in the Hollywood studios in the 1940s and in contemporary women's films. Predominantly archaeological, work in this vein is also important for how it recasts issues at the heart of cinema studies, such as authorship, reception and genre. From there I turn to lesbian evaluations of the hegemonic, foregrounding work that assesses the cinematic construction of heterosexuality as well as self-identified lesbian films. Finally, I conclude by discussing lesbian theories of spectatorship, particularly theories that draw from psychoanalysis.

Queer characters and dyke directors: historical reclamation

Where are the lesbians? This is perhaps the question that animates all reclamation studies, devoted to 'finding' the lesbians, both across the historical spectrum and contemporarily. Historical reclamation alerts present-day readers to the presence of lesbians in cinema before the demise of the Code, and subverts conventional histories of censorship that tell us that heterosexuality has gone uncontested. Involving the amassing and dissemination of data that conventional film historiography has overlooked, historical reclamation counters the notion that lesbianism is a topic of exclusive interest to 'other' disciplines, or one that has come into being only since the second wave of feminism. Chon Noriega's 1990 essay on the representation of homosexuality and lesbianism in Hollywood cinema during the Code years is an excellent example of such an approach. Focusing on reviews of films that featured lesbians or gay male characters, the piece is a counter-discursive genealogy of the shifting attitudes towards homosexuality from *These Three* (1936) through *Advise and Consent* (1962). For Noriega, the issue is not 'whether certain films have – in retrospect – gay and lesbian characters, subtexts, stars, or directors as an anodyne to censorship, but how homosexuality was "put into discourse", and the role censorship played during the Code era' (p. 21). An elegant negotiation of the problem of paucity, the essay demonstrates the benefit of looking beyond the superficial histories of cinema that equate censorship with absence.

In her 1993 bibliographic essay on queer theory and cinema, Fabienne Worth points out the tendency for different 'types' of queer cinema work to divide up according to sex, with gay men being drawn to historiographic matters, and lesbians conducting text-based, psychologically oriented analyses. Worth's claim is more subtle and well argued than perhaps it appears here, and it is one I would concur with: I am not saying that women haven't conducted historical research in cinema studies, or at the very least work on historically specific audiences. Antonia Lant's 1991 investigation of women in wartime Britain and Shelley Stamp Lindsey's 1996 study of American women viewers in their teens convincingly attest to the presence of women in the archives, as does Lea Jacobs's fine 1991 study of the negotiations between directors and censors over the 'sensitive' subject of adultery and prostitution. However, none of these estimable historical projects has been a 'lesbian' project *per se*. More curious, when lesbian scholars have produced 'historical' studies, such work has not prioritized lesbian matters.[5] The issue, here, is not why lesbians have been 'excluded' from any of these analyses; rather, it is why they have conducted so few of their own.[6] While I could well imagine a number of compelling lesbian historiographic projects, ranging from lesbian ethnographies to archival projects that would scrutinize censorship files for conversations about 'sex perversion', such studies have been slow to materialize.

The exception to the general dearth of lesbian historiographic work is biographical research. Essays on actresses Greta Garbo (Erkkila, 1985) and Agnes Moorhead (White, 1995b), along with Judith Mayne's (1994) book on Dorothy Arzner, have done much to redress the imbalance that Worth noticed. At its best, information about the life of a director, star or supporting actress broadens out to larger considerations of the historical climate in which she lived. Touching upon experiences of marginalization and self-censorship, lesbian biographical research optimally investigates the social circumstances of a particular period, asking about historical attitudes to feminism, gender and single womanhood, as Ruby Rich's 1981 study of the lesbian classic *Maedchen in Uniform* (Leontine Sagan, 1931) does. No longer simple excavations of the historical 'real', the most interesting biographical projects also openly acknowledge the stakes of the contemporary researcher.

The best and most recent example of such an approach is Judith Mayne's *Directed by Dorothy Arzner*. Not a traditional biography, Mayne's book is, in her words, a study in portraiture, an examination that names the director's sexuality as the key but not sole salient epistemological framework through which to consider her films. Less interested in plotting every aspect of the director's life than in cataloguing a wide range of themes in Arzner's work, the book is upfront about Mayne's investment in the project. She writes, 'films are not isolated objects, and film studies of the last decade have challenged fetishizations of the individual film as the privileged object of analysis. Lives are never so accessible' (p. 3). As a postmodern negotiation of the biographical referent, the book looks at all aspects of the director's life and work, including the kinds of films she made, how those films were talked about and how her image was received, all within the context of how Arzner, her films and images of the director circulate today.

Interestingly, one of the by-products of Mayne's and others' archival work has been a return to the problem of authorship. A central area of cinema analysis since the mid-1950s *auteur* or author studies looked at a series of films by a single director for thematic and formal commonalities, thereby significantly elevating film's status to the level of 'art'. However, since Roland Barthes's famous 1968 proclamation, the issue had been falling steadily out of favour.[7] Due in part to Mayne's interest in the issue in the Arzner book and elsewhere (1991), the topic is currently enjoying something of a revival. In contrast to Barthes, Mayne and notably Richard Dyer (1991) have named the author's death premature, arguing that a director's sexuality, along with her or his gender, race and class background, are indeed salient factors. For lesbians and gay men, the sexed, raced, classed and gendered body of the director is not an outmoded modernist dinosaur, but an idea that should never have been abandoned to begin with.

Virtually lesbian: reclaiming the present

Live bodies – specifically live *viewing* bodies – have also been important to contemporary reclamation projects. Research of this type has reassessed various characters for how they manifest lesbian characteristics and revisited different films and genres for how they suggest lesbian themes or subplots. In the spirit of reclamation, new genres have been named, like the 'temporary transvestite film' and the 'deadly doll film', that do not necessarily depict lesbianism but productively expose the homophobia of classical Hollywood and are thus of interest to lesbian viewers (Holmlund, 1994; Straayer, 1992). More controversially, this type of work has also entailed the 'reclaiming' of those avowedly non-lesbian characters and genres (like the vampire film) which seem to suggest lesbianism at the same time as they are denotatively heterosexual. For these reclamation projects, critics have often relied upon a text's reception by lesbian-friendly audiences to counter a director's or a press kit's or a historian's anti-lesbian claim. Audience response, in other words, has been key.

The issue of audience is also central for many non-lesbian cultural-studies-styled projects with which lesbian reclamation work has been in conversation. Jackie Stacey's 1994 investigation of how women fans in 1940s and 1950s England related to female Hollywood stars is an excellent example of such work. Proceeding in the manner of Valerie Walkerdine and Ien Ang, Stacey derives her understanding of reception patterns from real women's responses to an audience questionnaire. Basing her findings largely on ethnographic material, Stacey assessed viewers' changing relations to Hollywood stars. The notion of 'audience' has most recently figured centrally for Jacqueline Bobo, whose emphasis on black women's interpretative abilities has productively shifted the critical emphasis away from the text to the dynamic and constantly changing interplay between viewers and films. In her 1995 ethnographic work on the cultural reading and viewing strategies of African-American women, Bobo showed how audiences cultivated resistance strategies and oppositional meanings to find pleasure and power in a white-authored and potentially reactionary text – specifically, Steven Spielberg's *The Color Purple*.

During the late 1980s, several articles appeared wrestling with the analogous issue of the merits of ambiguous representations of 'lesbianism'. Simultaneously irritated and inspired by the materialization of the popular films *Lianna* (John Sayles, 1983), *Desert Hearts* (Donna Deitch, 1985), *Personal Best* (Robert Towne, 1982) and *Entre Nous* (Diane Kurys, 1983), each of which depicted women's relationships in a positive but not necessarily lesbian-positive way, Chris Straayer (1990) and Christine Holmlund (1991) analysed the contradiction between what were considered affirmative representations of female friendship on the one hand, and homophobic elisions or misconstruals of homosexuality, on the other. While the constructive representations of women in the films seemed a good thing, both Straayer and Holmlund expressed frustration with the phenomenon that I would call 'lesbian lite', or the soft-pedalling of lesbianism.[8]

Coining the term 'hypothetical lesbian heroine' to mark the oscillation she saw in the films, Straayer criticized the coy 'now you see it, now you don't' representation of lesbian eroticism within both the arty women's film *Entre Nous* and the soft-porn *Voyage En Douce* (Michele Deville, 1980). However, in spite of the problems the films demonstrated, Straayer concluded the essay on a redemptive note, proposing optimistically that the films' vision of female bonding is a deviant form of heterosexual masquerade and a lesbian-specific alternative to the conventional, heterosexual trope of love-at-first-sight. Like Straayer, Holmlund also lamented cinema's squeamishness in depicting female sexuality, particularly lesbian sexuality – including its feminization of lesbians and independent heterosexual women as well as its exclusive preference for soft-focus and formulaic sex. However, rather than seeing this as a liability, Holmlund claimed it as an asset and basis for a new genre – what she called 'the mainstream femme film'.[9] Directly countering the idea that only masculine-looking women tend to be understood as lesbians, Holmlund read each of the main characters within four recent women's films, *Desert Hearts*, *Personal Best*, *Entre Nous* and *Lianna*, as 'femmes'.

With their reliance on reading against the grain, these two articles exemplify the reclamatory gesture at its most enthusiastic, downplaying differences in nationality and self-claimed outness (the avowedly lesbian American *Desert Hearts* versus the straight-identified French *Entre Nous*) in order to classify films in a lesbian-relevant way. Bold mobilizations of lesbian-specific discourse (the word 'femme' does not typically appear on the pages of *Camera Obscura*, where Holmlund's article was published), the essays mitigate the heterosexist ambiguousness in contemporary representations of lesbianism by openly drawing attention to it. Despite their criticisms of the representational contortions mainstream cinema undergoes in order to avoid showing lesbianism, both writers find something redeemable in such representations, demonstrating how to appropriate them.[10]

Andrea Weiss's (1992) chapter on the vampire film is a good example of how lesbians have reclaimed pre-existing genres. A more popular account of the value of a traditionally heterosexual genre for lesbian viewers, Weiss tracks several decades of English-language films featuring female vampires with lesbian tendencies.[11] Touching upon the historical circumstances that initially gave rise to lesbian vampire imagery, Weiss positively appraises the genre's representation of strong, powerful women. A re-evaluation of a genre often thought violent, male-centric and misogynous, vampire films, Weiss found, provide important and readily available examples of the power women wield in a male-dominated world.

Precisely because of the vague way popular, mainstream cinema has always represented lesbianism, writing that decisively claims an ambiguous character or film as 'lesbian' lays itself open to charges of voluntarism, that is, to the accusation that it is *too* interpretation-dependent and not sufficiently empirical. Anyone who has ever tried to teach a class on lesbian cinema has had to deal with complaints of this nature, namely, students' frustrations about the dearth of 'straightforward' lesbian imagery, and irritation with the amount of time spent reading against the grain. While the charge of voluntarism is itself never other than a subjective matter (what makes a particular reading 'too' subjective is clearly in the eyes of the beholder), there can be a problem with readings that suggest that the critic is the *sole* determinant of a text's meaning that lesbians would do well to remain aware of.[12]

Racing whiteness, sex matters: deconstructions

One way lesbians have avoided charges of voluntarism is by tilting the agenda away from reclamatory work towards critiques of the hegemonic. Early lesbian film criticism is strongly deconstructive in aim, not yet concerned with figuring the specificity of lesbian representation but rather with understanding Hollywood's depiction of women's relationships in general – heterosexual as well as lesbian. Like the heterosexual feminist film theory with which it was still very much in conversation, early lesbian film criticism examined the gendered operations of seeing and acting in classical Hollywood cinema. Although the introduction to the 1981 *Jump*

Cut eventually went on to discuss lesbian-specific issues, the departure point was the representation of female friendship – something that was a matter of interest to *all* feminists. Images of male friendship, the editors noted, receive considerably more screen time than images of female friendship, suggesting that what is threatening to Hollywood is not necessarily lesbianism, but women's relationships in general – *pace* Eve Sedgwick.[13]

The deconstructive impulse in the 1981 issue of *Jump Cut* did not emerge *dea ex machina*, but in a space carved out by feminist film theorists working at roughly the same time. This theory constitutes an important antecedent to a good deal of contemporary lesbian film criticism, deconstructive criticism included. Though not written from an explicitly 'lesbian' point of view, Teresa de Lauretis's 1984 chapter 'Desire and Narrative' from her book *Alice Doesn't* is one example of such work. An articulation of the heterosexual and heterosexist nature of the narrative operation, the article significantly added sexuality to the critical agenda. Although the essay doesn't explicitly foreground a lesbian perspective, its identification of the heterosexualness of narrative – the male hero's movement through and conquest of space that is gendered as feminine – opened up room for considerations of what difference lesbianism might make to such a paradigm.[14]

Taking off where de Lauretis and *Jump Cut* left off, subsequent lesbian film criticism has focused on how the addition of lesbian characters or themes might alter formal and narrative cinematic structures. Judith Roof (1991), for example, has analysed the representation of lesbianism in the soft-core porn film, finding that it is an essential part of the story's trajectory, the fuel that drives the narrative engine. In Roof's description, soft-porn films typically represent the lesbian affair as necessary to the protagonist's 'education', with the erotic involvement of two women functioning as a teaser for the heterosexual climax. In her analysis of the 1988 action cop movie *Internal Affairs*, Cindy Patton noted how the lesbian character functions to confirm the heterosexuality of the two male leads by deflecting anxieties about homoeroticism typically present within the action genre. In Patton's words, the lesbian 'allows the plot to move forward not because her sexuality is a narrative problematic, but because she is the last kind of character left when the cop film goes politically correct and recognizes its prior dependence on misogyny and homophobia' (1995, p. 33).

Both essays reveal the structuring anxieties and representational limits of cinema as a whole. Unlike many reclamation studies, lesbian deconstructive work is not concerned with the exceptional, but strives to expose the gendered underpinnings of mainstream narrative film, be it soft-porn, art-cinema, action-adventure or some combination thereof. While much reclamation work principally concentrates upon 'finding' the lesbians (or strong women, or positive role models), work that sets out to evaluate heterosexual cinema reveals the homophobia that circumscribes representations of lesbianism to begin with.

As lesbian cinema studies matures, criticism of self-identified lesbian and/or lesbian-directed and produced films has begun to appear. In addition to Holmlund, others have been critical of Deitch's film (Stacey, 1995; Merck, 1993), as well as of *Lianna* (Merck, 1984). As yet however, few have ventured into the territory Ruby Rich covers in her important 1993 article on the representation of race within films by lesbians and gay men. Noticing the increasing popularity of the trope of cross-raced couples in films by lesbians, Rich wonders to what extent racial difference in queer cinema performs the work of gender difference within heterosexual films. While she applauds the rupturing of the frequently monochromatic queer colour spectrum, she expresses wariness about some white film-makers' representations of racial difference, questioning whether the issue commands the seriousness and attention it fully deserves.

Rich's essay is important for how it foregrounds a matter that too infrequently comes up in lesbian cinema studies scholarship, which is the question of the difference that race – or nation, or class, or age – makes to lesbian analyses. While critical work has appeared on films by lesbians of colour (Onodera, 1994; Parkerson, 1993; Parmar, 1993), and on films by white film-makers featuring actresses of colour (White, 1995a; de Lauretis, 1991), there haven't been nearly enough such analyses; furthermore some of the latter have received criticism for not engaging with the question as fully as they might have (de Lauretis, 1991). It is not my intention to rehearse such criticisms once again, but to draw attention to the need for more cross-category analyses of lesbianism and race, lesbianism and nationality, and lesbianism and class.[15] How lesbianism might be a metaphor or trope focalizing racial or national issues is an area awaiting exploration.

One important piece that embodies the concerns of black lesbian spectators is an essay by Z. Isiling Nataf (1995). Nataf analyses the pleasures and feelings of ambivalence available to black lesbian spectators, reading four films against the grain: the independent British thriller *Mona Lisa* (Neil Jordan, 1986), the low-budget black action film *Sweet Sweetback's Baadasssss Song* (Melvin Van Peebles, 1971), the Hollywood blockbuster *Ghost* (Jerry Zucker, 1990) and the Sandra Bernhard comedy vehicle, *Without You I'm Nothing* (John Boskovich, 1990). Focusing particularly upon what she calls 'the undecidable signs in queer subtexts', Nataf construes the indeterminacy of the films positively, suggesting that it opens a space for appropriation of different types of images by black lesbians.

They must be theorizing things: spectatorship

In contrast to the scant attention nationality or race have received, spectatorship is one of the most animated domains in lesbian film scholarship currently. In overall aim and methodology, lesbian spectatorship work builds on feminist film theory of the 1970s and early 1980s, which in turn was committed to qualifying, for the woman spectator, many of the concepts set forth by writers such as Christian Metz, Jean-Louis Baudry and Stephen Heath. Both the 'apparatus theorists', as Baudry, Metz and Heath were called, and their feminist colleagues, such as Laura Mulvey and Claire Johnston initially, and Mary Ann Doane, Teresa de Lauretis and Tania Modleski later on, relied on psychoanalytic, frequently Lacanian, precepts for their research. The spectator's racial, class, national or sexual orientation attributes typically went unnamed, and the term generally referred to an idealized female subject rather than to any socially located or empirically determined viewer – at least in its initial formulation, although there is good evidence that this is changing.[16]

While the articulation of a non-male spectator has been useful to lesbians, many of them have taken feminist film theory to task for failing further to qualify the lesbian spectator and for its unhelpful and, many have felt, homophobic binarization of spectatorship. Even as they have profited from the efforts of feminists, lesbians have upbraided earlier writers for theorizing – some have said proscribing – a system of viewership that unexceptionally assigns desire, vision and agency to the male, and desiredness and passivity to the female. Lesbians have faulted feminist film theorists for failing to recognize that desire and identification need not be cut to the model of heterosexuality, even though much of Hollywood cinema suggests that they are (de Lauretis, 1991; Mayne, 1991; Roof, 1991; Straayer, 1990; Stacey, 1987; Becker *et al.*, 1981).

In spite of these criticisms, lesbians' debt to feminist work is clear. In no place is it more apparent than in those articles that invoke feminist psychoanalytic theory directly. Patricia White's reading of the British film *Nocturne* (Joy Chamberlain, 1991) and Lizzie Thynne's essay on the Canadian *Anne Trister* (Lea Pool, 1986) both rely extensively on heterosexual feminist readings of the mother/daughter relation for their speculations about lesbian spectatorship (White, 1995a; Thynne, 1995).[17] However, a key predecessor to those pieces, Teresa de Lauretis's (1991) article on *She Must Be Seeing Things*, bypasses feminist revisions of psychoanalysis altogether, returning to an earlier male-authored paradigm. Significantly invested in Laplanche and Pontalis's idea of primal fantasy as a scene or setting of desire, de Lauretis is interested in Sheila McLauchlin's 1987 film because of how it plays out such a scene; and specifically because it does so with women participants. Not, according to de Lauretis, a textual reading *per se*, the article focuses on the film's address to a lesbian subject in the terms that Laplanche and Pontalis outline. Its accomplishments are thus multiple: in bringing the independent film in conversation with a classical, psychoanalytic model of subject formation and fantasy, de Lauretis demonstrates the applicability of psychoanalytic theory for lesbian subjects *and* the theoretical qualities inherent in McLauchlin's film.

Ironically, the increase in lesbian work on spectatorship has coincided almost precisely with the subtle distancing of many non-lesbian feminists from psychoanalytically orientated spectatorship theory. In a 1989 issue of *Camera Obscura* entitled 'The Spectatrix', many of the contributors separated themselves from psychoanalytic theory, calling for an engagement with cultural and historical processes over semiotic and psychological ones (Doane and Bergstrom, 1989). While this is not the place to debate the merits of the contributor's comments, it is important to acknowledge the contrast between lesbian and heterosexual feminists' attitudes to psychoanalysis, a contrast that ironically became marked, as Judith Mayne (1993) notes, in the very journal that initially supported the psychoanalytic approach.

What does it mean that many lesbians are investing in a method that a number of non-lesbian feminists are turning away from? At the very least, lesbian spectatorship theorists, like their feminist predecessors, may face charges of being too text-based, and of disregarding the historical and cultural specificity of viewing experiences in favour of psychological processes. At worst, lesbian spectatorship theorists risk reifying individual lesbian spectators as 'the' lesbian spectator, in much the same way that feminist film theorists disregard differences between heterosexual and lesbian spectators. Whether other differences, such as nationality, race and class, can become salient to lesbian spectatorship theory remains to be seen.

Conclusion

To conclude, lesbians have been active and vocal contributors to many of the most vital areas of film studies, at the same time as they have successfully appropriated its critical tools for their own projects. To situate lesbian cinema scholarship in that context, however, is to tell only half the story: in addition to cinema studies, lesbian studies and queer theory have been instrumental in the field's development, providing vital analytical implements for the mediation of sexism, homophobia and representation. In turn, lesbian film work has succeeded in infusing fresh blood into queer theory, lesbian studies and women's studies, figuring importantly at national lesbian and gay and women's studies conferences. How much of this activity has made it through the gates of academia is not entirely clear, however, though the obvious political relevance and liberatory potential of claiming cinematic forebears, exposing the representational mechanisms of compulsory heterosexuality, and articulating lesbian spectatorial desire leave me hoping for a generous audience. How lesbians negotiate the mired terrain of popular culture, particularly cinema, which is both ubiquitous and powerful, spectacularly affirming and violently homophobic, which engages a multiplicity of desires, fantasies and fears, sometimes all at once – how lesbians continue to negotiate this realm is a theoretical as well as a political issue that lies at the heart of lesbian cinema studies, and one which all lesbians would do well to take notice of.

Notes

I would like to thank Victoria Smith and Yvonne Keller for their helpful editorial suggestions.

1. I am referring to the system of self-censorship that Hollywood adopted in 1934. Specifically, the censorship code was a twelve-point plan that acknowledged the responsibility of the film-making industry to, in their phrasing, uphold the sanctity of the institution of marriage and the home, by eliminating all representations of (again, their words) A. crimes against the law and B. low forms of sex relationship, specifically 1. adultery and illicit sex, 2. scenes of passion, 3. seduction or rape, 4. sex perversion, 5. white slavery and 6. miscegenation. The rescinding of these separate prohibitions was achieved gradually and in stages. For example, in 1956 the clause prohibiting representations of prostitution and miscegenation was repealed, followed in 1961 by the clause prohibiting the representation of 'sex perversion', i.e. lesbianism.
2. For recent commentary on the maleness implicit in the term 'queer', see Wilton (1995). For a critique of its whiteness, see Dhairyam (1994).
3. Compare Burston and Richardson (1995); Creekmur and Doty (1995); Grosz and Probyn (1995); Pietropaolo and Testaferri (1995); Carson *et al.* (1994). For lesbian-specific anthologies, see Hamer and Budge (1995); Wilton (1995); Doan (1994).
4. Compare Boffin and Fraser (1991); Hadleigh (1993, 1994); Weiss (1992).
5. This is the case for Jackie Stacey's 1994 study.
6. This is the approach I am trying to take in my essay on *The Children's Hour* (1996). Further exceptions are Judy Whitaker's ethnographic essay in the 1981 *Jump Cut* and Andrea Weiss's work on the 1930s film in *Vampires and Violets* (1992).
7. In his 1968 essay 'The Death of the Author', Barthes argues that the critical category of the 'Author' is a faded modernist concept of little use to contemporary criticism.
8. An earlier article by Elizabeth Ellsworth (1986) on *Personal Best* juggles many of the issues of reception and ambiguity that Holmlund's and Straayer's do.
9. I am of two minds about Homlund's neologism. While on the one hand I respect its invocation of lesbian-specific discourse, recognizing that it is no more subjective than word choices for other genres (the term 'Western' comes to mind), on the other hand, I am less certain about its imposition of a historically and subculturally specific term on two films (*Entre Nous* and *Personal Best*) that have actively refused membership in lesbian categories.
10. Other self-declared heterosexual films that lesbians have attempted to reclaim as 'lesbian' include *Black Widow* (Smyth, 1995; Traub, 1991); *All About Eve* and *Desperately Seeking Susan* (Stacey, 1987); *Fatal Attraction* (Holmlund, 1989); *Ghost*

(Nataf, 1995); *Rebecca* (Berenstein, 1992); *Marnie* (Knapp, 1993); and the *Alien/s* trilogy (Jennings, 1995).

11. For additional work on lesbian vampires in film, see Krzywinska (1995) and Zimmerman (1981).
12. Fortunately, awareness of and insight into the dilemma I am outlining here is as old as the problem itself (see Becker *et al.*, 1981; Miller, 1991).
13. I am referring to Sedgwick's claim that homosocial desire between women is more socially acceptable than homosocial desire between men.
14. Victoria Smith (1994) also makes this point.
15. One example is Lynda Hart's chapter on *Single White Female* (Barbet Schroeder, 1992) in her 1994 book *Fatal Women*. One of the few critics, in addition to Rich, who tries to theorize race, lesbianism and film together (at least within this chapter), Hart rehearses the historical connections between the category of the lesbian, the prostitute and the woman-of-colour to discern the anxieties that motivate the film's representation of murderousness in the woman protagonist. Chris Holmlund's (1994) work on the 'deadly doll' film similarly pursues other factors – race and age – that join together in addition to lesbianism to animate the cultural fantasy of women who are alternately aggressors and victims.
16. That Jackie Stacey adopts the word 'spectator' for her 1994 ethnographic study is an indication that the meaning of the term may be expanding to include different types of subjects in addition to that defined by psychoanalytic theory.
17. Christine Holmlund's 1989 article on *Fatal Attraction* invokes Luce Irigaray, as does Thynne's.

References

Barthes, R. (1968) 'The Death of the Author.' In *Image, Music, Text* (1977) trans. Stephen Heath. New York: Hill.

Becker, E., Citron, M., Lesage, J. and Rich, B. Ruby (eds) (1981) 'Special Section: Lesbians and Film.' *Jump Cut*. 24–5: 17–44.

Berenstein, R. (1992) '"I'm Not the Sort of Person Men Marry": Monsters, Queers, and Hitchcock's *Rebecca*.' *CineAction*. 29: 82–96.

Bobo, J. (1995) *Black Women as Cultural Readers*. New York: Columbia University Press.

Boffin, T. and Fraser, J. (eds) (1991) *Stolen Glances: Lesbians Take Photographs*. London: Pandora.

Burston, P. and Richardson, C. (eds) (1995) *A Queer Romance: Lesbians, Gay Men and Popular Culture*. London: Routledge.

Carson, D., Dittmar, L. and Welsh, J. (eds) (1994) *Multiple Voices in Feminist Film Criticism*. Minneapolis: University of Minneapolis Press.

Creekmur, C.K. and Doty, A. (eds) (1995) *Out in Culture: Gay, Lesbian and Queer Essays on Popular Culture*. Durham, NC: Duke University Press.

de Lauretis, T. (1984) *Alice Doesn't: Feminism, Semiotics, Cinema*. Bloomington, IN: Indiana University Press.

de Lauretis, T. (1991) 'Film and the Visible.' In Bad Object Choices (eds) (1991) *How Do I Look?: Queer Film and Video*. Seattle: Bay Press.

Dhairyam, S. (1994) 'Racing the Lesbian, Dodging White Critics.' In Doan (1994).

Doan, L. (ed.) (1994) *The Lesbian Postmodern*. New York: Columbia University Press.

Doane, M.A. and Bergstrom, J. (eds) (1989) 'The Spectatrix.' *Camera Obscura*. 20–1.

Dyer, R. (1991) 'Believing in Fairies: The Author and the Homosexual.' In Fuss (1991).

Ellsworth, E. (1986) 'Illicit Pleasures: Feminist Spectators of *Personal Best.*' *Wide Angle.* 8/2: 45–58.

Erhart, J. (1996) '"She Could Hardly Invent Them!" From Epistemological Uncertainty to Discursive Production: Lesbianism in *The Children's Hour.*' *Camera Obscura.* 35: 85–105.

Erkkila, B. (1985) 'Greta Garbo: Sailing Beyond the Frame.' *Critical Inquiry.* 11/4: 595–619.

Fuss, D. (ed.) (1991) *Inside Out: Lesbians Theories, Gay Theories.* New York: Routledge.

Gever, M., Greyson, J. and Parmar, P. (eds) (1993) *Queer Looks: Perspectives on Lesbian and Gay Film and Video.* New York: Routledge.

Grosz, E. and Probyn, E. (eds) (1995) *Sexy Bodies: The Strange Carnalities of Feminism.* London: Routledge.

Hadleigh, B. (1993) *The Lavender Screen: The Gay and Lesbian Films, Their Stars, Makers, Characters and Critics.* New York: Citadel.

Hadleigh, B. (1994) *Hollywood Lesbians.* New York: Barricade.

Hamer, D. and Budge, B. (eds) (1995) *The Good, the Bad, and the Gorgeous: Popular Culture's Romance with Lesbianism.* London: Pandora.

Hart, L. (1994) *Fatal Women: Lesbian Sexuality and the Mark of Aggression.* Princeton, NJ: Princeton University Press.

Holmlund, C. (1989) 'I Love Luce: The Lesbian, Mimesis, and Masquerade in Irigaray, Freud and Mainstream Film.' *New Formations.* 9: 105–24.

Holmlund, C. (1991) 'When Is a Lesbian Not a Lesbian? The Lesbian Continuum and the Mainstream Femme Film.' *Camera Obscura.* 25/6: 145–80.

Holmlund, C. (1994) 'Cruisin' for a Bruisin': Hollywood's Deadly (Lesbian) Dolls.' *Cinema Journal.* 34/1: 31–51.

Jacobs, L. (1991) *The Wages of Sin: Censorship and the Fallen Woman Film, 1928–1942.* Madison, NJ: University of Wisconsin Press.

Jennings, R. (1995) 'Desire and Design – Ripley Undressed.' In Wilton (1995).

Knapp, C. (1993) 'The Queer Voice in *Marnie.*' *Cinema Journal.* 32/4: 6–23.

Krzywinska, T. (1995) 'La Belle Dame Sans Merci?' In Burston and Richardson (1995).

Lant, A. (1991) *Blackout: Reinventing Women for Wartime British Cinema.* Princeton, NJ: Princeton University Press.

Lindsey, S. Stamp (1996) 'Is Any Girl Safe? Female Spectators at the White Slave Films.' *Screen.* 37/1: 1–15.

Mayne, J. (1991) 'A Parallax View of Lesbian Authorship.' In Fuss (1991).

Mayne, J. (1993) *Cinema and Spectatorship.* London: Routledge.

Mayne, J. (1994) *Directed by Dorothy Arzner.* Bloomington, IN: Indiana University Press.

Merck, M. (1984) '"Lianna" and the Lesbians of Art Cinema.' In C. Brunsdon (ed.) (1986) *Films for Women.* London: BFI, pp. 99–108.

Merck, M. (1993) 'Dessert Hearts.' In Gever *et al.* (1993).

Miller, D.A. (1991) 'Anal *Rope.*' In Fuss (1991).

Nataf, Z.I. (1995) 'Black Lesbian Spectatorship and Pleasure in Popular Cinema.' In Burston and Richardson (1995).

Noriega, C. (1990) '"Something's Missing Here!": Homosexuality and Film Reviews during the Production Code Era, 1934–1962.' *Cinema Journal.* 30/1: 20–41.

Onodera, M. (1994) 'Dishing It Out and Taking It.' In W. Waring (ed.) (1994) *By, For, and About: Feminist Cultural Politics.* Toronto: Women's Press.

Parkerson, M. (1993) 'Birth of a Notion: Towards Black Gay and Lesbian Imagery in Film and Video.' In Gever *et al.* (1993).

Parmar, P. (1993) 'That Moment of Emergence.' In Gever *et al.* (1993).

Patton, C. (1995) 'What's a Nice Lesbian Like You Doing in a Film Like This?' In Wilton (1995).

Pietropaolo, L. and Testaferri, A. (eds) (1995) *Feminisms in the Cinema*. Bloomington, IN: Indiana University Press.

Rich, B. Ruby (1981) 'From Repressive Tolerance to Erotic Liberation: *Maedchen in Uniform*.' *Jump Cut*. 24/5: 44–50.

Rich, B. Ruby (1993) 'When Difference Is More than Skin Deep.' In Gever *et al.* (1993).

Roof, J. (1991) *A Lure of Knowledge: Lesbian Sexuality and Theory*. New York: Columbia University Press.

Russo, V. (1981) *The Celluloid Closet*. New York: Harper.

Smith, V.L. (1994) 'Loss and Narration in Modern Women's Fiction.' Dissertation, University of California, Santa Cruz.

Smyth, C. (1995) 'The Transgressive Sexual Subject.' In Burston and Richardson (1995).

Stacey, J. (1987) 'Desperately Seeking Difference.' *Screen*. 28/1.

Stacey, J. (1994) *Star Gazing: Hollywood Cinema and Female Spectatorship*. London: Routledge.

Stacey, J. (1995) '"If You Don't Play, You Can't Win": *Desert Hearts* and the Lesbian Romance Film.' In Wilton (1995).

Straayer, C. (1990) 'The Hypothetical Lesbian Heroine.' *Jump Cut*. 35: 50–7.

Straayer, C. (1992) 'Redressing the "Natural": The Temporary Transvestite Film.' *Wide Angle*. 14/1: 36–55.

Thynne, L. (1995) 'The Space Between: Daughters and Lovers in *Anne Trister*.' In Wilton (1995).

Traub, V. (1991) 'The Ambiguities of "Lesbian" Viewing Pleasure: The (Dis)articulations of *Black Widow*.' In J. Epstein and K. Straub (eds) (1991) *Body Guards: The Cultural Politics of Gender Ambiguity*. New York: Routledge.

Tyler, P. (1972) *Screening the Sexes: Homosexuality in the Movies*. New York: Holt.

Weiss, A. (1992) *Vampires and Violets: Lesbians in Film*. London: Penguin.

Whitaker, J. (1981) 'Hollywood Transformed.' *Jump Cut*. 24/5: 33–5.

White, P. (1995a) 'Governing Lesbian Desire: *Nocturne*'s Oedipal Fantasy.' In Pietropaolo and Testaferri (1995).

White, P. (1995b) 'Supporting Character: The Queer Career of Agnes Moorehead.' In Creekmur and Doty (1995).

Wilton, T. (ed.) (1995) *Immortal, Invisible: Lesbians and the Moving Image*. London: Routledge.

Worth, F. (1993) 'Of Gayzes and Bodies: A Bibliographical Essay on Queer Theory, Psychoanalysis and Archaeology.' *Quarterly Review of Film and Video*. 15/1: 1–13.

Zimmerman, B. (1981) 'Lesbian Vampires.' *Jump Cut*. 24/5: 23–4.

7

Coming in the Classroom: Explicitly Sexualized Lesbian and Gay Representations in the Academy

Jane Gardner and Sarah Oerton

Debates about the impact on the academy of teachings on lesbian and gay identities, politics and cultures are already taking place, both in North America and in the UK (Wilton, 1995; Garber, 1994; Abelove *et al.*, 1993). In these discussions, issues ranging from the disclosure of lesbian or gay sexual identities in classrooms, to the content and form of lesbian and gay curricula in the humanities and social sciences (Epstein, 1994; Harbeck, 1992) are addressed. This cannot be said of the placing and integrating of explicitly sexualized (including allegedly sadomasochistic and 'shocking') lesbian and gay materials into academic courses. Drawing upon our experiences of teaching as sociologists and feminists interested in a radical sexual politics, we would like to explore the ways in which secure (and dangerous or forbidden) spaces for the interactive viewing of sexually charged lesbian and gay representations operate in classroom settings with diverse student bodies. Specifically, we would like to explore some of the creative tensions and intimacies that resulted from the inclusion of explicitly sexualized lesbian and gay photographs on two second and third level undergraduate courses in sociology which the two of us recently designed and taught. Neither of these courses was a lesbian- or gay-only forum, although the extent to which they were safer spaces in which to disclose a plethora of sexual identities and practices (both for students and facilitators) is a point to which we shall return later.

The institutional context in which these sociology courses are located gave rise to particular characteristics. The courses were not compulsory core ones; they formed part of a modular humanities and social science scheme, taught on a semester basis, and as such they attracted students with diverse disciplinary backgrounds. In the case of both courses, numbers tended to be small (between ten and twenty) with some students having considerable experience of women's studies courses, and/or familiarity with the history and sociology of sexuality, while others had neither. Although students would have had the option to take other (non-sociology) courses dealing with theories of representation, such as ones on feminist film theory and cultural politics, most of the students were unfamiliar with the theoretical debates concerned with the 'gaze' and with spectatorship. While women predominated in numerical terms on the courses, there were also a few heterosexual and gay men. All but two of the students in the cohorts (and both of us) were white. The courses ran for thirteen weeks, with two-hour, workshop-style sessions taking place each week, and two weeks for coursework-based assessment. The course descriptions made clear mention of the focus upon representation, but not of their explicitly sexualized content. Despite framing many of the workshop sessions as a series of questions, power to construct these courses (as well as assign grades) clearly lay with those teaching them. On both courses, and among other things, space was created for a critical consumption of 'erotic'/ 'pornographic' lesbian and gay cultural productions, drawn from a number of lesbian and gay photographers including contributions featured and/or reprinted in Ainley and Budge, 1993; Meyer, 1993; Boffin and Fraser, 1991; Grace, 1991; Haacke, 1991; Hoffman, 1991; and JEB, 1979. We wish to explore the selection and handling of, and response to, these materials, concentrating particularly on those sessions in which explicitly sexualized photographs were used to generate discussion. In this chapter we argue that the exploration and analysis of such photographs in sociology curricula can be vital, stimulating and subversive as well as very problematic. However, we are still working towards creating strategies to deal with the problems we identify. What we intend in this chapter is an exploration of some of the issues we encountered. We therefore raise more questions than we provide answers.

The sessions we want to concentrate on in particular took place when the courses were at least halfway through, and when, for both ourselves and the students, questions around safety and risk-taking were already explicitly on the agenda. The sessions were designed to encourage students to decode the signifiers of lesbianism/gayness, and to question the meaning of the lesbian or gay 'gaze'. This seemed particularly apposite given the developments from the 1970s onwards of work on the gaze, and particularly of work which has centred, but also critiqued, the power of the male gaze (Mulvey, 1975; Berger, 1972) and more recently, the female gaze (Gamman and Marshment, 1988). To some extent, this theoretical work on the gaze has reflected the stranglehold of sex/gender binaries and the limits of bipolar gendered spectator positions. This has been acknowledged by Williams (1991) and others. Evans and Gamman claim that 'gaze theory's universal focus on questions of gender has been applied wholesale to the extent that it cannot begin to address or explain how other dynamics of identity, in addition to gender – such as race, class, and generation, and the complex ways these categories intersect – may influence representations' (1995, p. 27). With the destabilizing of the gendered gaze, the possibilities for fluid, fluctuating and even obscure gazes have been recognized (Stacey, 1988) and gazes involving sexualized and racialized ways of looking have been explored (Burston, 1995; Evans and Gamman, 1995; de Lauretis, 1993; Meyer, 1993). The acknowledgement that the gaze is tied up with social relations and is context-dependent has therefore gained ascendancy. This has opened up possibilities that subject positions (and gazes) are fractured and 'everyone has their queer moments' (Burston and Richardson, 1995, p. 6).

Nevertheless, the text itself still remains implicated in the construction of gazes. Dyer (1992) in his analysis of the male 'pin-up' argues that the production of the photograph is controlled by the photographer and model providing an image which is constructed through their work, in addition to the 'promiscuous' imagination and pleasure of the spectator's gaze. Hence the photography itself restricts what can actually be said by whom and about what in any given social context, at any one time (Dyer, 1993). What we want to explore here is one empirical example of how both ourselves and students on our sociology courses positioned themselves in relation to explicitly sexualized representations of lesbians and gay men, and what gazes were open to us/them. Clearly there are contradictions here, not only in terms of what is prohibited and what is acceptable in terms of which representations are constituted as 'sexualized', but also what constitutes a reading of a representation as 'lesbian' (or 'gay'). These last two may not be synonymous or equivalent. As Wilton argues: 'How to say "lesbian" in photography is perhaps the key problem' (1995, p. 148). Perhaps there is no such thing as lesbian or gay photography, only that some photographers are lesbian women or gay men and that their work is never open to a fixed, homogeneous reading. It can be elusive and can change, but not in a way that is easily disconnected from social context, legal regulation and political power.

The tension between the gaze as both embedded *and* free-floating gave rise to a number of related concerns for our purposes. For example, what sort of spectator positions do explicitly sexualized lesbian and gay representations construct for students? Do they invite a multiplicity of positionings (though clearly not an infinite number of them)? Do students have to be willing to view as lesbians and gays, or in being less specifically situated, what viewing positions are possible (and desirable)? What are the political implications of any discussion of (albeit commodified and stylized) photographs dealing with lesbian and gay sexualities among non-lesbian and non-gay students, especially when they are heterosexual men and heterosexual women? All of these concerns were predicated on the idea that in order to take up any informed position, students would have to be familiar, albeit in different ways, with the codes of reference at work in the photographs. In short, they would necessarily have to develop different 'cultural competencies' based upon subcultural knowledges (Evans and Gamman, 1995, p. 35). In short, if they didn't 'understand', then they didn't get it. Hence our inclusion of some very 'in yer face' photographs.

Decisions about how representations deemed to be sexually explicit are constructed, regulated and distributed takes place in a wider socio-political and legal context, and it is evident that the work of some lesbians and gay men has opened up various contradictions around decency and privacy, censorship and 'exploitation' (Grace, 1991; Mapplethorpe, 1988). Notwithstanding this, the politics of what was selected for inclusion in the sociology courses we taught centred in large part on our own objectives for students.[1] These objectives were neither unambiguous nor simple, but did include encouraging students to think critically (and, to an extent, respectfully) about the construction of lesbian and gay desires and passions. More precisely, we were neither seeking to elicit students' responses to the photographs based upon a single gender bipolarity (readings as women or as men) nor were we seeking a single, situated sexual self (readings as lesbian, gay, heterosexual, bisexual, camp, queer and so on). We were also not asking for students to respond in *any* way that they wanted to, since not just any spectator position is authorized or elicited by the text such that *any* photograph can become the object of 'queer moments'. In addition, we attempted to frame these sessions with reference to debates concerning feminist pedagogy. Coate Bignell has argued that 'one of the aims of feminist pedagogy is to give authenticity to students' experiences and to welcome their perspectives as a valuable resource for learning (1996, p. 315). This emphasis upon giving primacy to student's articulations at the experiential and 'feeling' level, however, was highly problematic in relation to the inclusion of explicitly sexualized lesbian and gay representations in the classroom, for reasons which we will go on to explore later.[2]

But first, what did we want and expect from these sessions? We anticipated that they would give rise to various challenges for both ourselves and the students. Debates around the 'inappropriate' hetero-sexualization of academic space are already taking place, but little attention has been given to how this 'inappropriateness' might operate in terms of sexual diversity (except in limited ways in equal opportunities policies and practices) or to the extent to which consideration of sexual 'perversities' can coexist with academic and political freedoms.[3] Given the silence and abhorrence which surrounds lesbian and gay sexual desires, not to deal with explicitly sexualized lesbian and gay texts in sociology courses dealing with subjectivities, identities and representations would be to render lesbian and gay sexualities invisible, to subject them to silence and subterfuge. We anticipated that the inclusion of explicitly sexualized lesbian and gay photographs on these courses would be both stimulating and contentious, since in spite of, or maybe because of, the homoeroticism and homophobia which is present in academic institutions (as elsewhere), we assumed both fascination with, and resistance to, representations of lesbian and gay sex (often based on an assumption that subjects are erotic and/or perverse because they belong to communities which are defined primarily as sexual). We also anticipated that making publicly available photographs which could be constructed as obscene and 'shocking' might be to expose students both to the problems and pleasures of lesbian and gay voyeurism/exhibitionism (with all the unruly passion, discomfort and anger that that might entail) and to invite critical commentary from students as to the purposes of including such material on sociology courses in the first place. In opening up the spaces in which to give students the opportunity to view and respond to representations of lesbians and gay men exercising active, self-determined sexual pleasures, we were also aware that we were subjecting them to materials which they might find arousing (or offensive and degrading), and which might encourage 'positive' (or 'negative') reactions in them.[4] At the very least, we anticipated that these sessions would be provocative, vibrant and galvanizing; in short, that we would engage students and that they would 'jump in and get going'.

In the event, a different set of challenges presented themselves and fell short of our expectations in unanticipated ways, since they were not typical of students' engagement in other sessions on the courses. Students on both courses, in both years, generally responded to the photographs with overwhelming silence and immobilization. At the extreme, this silence took the form of a complete refusal to engage in any discussion, such that when little in the way of informed debate was taking place, even an appeal for students to voice *some* thoughts or feelings met with painful non-engagement. To begin with we struggled to make sense of what was going on and why. Was it all simply the result of situating explicitly sexualized (and often *privately* consumed) lesbian and gay representations in a specific and unfamiliar *public* forum, namely the academy, with students required to voice publicly their responses to the photographs in an immediate and spontaneous way? While offering one possible explanation, this ignores the very public (but also restricted) spaces in which, for example, Grace's and Mapplethorpe's photographs have been infamously exhibited, published and discussed (Hoffman, 1991). Was this silence the result of the conditions under which we were all working, not least that lecturers/facilitators (ourselves included) require that students demonstrate some 'cultural competencies' commensurate with the academic context in which we/they are situated? In our attempts to give meaning to this silence, we want to critique the impositions made upon both ourselves and students, such that we/they were only allowed to speak certain responses publicly, and to suggest that the processes of being both silent and silencing in these sessions operate in complex and contradictory ways which require systematic exploration and analysis by sociologists and others.

We want to explore a number of interrelated issues which may have had some bearing upon what was happening. First, the potential legal implications of publicly exhibiting explicitly sexualized lesbian and gay photographs has resulted in overt attempts (by gallery and bookstore directors and owners) to present such work as professional 'works of art'. This then allows for a distancing of the (pseudo-professional) reader/spectator, since what is being looked at is 'art' rather than 'obscenity', 'erotica' or 'pornography'. The marking of such representations as 'art' confounds the 'chain of hysterical association' (Vance, 1990, pp. 49–55) or homophobia explicit in Senator Jesse Helms's claims that homoerotic sadomasochistic material is 'obscene' and 'sick' (Haacke, 1991). It also allows 'patrons of the San Francisco art circuit [to] "rub shoulders" with the "men in black leather" while safely installed within the chic propriety of the art opening' (Meyer, 1993, p. 362). When giving the photographs to students, however, we were demanding, to a certain extent, personal-political responses, without the protection of the pseudo-professional position claimed by others. It is naive to expect both responses to coexist, but which one would we want to sacrifice? In not necessarily asking students to bring their *own* perspectives/viewing positions to the photographs but requiring that they did at least attempt to 'construct' a spectator position themselves which would enable them to deal with 'difficult' material, we *were* asking them to make a political investment which may have impacted upon them personally. However, personal-political responses may be extremely uncomfortable for students. Yet few of them in the contained environment of the classroom seemed willing to admit to difficulties with the material or to finding it disturbing or distasteful. This was clearly silencing for both them/us.

Second, there are issues of student 'safety' at stake here. As was pointed out to us, students on modular degree schemes do not attend these classes exclusively; they meet in other areas in the academy (some of them social) and this awareness may have affected their responses to the photographs, since there might have been repercussions for them beyond the classroom. No doubt in other interactions, for example, with lovers and friends on an equal footing or in 'one-off' encounters, students would respond to the same photographs very differently. This may have been compounded because, in general terms, sociology does not tend to offer students access to critically informed debates around the liberal, anti-censorship positions that may be more easily taken up by students in, for example, cultural studies or art history. This may give students in other disciplines a more 'protected' position from which to speak, which students with backgrounds primarily in sociology tend not to have access to. As a result, this left both ourselves and the students in dangerously exposed positions, without 'safe' discourses upon which to call.[5]

Third, and perhaps more telling, there were our own positions in the classroom; how safe (or dangerous) a position is assumed by those facilitating the exploration of explicitly sexualized lesbian and gay representations, as students openly view and discuss work? Did we inevitably restrict spectatorship by filtering and masking materials we selected for inclusion in our courses, particularly given the illegality of certain of the representations used? How implicated were we in this silence? Our mediation of the photographs used also took the form of concerns over 'censorship' and control which, when used in this context, were informed by the risks taken by lecturers/facilitators. We were also concerned with viewing 'choice' and the methods via which representations were actually presented to students. The positioning of materials was therefore crucially important; placing representations on slides or OHPs, setting the photographs up in 'gallery' situations (where students could not escape viewing them) is clearly different from placing those same representations on hard copy A4 paper on flat surfaces in the corner of a classroom (where students have to actively access them) or having them in stapled workpacks which were distributed in batches. In the event, we used a combination of these last two methods, and we also retained control over the timing and the order of the dissemination process. However, these latter 'choices' do contain an implicit form of coercion for *all* students to look, as, in the event, it was difficult for any one individual student to refuse to do so. This problematizes issues of viewing 'choice', censorship and control, and this may have contributed to the silencing processes which operated in the sessions.

But even with the problems identified above, the students' public non-engagement was still somewhat baffling, especially given our expectation that they would get 'turned on' by the photographs and that they would generate lively discussion. Some rather tentative responses were voiced by students. To begin with, and not surprisingly, when the silence was broken there were persistent attempts to assign gendered categories to certain of the subjects depicted in the photographs, so that the question, for example, of whether photographs of lesbians were really of men's bodies arose repeatedly. In the case of one student (who had self-consciously defined himself as heterosexual) an authoritative position on lesbian sex was assumed by means of proscribing lesbian sexual desires in terms of what he thought lesbians do or do not find arousing. On other occasions there were, interestingly, overt attempts at heterosexist reinscription, often involving phenomenal amounts of work in recording lesbians as heterosexual women, when they were engaging in active sexual exchanges such as kissing, touching and embracing (and even where they were bare-breasted). It appeared that a blurring and erasure of representational difference was occurring, but primarily in the context of *lesbian* representations alone. To be more precise, several of the photographs of lesbians were likened by students to Madonna's *Sex*, and even to some fashion advertising involving androgynous, look-alike, embracing women and girls. Certain of the photographs involving lesbians touching and kissing were thereby read as safe, 'clean' (even romantic?). Such responses do not allow for representations of lesbian sex to be read as 'polluted' in the way that representations of homosexual sex have been (Meyer, 1993). Even some of Della Grace's most explicitly sexualized photographs were 'sanitized' in a similar vein so that students' responses appeared to mirror responses to explicitly sexualized heterosexual representations of women, namely, what was disturbing or worrying to some students was the implicit violence/pleasure of *women* getting fucked. Hence some students' readings of 'chick-on-chick pornography' assumed the omnipresence of men's power and control over representations of *all* women.

Perhaps because of the heterosexism of most mainstream media and genres, the 'cultural competencies' available to many students are likely to be framed in narrow ways, hence this heterosexist reinscription. Virtually all the students in the cohorts we taught had great difficulty in specifying exactly what lines get crossed in order to read something (anything?) as 'lesbian', something that incidentally (most students asserted) *Sex* and the fashion photographs were not. However, in inscribing rigidly gendered and heterosexualized readings into the photographs, students were tending to foreclose discussion. We would want to argue that explicitly sexualized lesbian and gay representations cannot and should not be drawn upon to constitute a visible 'Otherness' against which heterosexuality can be contrasted, but at the same time we are not suggesting that difference cannot or should not be marked. How this is done should be a major concern both for sociologists and for students, who need the tools to engage in aspects of the construction of our/their identities which move beyond the limited dichotomies of gender, thereby providing us/them with opportunities to voice the pleasures and contradictions of our/their 'queer moments'.

Conversely, Mapplethorpe's S/M photographs were never read as anything other than homosexual representations, and there were no attempts at heterosexist reinscription of men's bodies in these poses, nor any attempt to seek signifiers of 'femininity' or a feminized body (for example, 'Is that a man or a woman?'). The deliberately posed and stylized content of Mapplethorpe's representations of S/M homosexual sex follow neither the conventions of heterosexist coding nor those of gay pornography as identified by Burston (1995). In terms of heterosexist mainstream media, representations of men have not allowed for readings of them as 'romancing' or 'buddying' each other in the ways that representations of women have (*Thelma and Louise*, 1991; *Fried Green*

Tomatoes at the Whistlestop Cafe, 1991). Burston has argued that in gay pornography even homosexuality tends to be 'screened out of the picture', so that representations of men engaged in 'erotic' behaviour typically involve them in accidentally sharing communal showers, where they 'just fool about' with each other and make reference to 'girlfriends' (1995, p. 2). Mapplethorpe's S/M photographs on the other hand, characterized by 'audacious anality' as Meyer (1993, p. 363) has described it, do not allow for any configuration of women's (absent but implicitly present) sexual power or prowess; neither women nor heterosexuality are the referents, and so it was harder for students to recode any of Mapplethorpe's S/M photographs as 'heterosexual'.

We would like to tentatively explore some of the implications of the differences in students' responses to the explicitly sexualized lesbian photographic work as opposed to the gay work. In the case of inclusion of explicitly sexualized photographs of lesbians in our courses, we have argued that women's bodies tended to be viewed in terms of the cultural currency available in heterosexualized and phallocentric discourses: namely, women as objects for men's gazes and desires. As was pointed out to us, representations of lesbians and lesbianism are thus subject to incorporation into these existing discourses and are further allied with other signifiers of women's sexual transgression such as frigidity, insanity and nymphomania, all of which are constructed to indicate the consequences for women who stray too far from the patriarchal order. The scarcity of representations of 'autonomous' lesbian sex between women indicates the disinclination to take women seriously as sexually active agents. This contrasts with a willingness to accept 'gay sex' texts as autonomous, as narratives of oppression and exclusion (particularly when they are not *too* sexually provocative). But, with a few notable exceptions (Grosz and Probyn, 1995; Jay, 1995), there is little scholarship which examines lesbian erotica in terms of 'forms of fascination between women available to *all* women' (Stacey, 1994, p. 29, original emphasis). We would argue that this has the effect of denying students the possibilities for any 'lesbian' (in addition to 'queer') moments that they might experience in the classroom. In this respect, we would concur with Stacey's claim that 'identification between femininities contains forms of homoerotic pleasure which have yet to be explored' (Stacey, 1994, p. 29).

In the light of this, it is understandably difficult to analyse responses to 'lesbian' representations. To accept spaces in which lesbians 'speak' to lesbians, and to grant to the explicitly sexualized 'lesbian' photographs the same autonomy as that seemingly granted (albeit within limits) to the 'gay' photographs, is very problematic. These difficulties are further compounded by portrayals of the sexualized activities of lesbians as forbidden and outlawed, as supplementary foreplay and/or as masculinized and phallocentric, all readings which maintain dominant discourses of self-directed and active lesbian sexuality as 'narcissistic' and 'male'. Notwithstanding this, it is important that lesbianism is not represented solely in terms of physical sexual practices, since lesbians have historically been defined in limited ways, most commonly in terms of what lesbians do sexually. 'Lesbian sex' has also been used as a standard form of titillation in heterosexual men's pornography. But erasing lesbians' sexual desires perpetuates the notion that lesbians are unable to define and articulate those desires in ways that would mark 'difference'. In the case of some photographs of lesbian sex, for example, there have been criticisms that they are simply too tame and 'vanilla' (Smyth, 1992). These problems are not so evident in the construction of homosexual desires and practices where 'difference' is overtly and negatively marked, so that, for example, concern has been publicly expressed over the extent to which dirt and disease, violence and death surround Mapplethorpe's explicitly (homo)sexualized representations (Meyer, 1993, p. 373). The unresolved difficulties here create tensions for student responses in the classroom.

Finally, we are aware that within sociology as currently constituted, there is an assumption that the exploration and theorizing of explicitly sexualized representations (whether 'lesbian' and 'gay', or not) is taking place elsewhere in the academy, namely in those disciplines where theories of representations are centre-stage (film studies, cultural studies, media studies, literature, etc). We would argue that this is a strange position for sociologists to take, given the postmodernist 'turn' towards theorizing identities and subjectivities and the growing interest in sexualities and bodies. But even if the discussions are taking place in other disciplines, we would want to argue that it is vitally important that we put our concerns, as we have identified and argued them in this chapter, at the centre of sociological debates surrounding representations, identities and subjectivities in the 1990s. Across the disciplinary board, the theoretical tools upon which students can draw in order to elicit 'lesbian' as well as 'queer' 'moments' need to be in place. We suggest that those working in the academy with an interest in interdisciplinarity need to take issue with the problems of non-engagement in this area and develop strategies for overcoming them. Sociologists are in a unique position to engage in and analyse these unfolding processes, since there may be commonalities and difference in terms of being silenced and silencing which have been explored in relation to class, 'race' and able-bodiedness, and which may be highly pertinent to the project we identify. It is thus of key importance that sociology as a discipline uncovers and explains the operation of these processes as they are constituted in and between interweaving subject positionings. We hope that our contribution will go some way to addressing the inattention paid so far to this subject.

Notes

We would like to thank Lesley Gannon, Sophie Nield and Jo Phoenix for their helpful comments and constructive input during the writing of this chapter.

1. The intentions of both producers of explicitly sexualized representations and those making use of them in the classroom are linked in complex ways. As Lewis maintains: '*Love Bites* [the title of Della Grace's lesbian erotic photographs], which is self-consciously illicit and transgresses the boundaries of taste and acceptability, not only would be harder to incorporate into teaching syllabi but is also profoundly ambivalent about whether it would want to be there' (1994, p. 77).
2. Clearly it would be naive to suggest that all feminist practitioners give primacy to students' own (sometimes very problematic) perspectives in classroom settings. Students do not have a homogeneous or even individually unified perspective and they may in addition openly articulate racist, homophobic and disablist views. Interestingly, as Coate Bignell points out, scant attention has been given to the perspectives and experiences of students in women's studies publications (1996, p. 315). While we welcome the need to foreground students' involvement in informed debates in the classroom, we would argue that they must also be allowed access to critiques of the complex working of power relations, if they are not to be left with little to say beyond the anecdotal and experiential.
3. The inclusion of explicitly sexualized lesbian and gay photographs in one of the sociology courses we taught was intended to problematize debates around pornography. Up until then, the students tended to take on very polarized positions in relation to the production and distribution of ('heterosexual') pornography. The introduction of lesbian and gay 'pornographies' had the intention (and the result?) of provoking students into less simplistic readings.
4. For our purposes here the issue is less one of how 'positive' or 'negative' expressions of lesbian and gay sexualities are disseminated in the classroom, as this in itself is problematic. To begin with, the concern to present a 'clean', respectable public image of lesbian and gay sex has been seen as politically reactionary by some queer theorists (Smith, 1992). There is also a tendency to assume that an 'authentic' lesbian and gay voice or perspective is necessarily positive in that it avoids perpetuating exaggerated, stereotyped and distorted representations of lesbians and gay men. Hantzis and Lehr, however, reject the notion that *any* positive portrayal of lesbian and gay characters (on television) merits celebration, and argue that, even if they appear to display the goodwill of various directors, producers and writers towards lesbian and gay issues, many 'positive' portrayals serve as mechanisms to perpetuate heterosexism by presenting a 'positive' lesbian and gay character as one who is not threatening to heterosexuals (1994, p. 118).
5. This is not to argue that we were insensitive to the ways in which our intentions for and requirements of students ruptured and contravened 'safe' discourses. This awareness of the lack of 'protection' further informed our selection of the photographs to be shown on these courses, while at the same time it mediated our attempts to encourage students to call upon academic and discursive knowledges which they had gained prior to these sessions. In short, it was not our intention to expose students in such a way that left them with *no* positions from which to articulate their responses.

References

Abelove, H., Barale, M.A. and Halperin, D.M. (1993) *The Lesbian and Gay Studies Reader*. New York: Routledge.

Ainley, R. and Budge, B. (eds) (1993) *Lesbian Looks: Postcards from the Edge*. London: Scarlet Press.

Berger, J. (1972) *Ways of Seeing*. Harmondsworth: BBC Publications and Penguin Books.

Boffin, T. and Fraser, J. (eds) (1991) *Stolen Glances: Lesbians Take Photographs*. London: Pandora.

Burston, P. (1995) *What Are You Looking At? Queer Sex, Style and Cinema*. London: Cassell.

Burston, P. and Richardson, C. (eds) (1995) *A Queer Romance: Lesbians, Gay Men and Popular Culture*. London and New York: Routledge.

Coate Bignell, K. (1996) 'Building Feminist Praxis out of Feminist Pedagogy: The Importance of Students' Perspectives.' *Women's Studies International Forum*. 19/3: 315–25.

de Lauretis, T. (1993) 'Sexual Indifference and Lesbian Representation.' In Abelove *et al.* (1993).

Dyer, R. (1992) 'Don't Look Now: The Male Pin-Up.' In Screen Editorial Collective (eds) *The Sexual Subject: A Screen Reader in Sexuality*. London and New York: Routledge.

Dyer, R. (1993) *The Matter of Images: Essays on Representations*. London and New York: Routledge.

Epstein, D. (ed.) (1994) *Challenging Lesbian and Gay Inequalities in Education*. Buckingham: Open University Press.

Evans, C. and Gamman, L. (1995) 'The Gaze Revisited, Or Reviewing Queer Viewing.' In Burston and Richardson (1995).

Gamman, L. and Marshment, M. (eds) (1988) *The Female Gaze: Women as Viewers of Popular Culture*. London: The Women's Press.

Garber, L. (ed.) (1994) *Tilting the Tower: Lesbians Teaching Queer Subjects*. New York and London: Routledge.

Grace, D. (1991) *Love Bites*. London: GMP Publishers.

Grosz, E. and Probyn, E. (eds) (1995) *Sexy Bodies: The Strange Carnalities of Feminism*. London and New York: Routledge.

Haacke, H. (1991) 'In the Vice'. *Art Journal*. (Fall) 50/3: 49–55.

Hantzis, D.M. and Lehr, V. (1994) 'Whose Desire? Lesbian (Non)Sexuality and Television's Perpetuation of Hetero/Sexism.' In J. Ringer (ed.) (1994) *Queer Words, Queer Images: Communication and the Construction of Homosexuality*. New York and London: New York University Press.

Harbeck, K.M. (ed.) (1992) *Coming Out of the Classroom Closet: Gay and Lesbian Students, Teachers and Curricula*. London: The Haworth Press.

Hoffman, B. (1991) 'The Thought Police Are Out There – Reflections on the First Amendment Protection of Offensive or Indecent Artistic Expression.' *Art Journal*. (Fall) 50/3: 40–5.

Jay, K. (ed.) (1995) *Lesbian Erotics*. New York and London: New York University Press.

JEB (Joan E. Biren) (1979) *Eye to Eye: Portraits of Lesbians, Photographs by JEB*. Washington, DC: Glad Hag Books.

Lewis, R. (1994) 'Dis-Graceful Images: Della Grace and Lesbian Sado-Masochism.' *Feminist Review* 46: 76–91.

Mapplethorpe, R. (1988) 'The Perfect Moment.' (Retrospective Exhibition) Institute of Contemporary Art, University of Pennsylvania.

Meyer, R. (1993) 'Robert Mapplethorpe and the Discipline of Photography.' In Abelove *et al.* (1993).

Mulvey, L. (1975) 'Visual Pleasure and Narrative Cinema.' *Screen*. (Autumn) 16/3: 6–18.

Smith, A.M. (1992) 'Resisting the Erasure of Lesbian Sexuality: A Challenge for Queer Activism.' In K. Plummer (ed.)

(1992) *Modern Homosexualities: Fragments of Lesbian and Gay Experience*. London and New York: Routledge.

Smyth, C. (1992) *Lesbians Talk Queer Notions*. London: Scarlet Press.

Stacey, J. (1988) 'Desperately Seeking Difference.' In Gamman and Marshment (1988).

Stacey, J. (1994) *Star Gazing: Hollywood Cinema and Female Spectatorship*. London and New York: Routledge.

Vance, C. (1990) 'Misunderstanding Obscenity.' *Art in America*. (May): 49–55.

Williams, L. (1991) 'Film Bodies: Gender, Genre and Excess.' *Film Quarterly*. (Summer) 44/4: 2–13.

Wilton, T. (1995) *Lesbian Studies: Setting an Agenda*. London and New York: Routledge.

8

Dyke Geographies: All Over the Place

Ali Grant

Recently, I had an excited discussion with another graduate student about the explosion of work in human geography on questions of identity, subjectivity, sexuality, difference and transgression, work that was reflective and constitutive of the general trend in progressive social thinking towards the production of more situated, partial and specific knowledges. At last, it was time for a Canadian 'Geo-Dyke' symposium for sure. However, our excitement quickly dissipated through cyberspace as we e-mailed back and forth, struggling to think of bodies other than our own that might constitute the elusive 'lesbian geographer'. Our correspondence veered off into discussions of gatekeeping and identity formation, and the more than academic question of, 'Well, is she or isn't she?' and 'Does it still matter?'

This illustrates the troubling something that is going on down in the discipline of the spatial: that is, the disjuncture between a burgeoning collection of exciting work on the unsettling of heterosexual hegemony and the mundane reality of the lack of lesbian bodies on the ground, so to speak. In this chapter I take a look at the development of lesbian interventions in geography and offer some thoughts on this disjuncture, as well as the good news that those symposia may soon become more than a mapper's fancy.

Off the map: the marginalized subject(s)

Sexuality has been a relative latecomer to the analysis of social, cultural, political and economic geographies, which is not surprising given the hegemony of masculinist knowledges in the discipline (Longhurst, 1995; Johnson, 1994; Pratt and Hanson, 1994; Rose, 1993a). As feminist geographers Loretta Lees and Robyn Longhurst point out, geographic knowledge 'has been constructed as that which is rational, reasonable, public, cultural, productive, masculine and of the mind' (1995, p. 218). More than two decades of feminist work in the discipline have somewhat disrupted this state of affairs[1] (McDowell, 1993a, 1993b; Rose, 1993b; Johnson, 1985; Mackenzie, 1984; Women and Geography Study Group,

1984; Tivers, 1978; Hayford, 1974); however, sexuality has, until quite recently, been kept off the map (Bell and Valentine, 1995; Bell, 1991).

The notion that space and sexuality might be mutually constitutive appeared initially in geographers' attempts to map 'gay ghettos' – the regions and neighbourhoods that were viewed as spatial expressions of distinct lifestyles and/or of marginalizing forces on deviant groups within the inner city (Winchester and White, 1988; Weightman, 1981). Gay geographer Larry Knopp's early work introduced some much-needed detail and political analysis to the study of the impact of lesbians and gays on the socio-spatial (re)structuring of the city (Knopp, 1990, 1987; Lauria and Knopp, 1985). Of course, most of this early work was urban and male in focus and the apparent invisibility of lesbian landscapes was explained in generalizing terms which feminist geographer Linda Peake criticized as 'smack[ing] of an inability to rise above the level of the patriarchal mire, of being unable to unpack the heterogeneity of class, "race", and other relations that characterize the lesbian community' (1993, p. 425).

Both this disappearance of lesbian under the sign 'gay' and the general heterosexism of the discipline were increasingly challenged from the late 1980s onwards (Bell and Valentine, 1995; Chouinard and Grant, 1995; Bell *et al.*, 1994; Peake, 1993; Valentine, 1993c; Adler and Brenner, 1992; Bell, 1991). It was clear that much of the work on sexuality in the 1980s had produced geographies of gay men and further, that feminist geography had been relatively slow in taking up the notion of a regulatory sexuality as central to male control of women's bodies, labour power and so forth. The work of lesbian geographer Gill Valentine was (and continues to be) pivotal in creating space for the emergence of critical lesbian interventions in the discipline in the 1990s. Her initial work (based on interviews with forty lesbians in a southern town in the UK) moved beyond a mapping and/or impact of the city approach to a detailed examination of the multiple ways lesbians experience, negotiate and transform everyday spaces.

Space is of course (hetero)sexed (Valentine, 1993a, 1993b, 1993c). The mutual constitution of sexualities and spaces is made most visible when the hegemonic heterosexuality of everyday environments is disrupted by the presence of deviant and/or unintelligible bodies. As cultural theorist Judith Butler has argued:

> The cultural matrix through which gender identity has become intelligible requires that certain kinds of 'identities' cannot 'exist' – that is, those in which gender does not follow from sex and those in which the practices of desire do not 'follow' from either sex or gender. (1990, p. 17)

Subversive spatial acts (Bell and Valentine, 1995) by organizations such as the Lesbian Avengers, Queer Nation and ACT UP disrupt the fabric of this cultural matrix, exposing (hetero)sexed space as an artefact; clearly not a natural backdrop which is 'just there', but something which must be produced and maintained through heteronormative repetition and regulation. Puncturing this 'thereness' is not simply a matter of the *presence* of unintelligible bodies; lesbians must work hard to *be and be seen* (Frye, 1983), to challenge the disappearing processes of the regulatory fictions of sex and gender (Butler, 1990; Valentine, 1996). This is especially so of the everyday spaces in which lesbians spend most of our time – workplaces, restaurants, public transport, the street and the home.

Intelligible sexualities are formed in place and time. Julia Cream notes:

> If, then, gender *and* sex are historically and geographically variable categories perhaps we need to think of different ways of understanding and talking about our bodies, our sex and our gender. We need to find new questions: questions that require a reappraisal of what it means to 'be' a woman or man. (1995, p. 36)

Geographers have been excited to see the centrality that spatiality is playing in these questions (Pratt and Hanson, 1994; Price-Chalita, 1994). Marginality, displacement, location and place are used both metaphorically and materially in the writings of many contemporary feminist theorists, in (re)thinking questions of difference, community, oppression and resistance. Recent lesbian interventions have played an important part in progressive geographic considerations of the roles that sex, bodies, desire and performance play in processes of regulation and transgression in place (Murray, 1995, Valentine, 1996).

Out and about: dykes make space at last

However, the treatment of lesbians in geography has been more often one marked by absences. The pervasive and enduring heterosexism of the discipline constructed 'women' as heterosexual-by-default. Lesbians made little appearance in early work on gays in the city. The aforementioned contention of Castells (1983) and others (for example, Lauria and Knopp, 1985) that a supposed lack of the lesbian mark on the city could be accounted for by men's greater territorial aspirations, needs and/or economic resources was challenged by the later work of geographers such as Linda Peake, Tamar Rothenberg and Gill Valentine. These authors have effectively illustrated that lesbian space is, of course, there if you know what to look for, and even if you don't – that in fact lesbians in certain places do create neighbourhoods and communities, both real and imagined. In her work on Park Slope, Brooklyn, for example, Tamar Rothenberg notes that 'In the process of creating a lesbian space, or perhaps more precisely a semi-lesbian or lesbian-congenial space, lesbians have been active participants in the gentrification of a neighbourhood' (1995, p. 165).

Further, geographical, historical and cultural variation in produced lesbian spaces reflects the embedded nature of these processes in place. In contemporary western societies, communities in smaller cities, towns and rural areas may leave relatively little institutional mark on the landscape, that is, one which can be easily read by *non-lesbians* – such as lesbian bookstores, restaurants and community centres – but this does not mean that they are not there. For example, feminist geographer Linda Peake's (1993) work in Grand Rapids, Michigan, found clusters of intentionally created lesbian households within the heterosexual fabric of the city. This lesbian landscape differs from that of big cities such as Vancouver where distinctive communities might be marked by lesbian co-ops, bars, a cultural centre and a very visible and insistent lesbian presence on the street.[2]

Then there are the more fleeting transgressive spaces created by temporary ruptures in the everyday heterosexual façade – two dykes kissing on the street – and the longer-lasting, but still temporary, spaces of lesbian pride marches, demonstrations, the production and consumption of music (Valentine, 1995), and of dances and culture in general. Whether or not they are actually widely read as lesbian spaces (the way a lesbian bar may be), they temporarily destabilize the fictional coherence of heterosexual environments. Although there has been much work inside and outside geography on the more visible and permanent types of urban and rural lesbian spaces,[3] these heterosexual and hostile environments are the ones most of us spend most of our time negotiating.

Spatial subversions: everyday negotiations

The ritualized performance of sexual identities, the regulatory force of the heterosexual imperative and the body as a site of oppression and resistance are at last firmly on the agenda of some of the more radical and progressive areas of the discipline (Bell and Valentine, 1995; Cream, 1995; Duncan, 1996; Longhurst, 1995; McDowell and Court, 1994). The publication of David Bell and Gill Valentine's edited collection *Mapping Desire: Geographies of Sexualities* marks the emergence of sexualized geographies as an insistent and expanding area of research in the discipline.[4] Although a timely and impressive collection of work by geographers and non-geographers, the editors recognize it is limited because the included geographies are 'primarily the experiences of "whites" within contemporary US and UK cities' (1995, p. 10). Within these limitations there is a certain variety in the multiple sexualized geographies presented including chapters by lesbian geographers – for example, Ali Murray's chapter on butch/femme and lesbian sex workers, Tracey Skelton's contribution on gay resistance and Jamaican Ragga and Lynda Johnston and Gill Valentine's collaboration on the multiple and contradictory meanings of 'home'.

Johnston and Valentine thoroughly destabilize geographers' use of notions of home as a haven and source of identity by illustrating the diverse senses of home that exist for many lesbians. The parental home, for example, can be a place of oppression and/or subversion for lesbians who are either living there or visiting. As the authors argue, 'it is a location where lesbianism and heterosexuality do battle' (p. 111). The performance of multiple lesbian identities can be seriously constrained by the parental gaze, out or not. Johnston and Valentine found that even if lesbians are out when they return 'home', the familiar process of de-dyking the apartment can be forcefully turned on the self as Julie, a New Zealand lesbian, reveals in this extract:

> When I came out to my parents, my mother said 'there's only one stipulation, you can bring your girlfriends home but they can't sleep in the same room with you' . . . That was it. When I have taken a lover home there she has just been really different. It's felt really uncomfortable. (pp. 101–2)

The sketches produced by New Zealand lesbians for Lynda Johnston of themselves 'at home', of 'my home' and of the heterosexual 'family home' capture, quite beautifully, the multiple and contradictory meaning that different 'homes' can have for lesbians who must perform so differently in different places.

Elsewhere, Gill Valentine (1993b) has illustrated how the performance of this multiplicity of identities in different places can be 'nerve-racking'. Being out in one place and not another can create a situation where running into straight colleagues on the way to a lesbian event with your girlfriend on your arm can create a certain tension. At times then, the 'lesbian home' becomes a refuge, one of the few places where the regulatory forces of heterosexuality can be temporarily kept at bay, and where lesbian identities and cultures can be developed and performed.[5]

Cyberspace is emerging as another possible refuge from the boring overwhelmingness of heterosexuality. Lesbian geographer Celeste Wincapaw's (forthcoming) work on women-only electronic mailing lists as sexualized spaces illustrates how these 'neighbourhoods', based on a mixture of essentialist and non-essentialist notions of gender, are not always apparent to the surfing heterosexual. Further, Wincapaw illustrates some of the local struggles that go on in cyberspace over the creation and maintenance of lesbian-only space. Gatekeeping can be used to a certain extent but requires a definition of what lesbians are. The frequent requirement by list-owners/moderators that subscribers should be biologically female and preferably lesbian and/or bisexual does not and cannot stop men from either identifying as or pretending to be lesbians and getting access to the list. Interestingly, Wincapaw concludes that lesbian space *is* created despite the presence of non- or questionable lesbians, to the extent that it is a space in which lesbian voices and issues dominate.

This is not to suggest some essentialized and false dichotomy of good lesbian space/bad heterosexual space. Neither cyberspace nor the home are uncomplicated backdrops to the playing out of lesbian lives. Lesbian space is always being produced, reproduced, negotiated, fought over. The meaning of the 'lesbian home' is not singular – refuge can quickly become isolation in destructive relationships; periodic de-dyking may be necessary to transform it against the intrusion of the heterosexual gaze. As Joanne, a New Zealand lesbian, succinctly put it, 'Things like *Macho Sluts* . . . would go down like a cup of cold sick. I freak out and run round and de-dyke the whole place' (in Johnston and Valentine, 1995, p. 107). De-dyking is not necessarily reactive – lesbians may choose to maintain the integrity of the lesbian space and/or performance either by keeping heterosexuals out altogether, or by denying them access to lesbian cultures through temporary removal of artefacts and so on.

When thinking about lesbian spaces, geographers have been drawn to Benedict Anderson's notion of 'imagined communities' where those who see themselves as belonging 'will never know most of their fellow-members, meet them, or even hear of them, yet in the mind of each lives the image of their communion' (1991, p. 6). When dykes in different places talk of 'the community' it is partly this notion of community that is being invoked, although as many a travelling dyke will tell you, the distinction between imagined and real is a slippery one, as friends of friends of friends provide floor space in faraway places. There is a sense that when you go to certain social and political events, or enjoy certain artists, members of 'the community' will be there. This is, of course not *the* or *a* community, but multiple communities marked by, among other things, 'race', class, sexual identities and politics. As Arlene Stein notes in discussing historical changes in lesbian 'movements':

> If the corner bar was once the only place in town, by 1990 in cities across the country [USA] there were lesbian parenting groups, support groups for women with cancer and other life-threatening diseases, new and often graphic sexual literature for lesbians, organizations for lesbian 'career women' and lesbians of colour, and mixed organizations where out lesbians played a visible role.[6] (1992, p. 35)

The lesbian spaces that are created when 'the community' comes together can be temporary and sporadic, having to be 'dyked' each time – for example, taking over the hall at the YWCA once a month for a dance. In the premier issue of a new lesbian rag out of Toronto, Lynda Scarrow offers a lighthearted guide to some of the better dyke-spotting places in that city. Some are geographically bounded, but others are a little more mobile and transient. For example, she reveals that 'Canadian Tire,[7] Ikea and Home Depot are hot spots to look for dykes who are good with their hands' (1996, p. 23). The particular flavour of these dyke spots will differ from place to place and certainly would not be easily read as such by non-lesbians. However, the spaces of the power tools aisle are easily 'dyked' by the presence of two or more women discussing the merits of the newest Black and Decker. They may not be dykes (although there's a good chance they will be) but these types of interactions can represent a subversive disruption of heterosexual space in the same way that arranging to meet twenty of your dyke friends down at the new Second Cup, or a dyke shopping night at Fortinos can be. By taking/making space in this way we expose the façade of the heterosexuality of that space and the requirement that it be *made* straight through repetitive heteronormative acts.

Dyking feminist geography: ending the ongoing non-examination

These types of lesbian interventions in the discipline have and will continue to unsettle central geographic notions of place, home, public/private, community, the asexuality of space and so on. These, together with wide-ranging influences from cultural studies and post-colonial and post-structuralist writings, have led to a rethinking of questions central to feminist geography – of gender, sex, femininity and masculinity. Bell and Valentine note however that 'A big absence from geographies of sexualities is, ironically, the dominant sexuality within contemporary societies – heterosexuality' (1995, p. 12). Happily, I think this may be changing with, for example, work by straight feminist geographers on sexualized performances, such as Linda McDowell's (1995) incisive work on heteronormative bodywork in the sexualized spaces of City banking (also with Gill Court, 1994). As feminist geographers move to 'contextualise and localise feminist theorising within the discipline' (Larner, 1995, p. 177), critical lesbian geographies offer much from multiple sites of resistance located inside and outside academic knowledges and practices.

However, Bell and Valentine argue that as geographies of sexuality start to spill out from their locations on the margins of social and cultural geography into political and economic geography, feminist geography is in fact the one area which is in need of a 'divorce' from this emerging work. While I agree that there is indeed a problem of automatically tagging sexuality on to gender (which is certainly the case at conferences for instance, where they tend to be joined in sessions), I disagree on the need for separation when it comes to *lesbian* geographies specifically. There was never a 'marriage' in the first place. That is, the historical, theoretical separation of sex and gender has not only 'allowed society to believe that it can change its sexist behaviour (because gender is a social construction) without challenging the more deeply naturalized idea that men and women are essentially different' (Kobayashi and Peake, 1994, pp. 233–4), it has also allowed areas of feminist geography to imagine that sexist oppression can be challenged without breaking the heterosexual contract. As feminist geographers delve deeper into investigations of the regulatory role that a compulsory heterosexuality plays in the construction of normative femininity and masculinity, our central tenets need a good dose of lesbian intervention rather than a separation from it.

As we have seen 'the unifying objects of our research dissolve before our eyes' (Gibson-Graham, 1994, p. 206), the recognition that Woman has always equalled Heterosexual is an exciting one, full of possibilities. Both Monique Wittig and Judith Butler make convincing cases for theoretical and practical conceptualizations of the categories Women and Men as only making sense within the regulatory heterosexual order – an insight that surely forces an end to what Louise Johnson so nicely calls the 'ongoing non-examination of compulsory heterosexuality in geography' (1994, p. 110). The continuing development of thoroughly embedded, contextualized feminist geographies bodes well for critical recognition of the heterosexual and otherwise positionality of those knowledges (for example, see England, 1994).

Lesbian knowledge which illustrates the substantive challenge that multiple lesbian lives might pose to the reproduction of gender oppression offers much for the geographical investigation of specific processes of oppression, resistance and identity formation in particular places. For example, my own work on local, white, feminist anti-violence activism reveals concretely the various ways in which processes of discipline and punishment are deployed through the regulatory fiction of gender (manifested most obviously in the tired old 'lesbian threat'). In these particular geographies the transformative potential of local feminist activism continues to be effectively defused by the use, not only of the term 'lesbian' but also of the term 'woman'. By constructing (and punishing) certain types of activism as UnWomanly Acts, regulatory bodies use discipline to force the proper 'doing' of gender – thus stabilizing this fiction while simultaneously reducing the potential of such acts to reduce its regulatory power. Critical lesbian interventions offer up for scrutiny the results of the persistent denial of unintelligible bodies and practices: what does the removal and/or denial of lesbians and transgressive females from locations such as sexual assault centres and shelters mean for the development of multiple sites of resistance and identity formation in place; in what ways are the transformative possibilities of feminist movements unrealized by the internal policing of disruptive bodies which so often accompanies institutionalization; what does this kind of regulation in academia mean for the reproduction of regulatory fictions and normative hierarchies in those sites of knowledge production? What will feminist geographies/ers do with the theoretical and practical insight that the necessary refusal to 'do gender right' ultimately means the refusal to be a

Woman? And what does this mean for the invisibility of lesbian bodies in space?

Lesbian bodies: lost in space?

This brings me full circle to the initial conundrum: the case of the missing lesbians. Well, not exactly the missing lesbians, more the not-quite-as-visible-as-we-might-be lesbians. There is an incredible irony in the fact that as we move towards self-consciously situated, *embodied* geographies there has been an associated emergence of strangely migratory, *disembodied* queer geographies. That is, as I perused geographies of sexualities and sexualized geographies for this chapter, I encountered the following bodies during my search for the lesbian geographer (metaphorically, of course): lesbian geographers doing lesbian geographies; self-identified straight women doing lesbian geographies; self-identified lesbian geographers not doing lesbian geographies; professionally and/or otherwise not out lesbians who may or may not be doing lesbian geographies; lesbians who may or may not be doing lesbian geographies who choose politically to eschew that identity; queer geographers doing queer geographies who turned out to be straight bodies (in socio-economic contexts and consequences) and so on. This begs the inevitable question of what constitutes lesbian geographies/ers anyway.

In discussing her own feminist geographies, Louise Johnson refers to the 'complexities of naming' involved in considering positionality: 'I have agonised for years about the consequences – professional and otherwise – of "coming out" in print, declaring my own sexuality and building a feminist geography upon my lesbianism' (1994, p. 110). She wonders what all of the declared components of her identity bring to her feminist geography, noting that 'Clearly, being a woman does not automatically imply a gender-aware geography, nor does a sudden declaration of sexual orientation excuse or even make comprehensible the heterosexist bias in my own work or constitute it automatically as lesbian geography' (*ibid.*). This illustrates the reality that simply being a lesbian does not *automatically* mean transgression, disruption, displacement; nor does it ensure a radical or progressive politics. A lesbian identity is not a given, but one which has to be produced and maintained through repetitive performance (Butler, 1990).

What then is the difference between a straight feminist doing research on the development of lesbian neighbourhoods and a politicized lesbian doing work on lesbian negotiations and transformations of space? Are they both lesbian geographers? Are they both engaged in lesbian geographies? I don't ask these questions lightly and, like bodies, they do matter (Butler, 1993). In (occasionally) disembodied queer geographies, the particular contours of the lived relations of individual knowledge workers seem to fade away in arguments for more fluid conceptions of multiple and mobile sexual identities and subject positions. This travel is of course easier for bodies that have never been forcibly displaced, marginalized or kept out, and this argument, like many things, is most appealing when taken in moderation. Where it rubs like salt against the wound is when disruptive lesbians lose our jobs, find career progression blocked, our teaching disallowed or lacking legitimacy, our bodies ridiculed and denied. As the umbrella of *queer* falls away, forceful and often violent denial of human rights tends to quickly separate the lesbians from the Women. I agree then with Shane Phelan that 'We have to stand where we are, acknowledging the links and contradictions between ourselves and other citizens of the world, resisting the temptations to cloak crucial differences with the cloak of universality and to deny generalities for fear of essentialism' (1993, p. 786). Still, what does it mean, this lesbian geographer thing? It is of course, not a singular body,[8] but I lean firmly towards those Wittigian lesbians[9] – that to be a lesbian geographer is many things, not essentially anything, not a fixed, static identity but one that in the process of always becoming employs disruptive and destabilizing politics. Monique Wittig argues, 'Lesbian is the only category I know of which is beyond the categories of sex (woman and man), because the designated subject (lesbian) is *not* a woman, either economically, or politically, or ideologically' (1992, p. 20). So, I imagine the lesbian geographer to be, among other things, a disruptive body, always and everywhere destabilizing this category of sex and the power of the fiction of gender to regulate our lives. In this process we might make use of feminist geographers Audrey Kobayashi and Linda Peake's 'unnaturalizing discourse' which 'provides for a dismantling of naturalized categories and the imposition of disorder upon the orderly and normative worlds of sexism and racism, in which differences are constructed, organized and naturalized' (1994, p. 226). And as greater numbers of lesbian geographers take up space in the discipline, we can, I hope, move beyond infancy to create a forum where we can begin to engage in the kinds of debate over difference, identity and politics that feminist geographers have begun (see Penrose *et al.*, 1992).

I do of course recognize the partial, situated nature of this knowledge – my clearly positioned self in all of this, as a non-disabled white dyke. It is undoubtedly these locations which allow my privileging of particular lesbian geographies. It is also those privileges that insist I must be out, identified, visible and thus able to be in coalition with those who cannot or will not pass, against multiple and connected systems of oppression. As feminist geographer Wendy Larner notes, 'the goal is not unity based on a common experience, or even experiences, but rather some form of workable compromise which will enable us to coalesce around specific issues' (1995, pp. 187–8).

Lastly, there is another critical part to this visibility and identity issue. In processes of identity formation, coming to be politicized lesbian subjects involves interaction with and knowledge of *other* politicized lesbians. Being firmly of the 'lesbianism is catching' school of transformative politics, I want to suggest that it is critical to be out in academia to disrupt the processes which deny females a choice. As Adrienne Rich argued,

> it is impossible for any woman growing up in a gendered society dominated by men to know what heterosexuality really means, both historically and in her individual life, as long as she is kept ignorant of the presence, the existence, the actuality of women who, diverse in so many ways, have centred their emotional and erotic lives on women. (1986, p. 200)

Coming back down to earth, it is important to emphasize that disappearing processes do, of course, continue in geography. Gill Valentine noted that 'Within the academic community the lack of "out" gay [*sic*] geography students, researchers and staff suggests that many departments are as intolerant of difference as much as other employers' (1993b, p. 246). This is exacerbated by lesbians and lesbian studies being lost in queer space, when 'queer', on the way to indicating a very broad set of political and philosophical positions, has lost so much of its earlier political punch as well as clouding the particular threat that lesbian praxis continues to pose to gender and other hierarchies. However, lesbian spaces *will* continue to be carved out through several processes including the increasing importance of contextualized, situated knowledges in progressive areas of geography and the continuing influence of work from outside the discipline. However, it is critical to resist the potentially contagious elitism that plagues some of the most influential social thinking today and to stay engaged with grassroots activism and ideas, so that our interventions inside academia may have some meaning for our interventions outside it. And finally, this optimism arises from the increasing number of lesbian bodies appearing on the geographical horizon. Much of their work is forthcoming in as-of-yet unpublished dissertations, conference presentations and so on.[10] This and the development of Geo-Dykes, an international network of lesbian geographers,[11] promise to make geography a more attractive and fertile ground for ongoing critical lesbian interventions.

Notes

I would like to thank Joan Bridget, Linda Peake and Gill Valentine for their comments on an earlier draft.

1. See especially *Gender, Place and Culture: A Journal of Feminist Geography*.
2. On spatial variation in the UK, for example, see Sally Munt's (1995) journey from Brighton to Nottingham in *Mapping Desire*.
3. Most of this work in geography has been urban in focus, but see lesbian geographer Cassie Lyon's (1995) work on permanent and seasonal lesbian and women's communities in rural areas of the USA.
4. Having said that, when lesbian geographer Celeste Wincapaw went about recruiting participants for her work on lesbian cyberspaces, she had to work at convincing women on the Internet that she was genuine and that there was in fact such a thing as lesbian geography (personal communication, April 1996).
5. Indeed, Valentine found lesbian homes to be especially important in developing networks where there was a lack of (or no desire for) institutional lesbian spaces such as clubs.
6. Similarly, Becki Ross notes in her work on lesbian organizing in Toronto: 'In large urban centres across Canada and other Western countries, the 1980s have heralded the subdivision of activist lesbians into specialized groupings: lesbians of colour, Jewish lesbians, working-class lesbians, leather dykes, lesbians against sado-masochism, older lesbians, lesbian youth, disabled lesbians and so on' (1990, p. 88).
7. In case you plan a trip, Canadian Tire and Home Depot are hardware/homeware/automotive-type stores, Ikea sells assemble-at-home furniture, Second Cups are coffee shops and Fortinos a south-western Ontario grocery chain.
8. See the interesting responses by Walker (1995), Probyn (1995), Knopp (1995) and Kirby (1995) to the publication of David Bell, Jon Binnie, Julia Cream and Gill Valentine's (1994) 'All Hyped Up and No Place To Go', on the meaning of multiple lesbian and gay performances.
9. Monique Wittig argues that the 'refusal to become (or to remain) heterosexual always meant to refuse to become a man or a woman, consciously or not. For a lesbian this goes further than the refusal of the *role* "woman". It is the refusal of the economic, ideological, and political power of a man' (1992, p. 13).
10. For example, Lynda Johnston's work in New Zealand on embodiment, sexuality and tourism; Celeste Wincapaw's work on lesbian cyber-neighbourhoods; and my own work on geographies of transgressive females, sites of resistance and the regulation of feminist anti-violence activism. For information on these and other works in progress, contact the author.
11. This adds to networks already established in various countries. For information on lesbian geographies in: New Zealand – contact Lynda Johnston, Department of Geography, University of Waikato, Hamilton, NZ; the UK – Gill Valentine, Department of Geography, University of Sheffield, Sheffield, UK; the USA – Pat Farrell of the GLB Caucus of the AAG; Canada – Ali Grant, Department of Geography, McMaster University, Hamilton, Canada; for other countries and/or to join Geo-Dykes, the international network of lesbian geographers, please contact Ali Grant.

References

Adler, S. and Brenner, J. (1992) 'Gender and Space: Lesbians and Gay Men in the City.' *International Journal of Urban and Regional Research*. 16: 24–34.

Anderson, B. (1991) *Imagined Communities: Reflections on the Origin and Spread of Nationalism*, revised edition. London: Verso.

Bell, D. (1991) 'Insignificant Others: Lesbians and Gay Geographies.' *Area* 23: 323–9.

Bell, D. and Valentine, G. (eds) (1995) *Mapping Desire: Geographies of Sexualities*. London: Routledge.

Bell, D., Binnie, J., Cream, J. and Valentine, G. (1994) 'All Hyped Up and No Place To Go.' *Gender, Place and Culture*. 1: 31–47.

Butler, J. (1990) *Gender Trouble: Feminism and the Subversion of Identity*. London and New York: Routledge.

Butler, J. (1993) *Bodies that Matter: On the Discursive Limits of 'Sex'*. New York: Routledge.

Castells, M. (1983) *The City and the Grassroots*. Berkeley, CA: University of California Press.

Chouinard, V. and Grant, A. (1995) 'On Being Not Even Anywhere Near "The Project": Ways of Putting Ourselves in the Picture.' *Antipode*. 27/2: 137–66.

Cream, J. (1995) 'Re-Solving Riddles: The Sexed Body.' In Bell and Valentine (1995).

Duncan, N. (ed.) (1996) *Bodyspace: Destabilizing Geographies of Gender and Sexuality*. London: Routledge.

England, K. (1994) 'Getting Personal: Reflexivity, Positionality and Feminist Research.' *Professional Geographer*. 46: 80–9.

Frye, M. (1983) *The Politics of Reality: Essays in Feminist Theory*. New York: The Crossing Press.

Gibson-Graham, J.K. (1994) '"Stuffed If I Know!": Reflections on Post-Modern Feminist Social Research.' *Gender, Place and Culture*. 1/2: 205–24.

Hayford, A. (1974) 'The Geography of Women: An Historical Introduction.' *Antipode*. 6: 1–18.

Johnson, L. (1985) 'Gender, Genetics and the Possibility of Feminist Geography.' *Australian Geographical Studies*. 23: 161–71.

Johnson, L. (1994) 'What Future for Feminist Geography?' *Gender, Place and Culture*. 1/1: 103–13.

Johnston, L. and Valentine, G. (1995) 'Wherever I Lay My Girlfriend, That's My Home: The Performance and Surveillance of Lesbian Identities in Domestic Environments.' In Bell and Valentine (1995), pp. 99–113.

Kirby, A. (1995) 'Straight Talk on the PomoHomo Question.' *Gender, Place and Culture*. 2: 89–95.

Knopp, L. (1987) 'Social Theory, Social Movements and Public Policy: Recent Accomplishments of Gay and Lesbian Movements in Minneapolis, Minnesota.' *International Journal of Urban and Regional Research*. 11: 243–61.

Knopp, L. (1990) 'Some Theoretical Implications of Gay Involvement in an Urban Land Market.' *Political Geography Quarterly*. 9: 337–52.

Knopp, L. (1995) 'If You're Going to Get All Hyped Up You'd Better Go Somewhere!' *Gender, Place and Culture*. 2: 85–8.

Kobayashi, A. and Peake, L. (1994) 'Unnatural Discourse. "Race" and Gender in Geography.' *Gender, Place and Culture*. 1/2: 225–44.

Larner, W. (1995) 'Theorizing "Difference" in Aotearoa/New Zealand.' *Gender, Place and Culture*. 2/2: 177 - 90.

Lauria, M. and Knopp, L. (1985) 'Toward an Analysis of the Role of Gay Communities in the Urban Renaissance.' *Urban Geography*. 6: 152–69.

Lees, L. and Longhurst, R. (1995) 'Feminist Geography in Aotearoa/New Zealand: A Workshop.' *Gender, Place and Culture*. 2/2: 217–22.

Longhurst, R. (1995) 'The Body and Geography.' *Gender, Place and Culture*. 2/1: 97–105.

Lyon, C.E. (1995) *Exploring Desired Spaces: A Study of Feminist Activism and Spatial Organization*. Unpublished Master's thesis, North York, Ont.: York University.

McDowell, L. (1993a) 'Space, Place and Gender Relations: Part 1. Feminist Empiricism and the Geography of Social Relations.' *Progress in Human Geography*. 17/2: 157–79.

McDowell, L. (1993b) 'Space, Place and Gender Relations: Part 2. Identity, Difference, Feminist Geometries and Geographies.' *Progress in Human Geography*. 17/3: 305–18.

McDowell, L. (1995) 'Body Work: Heterosexual Gender Performances in City Workplaces.' In Bell and Valentine (1995), pp. 73–95.

McDowell, L. and Court, G. (1994) 'Performing Work: Bodily Representations in Merchant Banks.' *Environment and Planning D: Society and Space*. 12: 727–50.

Mackenzie, S. (1984) 'Editorial Introduction.' *Antipode*. 13: 3–10.

Munt, S. (1995) 'The Lesbian Flâneur.' In Bell and Valentine (1995), pp. 115–25.

Murray, A. (1995) 'Femme on the Streets, Butch in the Sheets (a Play on Whores).' In Bell and Valentine (1995), pp. 66–74.

Peake, L. (1993) '"Race" and Sexuality: Challenges to the Patriarchal Structuring of Urban Social Space.' *Environment and Planning D: Society and Space*. 11: 415–32.

Penrose, J., Bondi, L., McDowell, L., Kofman, E., Rose, G. and Whatmore, S. (1992) 'Feminists and Feminism in the Academy.' *Antipode*. 24/3: 218–37.

Phelan, S. (1993) '(Be)Coming Out: Lesbian Identity and Politics.' *Signs: Journal of Women in Culture and Society*. 18/4: 765–90.

Pratt, G. and Hanson, S. (1994) 'Geography and the Construction of Difference.' *Gender, Place and Culture*. 1/1: 5–29.

Price-Chalita, P. (1994) 'Spatial Metaphor and the Politics of Empowerment: Mapping a Place for Feminism and Postmodernism in Geography.' *Antipode*. 26/3: 243–54.

Probyn, E. (1995) 'Lesbians in Space: Gender, Sex and the Structure of Missing.' *Gender, Place and Culture*. 2: 77–84.

Rich, A. (1986) *Blood, Bread and Poetry: Selected Prose 1979–1985*. New York: W.W. Norton & Company.

Rose, G. (1993a) *Feminism and Geography: The Limits of Geographical Knowledge*. Minneapolis: University of Minnesota Press.

Rose, G. (1993b) 'Progress in Geography and Gender. Or Something Else.' *Progress in Human Geography*. 17/4: 531–7.

Ross, B. (1990) 'The House that Jill Built: Lesbian Feminist Organizing in Toronto 1976–1980.' *Feminist Review*. 35: 75–91.

Rothenberg, T. (1995) '"And She Told Two Friends": Lesbians Creating Urban Social Space.' In Bell and Valentine (1995), pp. 165–81.

Scarrow, L. (1996) 'Dyke Watch: A Fun Guide to Toronto's Best Woman-Watching Spots.' *Siren*. 1/1: 23.

Skelton, T. (1995) '"Boom, Bye, Bye": Jamaican Ragga and Gay Resistance.' In Bell and Valentine (1995), pp. 264–83.

Stein, A. (1992) 'Sisters and Queers: The Decentering of Lesbian Feminism.' *Socialist Review*. 22/1: 33–55.

Tivers, J. (1978) 'How the Other Half Lives: The Geographical Study of Women.' *Area*. 10: 302–6.

Valentine, G. (1993a) 'Desperately Seeking Susan: A Geography of Lesbian Friendships.' *Area*. 25/2: 109–16.

Valentine, G. (1993b) 'Negotiating and Managing Multiple Sexual Identities: Lesbian Time-Space Strategies.' *Transactions, Institute of British Geographers*. 18: 237–48.

Valentine, G. (1993c) '(Hetero)sexing Space: Lesbian Perceptions and Experiences of Everyday Space.' *Environment and Planning D: Society and Space*. 11: 395–413.

Valentine, G. (1995) 'Creating Transgressive Space: The Music of kd lang.' *Transactions of the Institute of British Geographers*. 20: 474–85.

Valentine, G. (1996) '(Re) Negotiating the "Heterosexual Street".' In Duncan (1996), pp. 146–55.

Walker, L. (1995) 'More than Just Skin-Deep: Fem(me)ininity and the Subversion of Identity.' *Gender, Place and Culture*. 2: 71–6.

Weightman, B. (1981) 'Commentary: Towards a Geography of the Gay Community.' *Journal of Cultural Geography*. 1: 106–12.

Wincapaw, C. (forthcoming) *On Line Flirts and Passionate Debates: Lesbian and Bisexual Women's Experiences in the Dyke World of Internet-Based Electronic Mailing Lists*. Unpublished Master's thesis, Ottawa: Carleton University.

Winchester, H. and White, P. (1988) 'The Location of Marginalized Groups in the Inner City.' *Environment and Planning D: Society and Space*. 6: 37–54.

Wittig, M. (1992) *The Straight Mind and Other Essays*. Hemel Hempstead: Harvester Wheatsheaf.

Women and Geography Study Group of the Institute of British Geographers (1984) *Geography and Gender: An Introduction to Feminist Geography*. London: Hutchinson.

9

'We Are Family': Lesbians in Literature

Gabriele Griffin

The historical bit

It's odd how you forget what happened – just how you came to be teaching lesbian texts by known lesbian writers, in predominantly heterosexual higher education classrooms. It now seems so familiar that it's quite a shock to go back to books like *Lesbian Texts and Contexts* or *What Lesbians Do in Books* and discover – again – that they were only published in 1990 and 1991 respectively. Not so long ago, after all. The emergence of lesbian literary texts and of lesbian literary criticism and theory in higher education in the UK – as opposed to adult education or lesbian studies courses offered outside institutional frameworks – is for me predominantly associated with the establishment of women's writing as a discrete and gender-conscious concern in academe.

I taught my first women's writing course within an English degree in 1984 and by then, already, everything was permissible – well, up to a point. The mid-1980s in English in the UK were to that subject what the Swinging Sixties are supposed to have been for sex, though, if one follows Sheila Jeffreys's (1990) line, this was not good news for women. But, in literary terms so to speak, the 1980s were good news for women in general and for lesbians in particular. The debates that were being fought in English Literature departments in the UK then, now mostly won, concerned the following issues:

- the introduction of critical theory (of any kind);
- the end of grand narratives (no more Darwinism in literature);
- the status of the canon (newly desanctified);
- the relativities of high and popular culture (can the latter be called 'culture' some asked);
- the inclusion or otherwise of genres other than drama, poetry and the novel such as (auto)biography;
- the place of women writers.

All proved enormously important and facilitated a climate, at least in relatively 'progressive' English departments, that enabled extensive reviews of what was taught – hence, *inter alia*, women's writing courses. The introduction of such courses also demanded a metadiscourse about their inclusion in curricula both to the academy and to students who had apparently subsisted – more or less entirely so it seemed – on the works of William Shakespeare and Philip Larkin. That demand meant talking about the sexual politics of the production and dissemination of texts, which in turn meant that you could introduce texts like Virginia Woolf's (1929) *A Room of One's Own* and Adrienne Rich's (1980) 'When We Dead Awaken: Writing as Re-Vision' which discuss just these subjects. Thus, lo and behold, there they were – lesbians in the classroom. Not that many students noticed straight away. One might, in fact, argue that the introduction of these texts 'naturalized' lesbian writers, did what many lesbians do in 'real' life, namely, adopt the 'get-to-know-me-first-and-then-I'll-tell-you' attitude. And one can argue both for and against this strategy.

A completely different line, and one that I think is much more to the point, is to suggest that lesbian writers speak within and beyond lesbianism towards issues which concern *all* women,[1] such as women's marginalization in patriarchal culture. In important ways, and as the song goes, 'we are family'.[2] As lesbians' investment in patriarchy is very different from heterosexual women's investment,[3] given that the latter need to negotiate a different range of (intimate) relations with patriarchy relative to the former, lesbians can (sometimes) afford to speak out much more strongly about women's position in heteropatriarchal society than their heterosexual counterparts may feel able to. This ability to speak out for/on behalf of[4] women was greatly facilitated in the academic context where such hitherto unheard voices were suddenly in demand – provided, as I shall discuss below, they stayed clear of *sexuality* as opposed to sexual difference, a crucial and, significantly, de-eroticizing difference.

The need to consider sexual difference, the difference on which women's writing as a category was founded and which, from a lesbian perspective, is the overtly determining factor of her existence, led to publications such as Elizabeth Abel's (1982) *Writing and Sexual Difference*. Here, essays like Nina Auerbach's 'Magi and Maidens: The Romance of the Victorian Freud' sat alongside texts like Catharine R. Stimpson's 'Zero Degree Deviancy: The Lesbian Novel in English', thus placing side by side writings about lesbian and non-lesbian subjects for all who bought the book. Subsequent milestones in feminist criticism like Judith Newton and Deborah Rosenfelt's (1985) *Feminist Criticism and Social Change* and Elaine Showalter's (1986) *The New Feminist Criticism* all contained essays on lesbian subjects, whether these be Sonja Ruehl's (1985) influential reappraisal of 'Inverts and Experts: Radclyffe Hall and the Lesbian Identity' or Bonnie Zimmerman's (1981) 'What Has Never Been: An Overview of

Lesbian Feminist Criticism'. The point is that lesbian feminist criticism, and with that lesbian writing, gained space on women's writing agendas and in publications on women's writing, and now became 'visible' both to lesbians and non-lesbians rather than just to a lesbian audience.

Simultaneously, lesbian literary scholars began to write histories of lesbian writing. Of these the best-known is perhaps Lillian Faderman's (1985) *Surpassing the Love of Men*, which, though it has been much contested since (for example, Castle, 1993), was very influential in raising the issue of how one might define 'lesbian' across time, an issue which became increasingly prominent among lesbians throughout the 1980s and 1990s as the idea of lesbian identity turned into lesbian identit*ies* and differences among lesbian positions were increasingly viewed in both synchronic and diachronic terms. Faderman's text was important too in providing an account of lesbian writing through history at a time when such projects were generally undertaken by those hitherto culturally and academically marginalized. In that sense both Jeannette Foster's (1956) *Sex Variant Women in Literature* and Jane Rule's (1975) *Lesbian Images* came too early and never received the attention (except possibly in lesbian circles) they deserved.

Acts of re-vision

In 'When We Dead Awaken' Adrienne Rich insisted that 'We need to know the writing of the past, and know it differently than we have ever known it; not to pass on a tradition but to break its hold over us' (1980, p. 35). This imperative (which echoed a claim made generally in university English Studies in the 1980s and, specifically, by feminists), and the requirement to discover writers hitherto marginalized, encouraged the review of the content of many literature courses and enabled the introduction of marginalized writers into staid and straight curricula. The impact of this as regards lesbian writers was predominantly felt on twentieth-century literature courses, partly because little was known about lesbian writers from before the twentieth century, still less in print. Courses focusing on the modernist period, for example, allowed greater scope for the introduction of lesbian writing. In my own day as an undergraduate, in the second half of the 1970s, modernism had meant T.S. Eliot with a bit of D.H. Lawrence thrown in. That is basically what I was taught. Lots of stuff about hollow men and skulking hulks. My own menu, by the time I taught 'Edwardians and Moderns', consisted of (among others, in no particular order) Gertrude Stein, Dorothy Richardson, Virginia Woolf, Katherine Mansfield, Charlotte Mew, Charlotte Perkins Gilman, H.D. and Djuna Barnes. Much research has been done on women in modernism[5] and the very important role that lesbians played, especially in their salons in Paris and New York, as literary writers, journalists and publishers in promoting modernist art. Indeed, when it came to reviewing the modernist canon it was very difficult for me to know what to choose from the large number of lesbian modernist texts available.

Many lesbians, none more so perhaps than Gertrude Stein, whose writing constituted part of the break with tradition which the possibilities of avant-garde work within the modernist period entailed, utilized their work to create new ways of encoding lesbian experience. Stein's (1989) *Lifting Belly*, her poetic account of life with her lover Alice B. Toklas, is a prime example of this. Similarly H.D.'s (1927) *Her* broke with the realist tradition of novel-writing through stylistic devices such as stream-of-consciousness narration and the use of multiple pronouns (first and third person) by the narrator in order to evoke her [*sic*] distance from the patriarchal world and perceptions which cannot support an emerging lesbian self. *Her*, as well as other texts, were widely available for use on modernist courses once republished in the 1980s.

An interesting aspect of these novels compared to the lesbian classic *The Well of Loneliness* (1928), written in realist mode in the same period, is that they present an altogether more optimistic view of the lesbian and her future. While alienation remains a dominant theme in these modernist texts, often enacted through spatial migrations which place the protagonist in foreign territory, there to live and enact their removal from their society of origin, it is not (invariably) coupled with self-derogation, self-doubt and self-abasement. What these texts also share in common is a focus on the construction of the female self in the modernist period – a self able to express and live doubts about the role of woman as heterosexual construct in twentieth-century society. This tied in well with women's preoccupations with the problematic of their roles as women in western society of the 1980s. However, it cannot be said that it led to an explosion of 'conversion' to lesbianism among students who, willing to negotiate ideas of stylistic divergence and female estrangement, were often far less willing to engage in debates about texts as 'lesbian' or lesbians in texts.

It was through French feminist theory, specifically the work of Hélène Cixous (Cixous and Clément, 1986; Cixous, 1981) and Luce Irigaray (1985a, 1985b), that the idea of a lesbian aesthetic was introduced into debates about women's writing. Their arguments, sexually – indeed erotically – charged, concerning female artistic practice as an articulation of the erotic structure, expression and response of the female body and its/her relation to the mother proved powerfully seductive to lesbians and to heterosexual women alike. For lesbians it confirmed our sexual attraction to women and validated the female body in terms of *jouissance*. For heterosexual women it validated women and spoke of the unrealized possibilities of the female body, unrealized within heterosexuality because of many women's experience of the icon of heterosex – penetrative intercourse – as gynophobic and unfulfilling. But to push these positions to their logical conclusion, to suggest lesbianism as the answer, was to invoke insecurity and rejection in heterosexually orientated students who were not sure that they wanted to know (this).

Mothers and daughters

A prime example of this problematic turned out to be the teaching of Radclyffe Hall's (1924) *The Unlit Lamp* which focuses on a theme that became very prominent in feminism in the 1970s and 1980s: mother and daughter relationships.[6] I taught that novel on a women's writing course because it illustrates very neatly some of the ideas central to Italian feminism and especially as expressed in the work of the Milan Women's Bookstore Collective. Their work is particularly interesting to lesbians because at the centre of their writing is the issue of relationships between women. This focuses on the idea that in a patriarchal society it is through their valorization by another woman, rather than a man, that women will gain their sense of identity and self-worth: 'It was a short step . . . from accepting the fact of inequality to thinking that we get value from a female source, the mother, in a symbolic sense' (1990, p. 111). Self-consciously aware of differences between women, the Milan Collective linked these to power differentials associated with the diverse positions that women in western society may inhabit by virtue of class, knowledge, money, etc. and concluded: 'Attributing authority and value to another woman with regard to the world was the means of giving authority and value to oneself, to one's own experience, to one's own desires: "In defending Stein, I am defending myself"' (p. 112). So, instead of denying these differences they sought to harness them in the idea of a social contract between women whereby two women of differential power status make a commitment towards the empowerment of the less powerful woman through the help she gains from the more powerful one, who adopts the position of 'symbolic mother' and is not necessarily the natural mother of the other woman.

In Hall's *The Unlit Lamp* the protagonist, Joan, is caught between two mothers, her natural one, who is constructed as selfish and self-seeking and who claims Joan as a substitute 'ideal' (because undemanding of heterosex and biddable) husband, and Elizabeth, initially Joan's governess and later her lover, who takes on the role of symbolic mother in an attempt to enable Joan to leave her natural mother and establish her independence and a life with Elizabeth. Joan, torn between her love for both, gets caught in a trap of perpetual oscillation between her commitment to her mother and her commitment to Elizabeth. She is ultimately unable to leave her natural mother and thus loses Elizabeth. The novel suggests that this inability to leave the natural mother, who is presented as disabling rather than enabling, destroys Joan's opportunity for happiness and a life of her own as well as any chance of leading an adult life as a sexually active lesbian. In the battle between a symbolic and the natural mother, the symbolic mother loses.

The mostly heterosexually identified students' response to this novel was always very interesting. They wholeheartedly empathized with Joan's plight in relation to her demanding, controlling, selfish mother, with many expressing similar feelings of guilt about the difficulties of separating from the mother, but when it came to discussing both the quasi-sexual interest of the natural mother in the daughter – which in this novel is to some extent surprisingly overt – and the erotic relationship between Elizabeth and Joan, they were less forthcoming. Between the taboo of incest and the taboo of homosexuality it was extremely difficult to achieve a sustained discussion on either topic. The text as mediated through a perspective centring on the demanding mother was unproblematic for the students and seemingly allowed partial vision or occlusion. When the focus was shifted to the sexual politics of those relationships, resistance set in.

Symbolic mothers and castrating fathers

The Milan Women's Bookstore Collective's starting-point for their construction of the symbolic mother was their experience of reading texts by women writers such as Virginia Woolf, Emily Dickinson and indeed Adrienne Rich, from whose 'When We Dead Awaken' the Italian feminists, according to Teresa de Lauretis, ultimately derived their concept of the symbolic mother (Milan Women's Bookstore Collective, 1990, p. 3). In 'When We Dead Awaken' the enabling female is contrasted with the disempowering male. Of her own situation Rich wrote: 'My own luck was being born white and middle-class into a house full of books, with a father who encouraged me to read and write. So for about twenty years I wrote for a particular man . . .' (1980, p. 38), a testimony to the power of patriarchal patronage. This combines with a discussion of how her situation compares with that of other women: 'I am aware of the women who are not with us here because they are washing the dishes and looking after the children . . . not to mention women who went on the streets last night in order to feed their children' (*ibid.*). Rich is making the point that we not only need to uncover the history of women's (cultural) work which has been silenced, to understand the conditions under which we labour – in every sphere – but also to interrogate the nature of women's sensibilities and their differences from men. In the new generation of women poets she finds, 'Women are speaking to and of women . . . out of a newly released courage to name, to love each other, to share risk and grief and celebration' (p. 49). Rich's project in this essay is of a particular kind, concerned both with the archaeology of women's cultural production and its specificity or difference from men's cultural work. It expresses the concerns which governed early Anglo-American feminist criticism and which encouraged and legitimated, *inter alia*, the establishment of many feminist and lesbian feminist publishing houses which became synonymous with the new availability of lesbian writing and women's writing in general, one prerequisite for teaching such material.

But what kind of family?

Where Anglo-American feminist criticism, intent upon discovering hitherto forgotten and marginalized women writers, enabled lesbian writers to appear on the cultural maps, French feminist criticism, especially through the works of Julia Kristeva, Hélène Cixous and Luce Irigaray,[7] invited debates about the idea of a specifically female form of writing, introducing notions of the disrupted text as evidence of the return of the repressed maternal, of the (other) woman, while simultaneously querying the family relations which had been established as norm for/in cultural production. Jeanette Winterson's (1985) *Oranges Are Not the Only Fruit* arrived just in time for such interrogations. Highly literary, it combined the quasi-confessional first-person narrative conventionally claimed as a specifically female form of writing with the tradition of the *Bildungsroman* or narrative of self-discovery, while utilizing a blend of genres and lesbian subject matter to disrupt both the text and the reader. In this respect it exemplified ideas of postmodern narratives which were gradually emerging on the literary scene. Both its sheer literariness and, as I have argued elsewhere (Griffin, 1993, pp. 63–9), its use of humour to unite readers, including heterosexual readers, with the lesbian protagonist against the small-minded community from which she eventually escapes, propelled this fiction into mainstream British culture as indexed by the novel's serialization for the BBC (Hinds, 1992).

I taught this novel predominantly from the perspective of stylistic divergence but, thinking back to all the lesbian texts I have taught and considering what they seemed to have in common – and hence, in part, the title of this chapter – one of the most interesting aspects of the book is how it constructs the family. The novel opens with a description of 'the family': 'Like most people I lived for a long time with my mother and father. My father liked to watch wrestling, my mother liked to wrestle; it didn't matter what' (p. 3). In contrast to the conventional patriarchal family, the father in this text is instantly sidelined (he may be watching but we hardly ever see him; he is not so much an absent presence as a present absence) and the major focus is directed instead at the relationship between mother and daughter. The protagonist is adopted; her mother is not her 'natural' mother and that in more senses than one: not only is she not her biological mother but she also does not share her adopted daughter's sexual orientation:

> [My mother] had a mysterious attitude towards the begetting of children; it wasn't that she couldn't do it, more that she didn't want to do it. She was very bitter about the Virgin Mary getting there first. So she did the next best thing and arranged for a foundling. That was me. (p. 3)

The mother rejects hetero*sexuality* rather than heteropatriarchy and her fights with her daughter, whom she desires to fashion in her own image, begin when the daughter starts to discover her own sexuality. As in Radclyffe Hall's *The Unlit Lamp* the daughter has to make a choice between living according to the natural mother's dictate or achieving independence. But unlike Joan in Hall's novel, Jeanette makes a bid for independence which offers a sense of a happy ending.

Female communities

In both *The Unlit Lamp* and *Oranges Are Not the Only Fruit* the threat to the lesbian protagonist's independent existence comes from the heteropatriarchally committed mother who acts as the instrument of that formation, rather than from the father directly. This is very different in the lesbian feminist science fiction which emerged in the 1970s and 1980s and which, at the same time as it engaged with questions of motherhood, constructed all-female communities as a means of countering men's threat to women and to the environment associated with men's apparent need to express the male self through domination and violence.

Lesbian feminist science fiction began to surface at a time when the idea of recovering a history of forgotten women writers had been widened to a consideration of women's investment in particular, and hitherto constructed as particularly male-centred, genres. Women writers were claiming new territories and, significantly, it was science fiction which triggered this move. This is significant because at the time (1985) when The Women's Press in London, through its editor Sarah Lefanu, established their – as it turned out short-lived – women's science fiction list, made up overwhelmingly and tellingly by feminist (lesbian) work done in the USA, there had been an extended public debate, triggered by advances in reproductive technology, about fertility, women's control or otherwise over their bodies, motherhood and its (dis)contents and 'the family'. This culminated in publications such as *Test-Tube Woman* (Arditti *et al.*, 1984), whose contributors included many lesbians (and for lesbians who wish/ed to be mothers artificial insemination is/was an important topic), and in the Warnock Report (1984) on the ethical implications of reproductive technologies.

Sonya Andermahr (1992) has argued persuasively in favour of the interrelationship of political separatism and lesbian feminist science fiction as one cultural vehicle which gave the separatism demanded by radical lesbian feminists expression. The lesbian science fiction which emerged in the 1970s and 1980s, such as Sally Miller Gearhart's (1978) *The Wanderground,* certainly constructed a separatist world based on an embrace of the supposedly feminine values[8] of nurturance, co-operation, in-tune-ness-with-nature and empathy which apparently constitute women's identity. It combined concerns for the world's ecosystems with discussions of the social formations in which we live to advocate new communal lifestyles which excluded men. The debates that took place about these sci fi texts at women's and literature conferences of various kinds were surprisingly fierce, often centring on the question of how 'authentic' such representations of women were in relation to 'real' women.

The interrogation of ideas of femininity which became increasingly important in the second half of the 1980s and in the 1990s had begun and where, through sci fi, women appropriated a particular genre to reject many of its 'traditional' premises (preoccupation with advances in science/technology; reproduction of hierarchized social structures; imperialism, etc.), women's, particularly lesbians', appropriation of the thriller/detective fiction, turned on the appropriation of a specific conventionally male figure (Palmer, 1991). The arrival on the scene of the lesbian hero in the shape of the lesbian detective, as in Sarah Dreher's work for example, heralded the re-individualizing of lesbian protagonists, away from ideas of community other than very small social formations encapsulated in the bar scene or some such configuration. I never taught lesbian detective fiction and I can't quite say why, despite the fact that the teaching of so-called popular culture had become commonplace within academe by the time these appropriations took place.

A widening sphere

In 1980 Martha Vicinus, now firmly associated with lesbian scholarship, brought out two works in the UK: *A Widening Sphere* and *Suffer and Be Still* (both originally published in the USA in 1972). Both were concerned with Victorian women and both became very influential texts in the UK. In 1985 Eve Kosofsky Sedgwick published her equally influential text, *Between Men: English Literature and Male Homosocial Desire.* During the 1980s I found myself shifting increasingly from teaching lesbian texts to teaching lesbian literary criticism and theory. I was not the only one. By the end of that decade I had moved into women's studies. Somehow lesbian writings became a pastime, with lesbian theorizing attracting the serious academic focus. The – as some see it – fetishization of theory in the academy without doubt contributed to this reorientation; the explosion of lesbian theoretical texts in the book market also helped. In film, performance and queer theory lesbian thinking became hugely influential, mostly imported from the USA. It lent a counter-weight to the relentless bombardment from Lacanian and Derridian positions as the boys (and some women) gathered their forces.

But while I contemplate the impact of lesbian theory on the teaching of lesbian texts, I am also reminded of reading Audre Lorde's (1982) *Zami: A New Spelling of My Name*, which was just one of the many influential (auto)biographical texts which were published, the debates about the lesbian quality of the relationship between Celie and Shug in Alice Walker's 1983 *The Color Purple* and the arrival of postmodern lesbian writers such as Jeanette Winterson and Sarah Schulman on the lesbian literary scene.

For lesbians books, indeed literature, have always been crucial as a source of identification of/with self and others. Lee Lynch's (1990) 'Cruising the Libraries' is just one text that reflects lesbians' need for books, often their first source of information about themselves and other lesbians. Many of the coming-out narratives reiterate this point. The text confirms what was (always) felt. But our need for books is not necessarily paralleled by a need for lesbian books in the wider population. As I ponder shifts in my teaching and reading practices, I also wonder what it was/is like for others, who, lesbians apart, teach and/or read lesbian texts. And this is a question about the impact of lesbian work in academe. For surely one way in which that might be measured is the extent to which non-lesbians engage with that material. One might argue that the overwhelming success of *The Color Purple*, which features routinely on all sorts of women's writing courses, suggests that lesbian (subject) matters have arrived on the literary scene to stay. Production of lesbian texts is currently at an all-time high. Maybe the tide has turned and we are family, at last.

Notes

1. Hence the possibility of Radicalesbians' assertion 'A lesbian is the rage of all women condensed to the point of explosion' (1970, p. 17).
2. I use 'family' here in part in the way in which Ludwig Wittgenstein talks of it in his 'Blue Book' where he discusses family likenesses (1958, p. 17). It is also, of course, a reference to the song by Sister Sledge, a hot favourite with lesbians, certainly in the UK, and to which we like to dance at every opportunity.
3. For an interesting range of viewpoints on this, see Wilkinson and Kitzinger (1993).
4. I am emphatically not suggesting a homogenizing view of women here; rather, I wish to indicate that lesbian women can sometimes speak of heteropatriarchy in ways which heterosexual women cannot.
5. See, for example, Benstock (1987), Hanscombe and Smyers (1987), Gilbert and Gubar (1988) and Griffin (1994) as well as the many (auto)biographies which exist by/about women such as Margaret Anderson, Janet Flanner, Jane Heap, Sylvia Beach and Adrienne Monnier, Nancy Cunard, Mabel Dodge, Peggy Guggenheim etc.
6. There were many publications by well-established (lesbian) feminist writers on this topic such as Rich (1977), Olsen (1985), Ferguson (1989) and – though neither lesbian nor feminist – Friday (1977).

7. Credit should be given here to texts such as Kristeva's (1980) *Desire in Language* and (1984) *Revolution in Poetic Language*, to Cixous's (1981) 'Laugh of the Medusa' and Irigaray's (1985a) *This Sex Which Is Not One* and (1985b) *Speculum of the Other Woman*, which were central to many women's writing courses in the 1980s.
8. As I regard femininity as a construct I find it difficult to subscribe to how it is presented in this novel, which seems to me to replicate ideas of femininity commonly found in heteropatriarchal ideology.

References

Abel, E. (ed.) (1982) *Writing and Sexual Difference*. Brighton: Harvester.

Andermahr, S. (1992) 'Separatism and Utopian Fiction.' In S. Munt (ed.) *New Lesbian Criticism*. London: Routledge.

Arditti, R., Klein, R. Duelli and Minden, S. (eds.) (1984) *Test-Tube Women: What Future for Motherhood?* London: Pandora.

Benstock, S. (1987) *Women of the Left Bank*. London: Virago.

Castle, T. (1993) *The Apparitional Lesbian*. New York: Columbia University Press.

Cixous, H. (1981) 'The Laugh of the Medusa.' In E. Marks and I. de Courtivron (eds) *New French Feminisms*. Brighton: Harvester, pp. 245–64.

Cixous, H. and Clément, C. (1986) *The Newly Born Woman*. Manchester: Manchester University Press.

Faderman, L. (1985) *Surpassing the Love of Men: Romantic Friendship and Love Between Women from the Renaissance to the Present*. London: The Women's Press.

Ferguson, A. (1989) *Blood at the Root: Motherhood, Sexuality and Male Dominance*. London: Pandora.

Foster, J.H. (1956; reprinted 1985) *Sex Variant Women in Literature*. Tallahassee, FL: Naiad Press.

Friday, N. (1977) *My Mother My Self*. New York: Delacorte Press.

Gearhart, S.M. (1978; reprinted 1985) *The Wanderground*. London: The Women's Press.

Gilbert, S.M. and Gubar, S. (1988) *No Man's Land: The Place of the Women Writer in Twentieth-Century Literature*. New Haven, CT: Yale University Press.

Griffin, G. (1993) *Heavenly Love? Lesbian Images in Twentieth-Century Women's Writing*. Manchester: Manchester University Press.

Griffin, G. (ed.) (1994) *Difference in View: Women and Modernism*. London: Taylor and Francis.

Hall, R. (1924) *The Unlit Lamp*. London: Jonathan Cape.

Hanscombe, G. and Smyers, V. (1987) *Writing for Their Lives: The Modernist Woman 1910–1940*. London: The Women's Press.

H.D. (1927; reprinted in 1984) *Her*. London: Virago.

Hinds, H. (1992) '*Oranges Are Not the Only Fruit*: Reaching Audiences Other Lesbian Texts Cannot Reach.' In S. Munt (ed.) *New Lesbian Criticism*. London: Harvester Wheatsheaf, pp. 153–72.

Hobby, E. and White, C. (eds) (1991) *What Lesbians Do in Books*. London: The Women's Press.

Irigaray, L. (1985a) *This Sex Which Is Not One*. Ithaca, NY: Cornell University Press.

Irigaray, L. (1985b) *Speculum of the Other Woman*. Ithaca, NY: Cornell University Press.

Jay, K. and Glasgow, J. (eds) (1990) *Lesbian Texts and Contexts: Radical Revisions*. New York: New York University Press.

Jeffreys, S. (1990) *Anticlimax: A Feminist Perspective on the Sexual Revolution.* London: The Women's Press.
Kristeva, J. (1980) *Desire in Language.* Oxford: Basil Blackwell.
Kristeva, J. (1984) *Revolution in Poetic Language.* New York: Columbia University Press.
Lorde, A. (1982; rpt 1990) *Zami: A New Spelling of My Name.* London: Sheba.
Lynch, L. (1990) 'Cruising the Libraries.' In Jay and Glasgow (1990), pp. 39–48.
Milan Women's Bookstore Collective (1990) *Sexual Difference: A Theory of Social-Symbolic Practice.* Bloomington, IN: Indiana University Press.
Newton, J. and Rosenfelt, D. (eds) (1985) *Feminist Criticism and Social Change.* London: Methuen.
Olsen, T. (1985) *Mother to Daughter, Daughter to Mother.* London: Virago.
Palmer, P. (1991) 'The Lesbian Feminist Thriller and Detective Novel.' In Hobby and White (1991), pp. 9–27.
Radicalesbians (1970) 'The Woman Identified Woman.' In S. Hoagland and J. Penelope (eds) (1988) *For Lesbians Only: A Separatist Anthology.* London: Onlywomen Press, pp. 17–22.
Rich, A. (1977) *Of Woman Born.* London: Virago.
Rich, A. (1980) 'When We Dead Awaken: Writing as Re-Vision.' In *On Lies, Secrets and Silence.* London: Virago, pp. 33–49.
Ruehl, S. (1985) 'Inverts and Experts: Radclyffe Hall and Lesbian Identity.' In Newton and Rosenfelt (1985), pp. 165–80.
Rule, J. (1975) *Lesbian Images.* Trumansburg, NY: Crossing Press.
Sedgwick, E. Kosofsky (1985) *Between Men: English Literature and Male Homosocial Desire.* New York: Columbia University Press.
Showalter, E. (ed.) (1986) *The New Feminist Criticism.* London: Virago.
Stein, G. (1989) *Lifting Belly.* Ed. R. Mark. Tallahassee, FL: Naiad Press.
Vicinus, M. (ed.) (1980a) *Suffer and Be Still.* London: Methuen.
Vicinus, M. (ed.) (1980b) *A Widening Sphere.* London: Methuen.
Walker, A. (1983) *The Color Purple.* London: The Women's Press.
Warnock, M. (1984) *A Question of Life: The Warnock Report on Human Fertilization and Embryology.* Oxford: Basil Blackwell.
Wilkinson, S. and Kitzinger, C. (1993) *Heterosexuality: A Feminism & Psychology Reader.* London: Sage.
Winterson, J. (1985) *Oranges Are Not the Only Fruit.* London: Pandora.
Wittgenstein, L. (1958; reprinted 1978) *The Blue and Brown Books.* Oxford: Basil Blackwell.
Woolf, V. (1929) *A Room of One's Own.* London: Hogarth Press.
Zimmerman, B. (1981; reprinted 1986) 'What Has Never Been: An Overview of Lesbian Feminist Criticism.' In Showalter (1986), pp. 200–24.

10

Revolting Lesbians in the Politics Department

Sheila Jeffreys

I teach a lesbian and gay politics course with the support of my department of Political Science in the University of Melbourne. My course is called 'The Politics of Sex Reform Movements' because the students pointed out that a title that included the words lesbian and gay might impede their chances of employment. The very fact that my course has to be closeted in this way suggests some of the political difficulties of such teaching. My course and my department are exceptional in Australia. Departments of Political Science often contain no teaching about women or feminism, let alone lesbians. In designing my course I had to invent just what I considered lesbian politics involved.

Feminism and traditional political science

Unlike history or literature, political science has tended to remain resolutely masculine in orientation. Women's history and women's literature have had an effect on what is understood to be history or literature while political science has remained fairly immune to feminist influence. Many political science departments in universities have few or even no women staff. Feminist political scientists have nonetheless developed certain well-defined areas which address the traditional concerns of the discipline: political theory, particularly the critique of liberalism; women and politics, covering women in parliamentary and party politics; women and the state; the gendering of international relations.

Political science has remained resolutely masculine because of its traditional focus on 'real' politics, the politics of political parties and of government. Women have been noticeably absent from such 'real' politics and from theorizing about them, for reasons well explored by feminist theorists such as Carole Pateman (1988) and Catharine MacKinnon (1989) in their work on the separation of the private and the public sphere. The difficulty women, let alone feminists, have (had) in making headway in political science has been a function of the replication of the rules of traditional masculinist politics within the academy.

Women were certainly in history and making history, even though the writing of men's history usually excluded them, and women have certainly been prolific writers of literature, though excluded from the canon. It is not so easy to 'put women back into' masculinist political science. The big question for feminists engaged in more traditional political science has been why and how women have been excluded from political processes. The way in which 'democracy' has failed women, more than half its constituency, has to be and has been a major question for feminist political science.

In order to explain the absence of women, feminist theories have needed to re-theorize political science, throwing into question its major premises. Where women have taken on a major traditional area of political science such as international relations, this is the work that has been done. Feminist theories have asked how and where women fit into the international economy (Enloe, 1989, 1983). They have used feminist analyses of anti-militarism to engage with men's assumptions as to the primacy and inevitability of war (Peterson, 1992). They have questioned nationalism from a feminist perspective and linked nationalism to masculinity (Jayawardena, 1986). Feminist theorists have asked questions about such basic concerns for political science as the nature of international relations, the state, nationalism and politics itself.

What is lesbian politics?

Not surprisingly lesbian politics has been conspicuous by its absence. Where it has appeared this has been on courses concerned with social movements, where lesbians have been considered as part of the 'lesbian and gay' movement. Gay politics courses which take gay men as their measure and focus are very rare, though beginning to develop in the USA. There are ways in which gay concerns could be included in traditional politics courses without too much disruption of the course strategy. The question of gays in the military will enliven courses concerned with masculine concerns in the public world such as war and international relations, for instance. But it is hard to see how *lesbian* concerns which arise from the oppression of women in the 'private' world can be slotted in without a feminist reconceptualizing of what politics is.

I designed a course in lesbian and gay politics without a great deal to go on as to what this should or might consist of. My course covers both lesbian and gay politics and is open to women and men. It shows how homosexuality was invented in the late nineteenth century, how it was politicized in early homosexual rights movements and by theorists such as Edward Carpenter, and how 1950s assimilationist homophile movements, gay liberation, lesbian feminism and queer politics have constructed homosexuality. It looks at the politics of these movements, how they are organized, and what the crucial controversies within them are. My concern is with how suited the internal politics and political strategies of these movements are to realizing the goal of lesbian, of women's or even of gay liberation.

I analyse the history and contexts of lesbian and gay movements of liberation. I particularly want to be able to explain how some examples of what I regard as the products of oppression – such phenomena as transsexualism, sadomasochism, lesbian role-playing – have come to be viewed by some as revolutionary in the present, even a challenge to heteropatriarchy. Lesbian and gay politics have developed within a culture which is misogynist, racist and classist and these forces shape lesbian and gay forms of resistance. Oppression and loss of family and community of origin, harassment, violence and the absence of any images (at least positive ones) can lead to a romancing of outlawry and a celebration of attacks upon the rogue body which seems to have occasioned such pain. The contemporary association of homosexuality with branding, piercing and transsexualism – all forms of self-mutilation – emerges from the historical development of lesbian and gay oppression and resistance.

A literature on lesbian and gay politics, mostly American, is just beginning to develop. It is, for the most part, feminism free, avoiding any recognition that lesbians and gay men might have different and even conflicting interests or that lesbians are not just a smaller and slightly less exciting version of gay men. The major controversy seems to be between assimilationism and 'radical' or 'queer' politics. The assimilationists are seen as seeking to merge seamlessly into the present structures and institutions of the state and to gain for gay men, and perhaps lesbians too, the privileges that heterosexuals have enjoyed. Those who see themselves as more revolutionary, as 'queer', consider that their forms and practices, sometimes centred upon 'in your face' displays of self-mutilatory practices, are 'transgressive'. These differences are well portrayed in two recent American books. *Virtually Normal* by Andrew Sullivan (1995) takes a conservative view, opposing queer politics and seeing the most important struggle as reversing the ban on gays and lesbians in the American military. *Virtual Equality* by Urvashi Vaid (1995) promotes a politics of difference which affirms drag queens and sadomasochists against the new right.

Within this debate about different ways in which mainly male gay interests might best be promoted, lesbian interests, feminism and women's liberation have been completely silenced. They are not usually mentioned. The interests of women have become almost as invisible within gay or queer politics as they are within traditional masculine politics, but the veneer of rebelliousness that adheres to 'queer' can make this less easy to spot. In addressing the questions raised in this anthology about how to modify 'straight studies' I find myself necessarily writing about how to modify 'gay' studies too. The 'subversive' potential of lesbian theory, knowledge and practice has a double task, a fight to overturn both a 'gay' *and* a 'straight' paradigm. This may seem curmudgeonly considering how little visibility has yet been achieved in traditional political science for the issues of gay men or lesbians, but the fight for lesbian and feminist space needs to be constructed from the very beginning.

Politics is about power: who has it, why and how it operates and how change might occur. Teaching a course within a politics department gives the opportunity to speak in terms of power about all those issues – such as sadomasochism and homosexual prostitution – which tend to be addressed within lesbian and gay culture as if they are simply about fashion or individual choice. Within mixed lesbian and gay political movements it is men who have power in numbers, economics and general influence. A feminist lesbian politics course needs to put this issue of men's power and influence at the centre of concern.

I teach and write about gay male politics as well as lesbian politics. I can understand that some students would prefer to concentrate on what is happening among lesbians, how to develop a code of lesbian ethics or what lesbian community can and should look like and so on. But lesbian politics is constantly shaped by the existence of most lesbians within a male gay culture and politics. A great deal of the rejection of, and hostility towards, feminism within lesbian politics derives from the confusion of lesbian with gay male interests and attempts by lesbians to take gay men as their measure for all things. For that reason an analysis of gay male politics helps an understanding of the debates and tensions in lesbian politics now. From a lesbian feminist perspective lesbians and gay men are not simply slightly different varieties of the 'homosexual' but occupiers of different class positions. It is this perspective which make my course particularly unusual. Lesbian and gay liberalism sees lesbians and gay men as forming a homogeneous disadvantaged group which requires equal opportunities. I do not just see lesbians and gay men as constituting a variety of citizens deserving and desirous of inclusion in a multicultural society. I see lesbians as members of the class 'women' and therefore as having a distinct and lesbian-specific history and politics. My teaching of lesbian and gay politics seeks to tease out the differences which result from these different class positions rather than assuming any similarity between lesbians and gay men. Gay men's occupation of ruling-class status, though flawed and precarious, is likely to affect their behaviour towards lesbians, to produce practices dominant within gay culture such as drag and transsexualism, to shape sexual practice. In lesbian and gay political theory all these practices need to be analysed from an understanding of the power differences between men and women. In the rest of this chapter I will suggest what I see as important areas for the teaching and writing of lesbian and gay politics.

The personal is political

It is the feminist understanding of the personal as political that is potentially transformative for straight and gay politics alike. Malestream gay politics replicates straight politics in its failure to recognize the politics of personal life. Traditional political science deals with the public world of states, parties and the military. The great breakthrough of feminist thought, this understanding that the personal is political, was crucial to explaining the circumstances of women's lives, issues of unpaid housework, battering and abusive sexual practice. An understanding of the politics of personal life also helped feminists understand how women are constrained emotionally, in their body language, concerning whom they may touch or look at. The absence of women in parliament, for instance, depends not just on male prejudice, working practices, the exigencies of childcare, but on the whole way in which men conduct their relationships and communications. An understanding of the personal as political, then, shows how shallow is the liberal ideal of equality of opportunities.

Gay theorists and activists tend to restrict their understanding of the personal as political to fighting the unreasonable restriction of 'private' and 'personal' sexual practice by the state. The strategy thus becomes the protection of the 'private' realm of sex, even when practised in public, from the intrusion of the state. The most profound differences in theory and practice between lesbians and gay men have occurred around the issue of sexual practice. Feminist consciousness-raising, theory and practice have indicated that sexual desire and practice are themselves politically constructed and political in their effects. Feminist anti-violence work has shown the importance of challenging male dominant, aggressive sexuality in order to end male violence against women and the sex industry. These are not always popular insights into gay male culture.

The issue of toilet sex – why men rather than women do this, how it relates to gay oppression – the construction of male sexuality and masculinity – whether it is a revolutionary form – is an exemplary one for lesbian and gay politics. Those who see the proper focus of politics as the 'important' activities of men, such as war, might not see the relevance of this but, of course, from a feminist perspective, male sexuality, masculinity and warfare are very much connected. My questioning of the political significance of the male sexual initiative in cruising behaviour is, I think, a fitting companion to the teaching of my male colleagues in international relations about nuclear warfare and the first-strike capacity.

Politicizing heterosexuality

The most revolutionary understanding to emerge from feminist political analysis of 'personal' life for lesbian and gay politics is the idea that heterosexuality is a political institution, rather than the result of biological or individual preference. The theorizing and politicizing of heterosexuality has come from radical lesbian feminist theorists. Gay male theorists have not engaged much with these issues. As Adrienne Rich (1983) argues, heterosexuality needs to be analysed as a political system which is as influential as capitalism and the caste system. The teaching of lesbian political theory should cover the main feminist theorists of heterosexuality such as Rich, Monique Wittig (1992), Janice Raymond (1986) and my own work in *Anticlimax* (1990). These analyses have been continued and deepened by recent lesbian feminist work from the UK such as the Wilkinson and Kitzinger (1993) anthology which emerged from the special issue of *Feminism and Psychology* and Diane Richardson's (1996) edited collection *Theorizing Heterosexuality*.

Race and racism

The teaching of lesbian and gay politics needs to include the contributions made by black, indigenous and ethnic minority lesbians and gay men to lesbian and gay theory. Black lesbian feminists were the first to contribute both a criticism of the racism and ethnocentrism of lesbian movements and politics and a specific black lesbian politics. This development has been followed more recently by very interesting work by black British and American theorists on racism and gay politics (Hemphill, 1991). Work by indigenous lesbians in Australia and the USA, Asian lesbians in the UK and in Sydney, Jewish lesbians in the UK and the USA as well as black American and British lesbians, shows how lesbian experience is shaped by different cultural backgrounds and the experience of exclusion and racism (Johnson, 1994, 1991; Tsui, 1991; Lee, 1991; Carmen *et al.*, 1987; Lorde, 1984b; Moraga and Anzaldúa, 1981).

The issue of racist sexual stereotyping is useful to illustrate the influence of racism in lesbian and gay culture. This has been particularly obvious in relation to gay male culture, and I discuss with students Robert Mapplethorpe's photographs of black men (Mercer, 1992). I use prostitution advertisements based on ethnicity, personal ads and a documentary on aboriginal lesbians and gay men which discusses the prejudice against aboriginal men as sexual partners to show how stereotyping works. It is the sex industry that has been most influential in marketing racist sexual practices. Until recently the industry had not targeted lesbians as consumers. This is changing and I use images of lesbian erotica magazines to discuss the impact of racism on the construction of lesbian sexuality.

I consider that the politics of appearance is an important one for lesbian and gay culture. This causes some lively discussion with students who inhabit a culture which encourages them to see 'fashion' as simply individual choice. I ask them to seek the origins of crew cuts or shaven heads, piercings, tattooings, lipstick, black leather or even the colour black in a racist and sexist history and analyse the impact of these practices in supporting that racism and sexism.

Essentialism, social construction and identity

Teaching and theorizing lesbian and gay politics is dependent upon a concept of lesbian or gay identity. Lesbian feminist work on the social construction of lesbian identity offers a fundamental challenge to malestream political science. Even the most liberal of traditional political theory is likely to see lesbianism and male homosexuality as given rather than chosen or constructed. The lesbian feminist perspective tends to be radically social constructionist while many contemporary gay activists and thinkers have adopted a biological determinist position (Rose, 1996; Rich, 1983). Presently gay male researchers such as Simon LeVay (1993) are throwing their energies into discovering the gay gene and gay brain. The female stars of queer theory, Diana Fuss (1990) and Judith Butler (1990), have gone to the other extreme and have applied postmodern and feminist perspectives to throw into question the whole idea of 'being' a lesbian or a gay man. I have argued that such radical deconstructionism might be in danger of throwing the baby out with the bathwater (Jeffreys, 1993).

The historical work on the origins of lesbian and gay identity has offered more of a challenge, perhaps, to traditional history than to politics, but is crucially relevant to understanding how a politics of homosexuality has developed. The early homosexual rights movement in the UK, for instance, based much of its argument on the work of sexologists like Henry Havelock Ellis. They used his biological arguments about 'hereditary taint' to argue that there should be toleration of those who could not help themselves (Carpenter, 1921; Ellis, 1913). These arguments have reappeared with a vengeance a century later and the dangers can only be fully appreciated with an awareness of this historical context. As Jeffrey Weeks (1991) argues, they provide an explanation for those who crave the security of knowing why they are different. It is lesbian feminist theorists who have made the major contributions to our understanding of how homosexuality has been constructed historically. Mary McIntosh's (1992) pioneering essay from the 1960s considerably predates the work of Michel Foucault, for instance. In the 1970s and 1980s lesbian historians pointed out that both homosexuality and heterosexuality are inventions of a particular historical period, generally identified as the late nineteenth century, and constructed by particular historical forces such as the science of sexology and the law (Sahli, 1979; Smith-Rosenberg, 1979). Lillian Faderman's (1984) *Surpassing the Love of Men* should be seen as a classic of lesbian politics as well as lesbian history.

Gender and lesbian and gay politics

While it might be acknowledged that traditional masculinist politics has been dominated by 'gender', the significance of 'gender' to lesbian and gay politics has been less seriously questioned. Indeed many lesbian and gay theorists vaunt the challenge to 'gender' constituted by lesbian and gay practice and theory, while I argue in my work that practices like drag, supposed to offer a challenge, in fact cement and reinforce gender differences. The confusion of 'gender' with same-sex love has gone deep into male gay culture and theory, through the practice and apologetics of drag, camp and transsexualism.

Recent radical feminist theorizing defines 'gender' as dominant behaviour in masculinity and subordinate behaviour in femininity rather than as amusing differences that can be swapped and eroticized (Delphy, 1993). Dee Graham (1994) in her wonderful recent book of lesbian feminist theory entitled *Loving to Survive* offers a useful approach to femininity. She extends the idea of the Stockholm syndrome, whereby hostages bond to their captors, to what she calls societal Stockholm syndrome. In societal Stockholm syndrome women bond with men in heterosexuality through fear of sexual terrorism and because individual men show them small kindnesses. They then behave in 'feminine' ways, that is, in ways that those afraid for their lives will seek to defuse the violence of a captor by making them feel favourably towards them. This is an interpretation of feminine gender as the behaviour of the fearful and oppressed rather than any naturally occurring form of behaviour.

From this perspective the enthusiasm for drag, and in some cases even transsexualism, within gay theory and practice is politically problematic. This radical feminist perspective explains why lesbians have found drag hard to stomach. Drag simply imitates the behaviour of the oppressed – namely women – making it look particularly spineless and wretched, for the purposes of sexual excitement in the form of dominant/submissive sexuality and for laughs. I encourage students to see the behaviours of drag, camp and transsexualism as arising from gay oppression and the oppression of women, and as unsustainable in a politics which aims to free women and lesbians from the thrall of 'femininity'.

'Gender' is a controversial issue within lesbian politics. Some lesbians have lauded the simple pleasures or even revolutionary possibilities of role-playing, while others, like myself, have seen it as a re-enactment and reinforcement of the dominant/submissive roles of institutionalized heterosexuality (Jeffreys, 1993, 1989; Nestle, 1992).

Gay liberation

To understand the 'queer' politics of the present it is necessary to analyse how they have been formed out of, and in opposition to, the ideas of gay liberation and lesbian feminism. Gay liberation tends to be derided, misrepresented or ignored in contemporary gay writings in the same ways as feminism is, so it is important to consider the ideas and practices seriously. Gay liberation is seen as puritanical and reactionary, too politically correct, foolishly concerned with the politics of everyday life, of sexual practice and the mechanisms of attraction (Jay and Young, 1992). In fact the study of gay liberation writings from the early 1970s is very illuminating (Jay and Young, 1992; Walter, 1980). Here can be found insights and understandings which have sadly been lost to contemporary gay politics. These include the importance of linking the gay struggle with that of women, with the anti-racist campaign, with socialism and opposition to capitalism in general, and the importance of the personal being political. Questioning of the construction of sexuality was central to early gay liberation concerns to an extent which greatly surprises students today. An important question for lesbian and gay politics is why these ideas were driven underground. I encourage my students, who are usually amazed that anyone could have been thinking these things twenty-five years ago, to try to understand the forces responsible, such as the development of the commercial gay sex industry.

There has not been a great deal of analysis of the reasons why lesbians separated, and continue to separate, from mixed gay organizations, but it does seem that the politics of gay male sexual practice have been a crucial stumbling block. It is important for lesbian politics to consider the nature and causes of the difficulties lesbians have faced from the 1970s onwards in working politically with gay men (Thompson, 1985; Frye, 1983; Stanley, 1982). This background will help in understanding why the very same difficulties, albeit with some new twists, persist in 'queer' organizing today.

Lesbian feminism

The teaching of lesbian feminist theory and practice must, I think, form the heart of any lesbian politics course. It is important to go back to the original texts of the early 1970s for the founding ideas. Unfortunately there is no comprehensive anthology of those texts. Some key ideas of early American lesbian feminism lie in books such as *Sappho Was a Right-On Woman*, *Lesbian Woman*, and *Lesbian Nation*, and many of the most radical are collected together in *For Lesbians Only* (Hoagland and

Penelope, 1988). Julia Penelope's (1993) *Lesbian Culture* gives some of the flavour of what is exciting about lesbian feminism but it is strictly American. Radicalesbians' (1970) 'The Woman Identified Woman' paper illustrates why lesbian feminists did and still do see lesbians as having revolutionary potential. The 1996 anthology *Radically Speaking* (Klein and Bell, 1996) contains the writings of many contemporary lesbian feminists. These texts show how lesbian feminists transformed the notion of what lesbianism was, fighting stereotypes of lesbians as sick, as butch/femme and sadomasochistic, as the characters of men's pornographic imaginations, and instead creating the idea of lesbians as the natural vanguard of women's liberation, as women persecuted precisely because we threaten men's control and exploitation of women. Unfortunately it is necessary now to understand how these ideas have been opposed by other varieties of lesbian thought in ways which would never have been expected in the 1970s. My book *The Lesbian Heresy* (1993) looks at how lesbian feminist ideas have been challenged by libertarian, queer and anti-feminist varieties of lesbian thought and practice in the 1980s and 1990s. A new and exciting collection, *All the Rage* (Harne and Miller, 1996), looks specifically at the challenges to lesbian feminism in the UK and reasserts the importance of radical lesbian feminist politics.

Few women's studies courses, let alone lesbian and gay ones, seem to cover the theory and practice of separatism, perhaps because the teachers disapprove or fear a backlash from the students. It is my experience that students can examine separatism very seriously and pay real attention to the question of why this political practice has created such a furore politically that it is the ultimate taboo for a woman to announce that she is a separatist, much worse than coming out as a lesbian. The work of Marilyn Frye and the anthology *For Lesbians Only* are the texts I find most useful for teaching the politics of separatism (Hoagland and Penelope, 1988; Frye, 1983). It should be central to any course on lesbian politics to teach some of the main thinkers of lesbian feminism such as Mary Daly, Audre Lorde, Marilyn Frye, Janice Raymond, Monique Wittig, Adrienne Rich and Sarah Hoagland, though a specialized course in lesbian feminist theory is really necessary to give adequate attention to their ideas. The work which is emerging from lesbian theorists such as Jeffner Allen (1990) and Claudia Card (1995, 1994) on lesbian ethics and lesbian community I see as part of lesbian political thought though it is labelled philosophy.

The lesbian equivalent of the so-called feminist sexuality debates is still of great importance in lesbian theory and practice. One element of this is the controversy created around feminist questioning of whether lesbianism must inevitably include sexual activity with women and if so what would 'sex' consist of (Rothblum, 1993; Frye, 1990; Jeffreys, 1989; Lorde, 1984a). The politics of sexual practice, namely, what construction of sexuality is best suited to achieving lesbian and women's liberation, remains a matter of heated dispute. I encourage students to look at lesbian pornography in the light of feminist criticism of straight men's porn and see if there is any difference (Jeffreys, 1993; Smith, 1988).

HIV/AIDS

I see the HIV/AIDS epidemic as a crucial factor in changing the climate of lesbian and gay politics in the 1980s. The phenomenon has shaped both public perceptions of lesbians and gay men and lesbians' and gays' perceptions of themselves. It has, I suggest, been significant in the construction of 'queer' politics (Jeffreys, 1994). One important concern for lesbians is the effect on lesbian politics of the direction of lesbian energies into the emotional and political care of gay men. That direction of lesbian energy was clearest in the USA; in recent years there have been some interesting writings about the appropriateness of this from lesbians who were involved (Maggenti, 1993; Schwartz, 1993). These lesbians talk about their puzzlement at gay male sexual practice and discomfort at the politics they encounter, which are conservative in their stances on race and class compared with lesbian feminism. They also ask why lesbians have directed energy into a disease that predominantly affects gay men while ignoring, until recently, the disease which affects lesbians in such dramatic numbers and with such dire effect, breast cancer. I have suggested that the HIV/AIDS epidemic has shaped the construction of lesbian sexuality through the promotion of 'safe sex' practices learned from gay male models and concentrated on objectifying and often sadomasochistic sex (Jeffreys, 1993). Through such 'safe sex education' the safety of what is disparagingly called 'vanilla' lesbian sex is never promoted to all women as splendidly safe in itself.

Queer politics

Gay commentators have suggested that the queer impulse emerges from the disillusionment caused by the epidemic, from a time when the word 'gay' seemed inappropriate (Watney, 1992). Many of the young students I teach describe themselves routinely as queer as if that were simply the new word meaning homosexual, though some see queer politics as specifically transgressive and confrontational. For lesbian feminists, though, 'queer' is a very controversial term. Lesbian feminist theorists have pointed out that the very word 'queer' excludes lesbians (Parnaby, 1996; Jeffreys, 1994). Lesbian feminist critics have reminded us that queer politics is based upon the categories of sexology and on a deviancy model, and that the idea that 'any women can be a lesbian', which lesbian feminists wore with pride in the 1970s, is not easily compatible with seeing lesbians as a minority. Some of the categories of sexual practice such as sadomasochism, paedophilia and transsexualism that lists of queer minorities commonly include have occasioned considerable disquiet among feminist theorists and activists.

The academic version of queer theory, as in the journal *GLQ*, often seems to be simply an application of postmodernist ideas to lesbian and gay theory and can look dauntingly obscure and irrelevant to queer practice on the streets (Sedgwick, 1993; Butler, 1993). I think that it is important for students and teachers of lesbian and gay politics to keep abreast of these ideas because they are influencing and being used to justify practices, such as lesbians having transsexual surgery, that are of real material concern. I encourage students to consider what both the theory and practice mean for lesbians and whether they offer a specific lesbian political way forward or just the adoption of a male gay political agenda.

Which way forward?

I am particularly interested in the internal politics of lesbian and gay movements and the way that these influence the strategies that gay activists undertake. But in the last couple of years a new body of literature on lesbian and gay activism in the public world, on policy-making and law reform, a literature which addresses the more traditional objects of political science has emerged. Two books from the UK, Davina Cooper's (1994) *Sexing the City*, and Angelia Wilson's (1995) edited collection *A Simple Matter of Justice?*, and one from Australia, Miranda Morris's (1995) *Pink Triangle* on gay law reform in Tasmania, for instance, examine these issues and even include such respectable political science topics as lesbian and gay approaches to Rawls's *A Theory of Justice*. Ruthann Robson's (1992) *Lesbian (Out)Law* is a very useful and specifically lesbian critique of law which is invaluable when considering policy-making. While I am delighted that such a literature which at last inserts lesbian and gay issues into the traditional agenda is developing, I remain committed to the importance of analysing the politics of lesbian and gay movements and not just the impact of lesbian and gay activism on the state.

Any politics which homogenizes lesbians into gay politics is fraught with difficulties. The issues of policy which lesbians and gay men have to confront such as lesbian and gay access to reproductive technology, the right to marry, sadomasochism and the law, and gays and the military need to be fully informed by feminist politics, by lesbian feminist theorizing and practice. An understanding that the personal is political, the crucial insight that feminism offers to traditional political science and to gay politics too, needs to underlie the teaching and practice of lesbian and gay politics if lesbians and gay men are not simply to demand inclusion in heteropatriarchy on equal terms. Equal terms would mean male dominance and female submission after all, and that is not very progressive.

References

Allen, J. (ed.) (1990) *Lesbian Philosophies and Cultures*. New York: SUNY.

Butler, J. (1990) *Gender Trouble: Feminism and the Subversion of Identity*. New York: Routledge.

Butler, J. (1993) 'Critically Queer.' *GLQ*. 1/1: 17–32.

Card, C. (ed.) (1994) *Adventures in Lesbian Philosophy*. Bloomington, IN: Indiana University Press.

Card, C. (1995) *Lesbian Choices*. New York: Columbia University Press.

Carmen, Gail, Neen and Tamara (1987) 'Becoming Visible: Black Lesbian Discussion.' In Feminist Review (ed.) *Sexuality: A Reader*. London: Virago.

Carpenter, E. (1921) *The Intermediate Sex*. London: George Allen and Unwin. First published 1908.

Cooper, D. (1994) *Sexing the City: Lesbian and Gay Politics within the Activist State*. London: Rivers Oram Press.

Daly, M. (1979) *Gyn/ecology*. London: The Women's Press.

Delphy, C. (1993) 'Rethinking Sex and Gender.' *Women's Studies International Forum*. 16/1: 1–9.

Ellis, Henry Havelock (1913) *Sexual Inversion*. Vol. 2 of *Studies in the Psychology of Sex*. Philadelphia: F.A. Davis. First published 1903.

Enloe, C. (1983) *Does Khaki Become You? The Militarisation of Women's Lives*. London: Pluto Press.

Enloe, C. (1989) *Bananas, Beaches and Bases: Making Feminist Sense of International Politics*. London: Pandora.

Faderman, L. (1985) *Surpassing the Love of Men*. London: The Women's Press.

Frye, M. (1983) *The Politics of Reality: Essays in Feminist Theory*. New York: The Crossing Press.

Frye, M. (1990) 'Lesbian "Sex"'. In Allen (1990).

Fuss, D. (1990) *Essentially Speaking: Feminism, Nature and Difference*. New York: Routledge.

Gomez, J., Peck, D., Segrest, M. and Dietcher, D. (1995) *Over the Rainbow: Lesbian and Gay Politics in America since Stonewall*. London: Boxtree.

Graham, D. (1994) *Loving to Survive: Sexual Terror, Men's Violence and Women's Lives*. New York: New York University Press.

Harne, L. and Miller, E. (1996) *All the Rage: Reasserting Radial Lesbian Feminism*. London: The Women's Press.

Hemphill, E. (ed.) (1991) *Brother to Brother*. Boston: Alyson.

Hoagland, S.L. (1988) *Lesbian Ethics: Toward New Value*. Palo Alto, CA: Institute of Lesbian Studies.

Hoagland, S.L. and Penelope, J. (eds) (1988) *For Lesbians Only: A Separatist Anthology*. London: Onlywomen Press.

Hui, Y. (1988) 'Living on the Fringes – in More Ways than One.' In B. Cant and S. Hemmings (eds) *Radical Records: Thirty Years of Lesbian and Gay History*. London: Routledge.

Jay, K. and Young, A. (eds) (1992) *Out of the Closets: Voices of Gay Liberation*. London: Gay Men's Press.

Jayawardena, K. (1986) *Feminism and Nationalism in the Third World*. London: Zed Books.

Jeffreys, S. (1985) *The Spinster and Her Enemies: Feminism and Sexuality 1880–1930*. London: Pandora.

Jeffreys, S. (1989) 'Does It Matter If They Did It?' In Lesbian History Group (eds) *Not a Passing Phase*. London: The Women's Press.

Jeffreys, S. (1990) *Anticlimax: A Feminist Perspective on the Sexual Revolution*. London: The Women's Press.

Jeffreys, S. (1993) *The Lesbian Heresy: A Feminist Perspective on the Lesbian Sexual Revolution*. Melbourne: Spinifex; (1994) London: The Women's Press.

Jeffreys, S. (1994) 'The Queer Disappearance of Lesbians: Sexuality in the Academy.' *Women's Studies International Forum*. 17/5: 459–72.

Johnson, E. (1991) 'Alison.' In C. Dunsford and S. Hawthorne (eds.) *Exploding Frangipani*. Dunedin North, New Zealand: New Women's Press.

Johnson, E. (1994) 'A Question of Difference.' In J. Scutt (ed.) *Taking a Stand: Women in Politics and Society*. Melbourne: Artemis.

Klein, R. and Bell, D. (eds) (1996) *Radically Speaking*. Melbourne: Spinifex; London: Zed Press.

Lee, A. (1991) 'For the Love of Separatism.' In Allen (1990).

LeVay, S. (1993) *The Sexual Brain*. Cambridge, MA: MIT Press.

Lorde, A. (1984a) 'Uses of the Erotic: The Erotic as Power.' In *Sister Outsider: Essays and Speeches by Audre Lorde*. Freedom, CA: The Crossing Press.

Lorde, A. (1984b) *Zami*. London: Sheba Publishers.

McIntosh, M. (1992) 'The Homosexual Role.' In E. Stein (ed.) *Forms of Desire: Sexual Orientation and the Social Constructions Controversy*. London: Routledge.

MacKinnon, C.A. (1989) *Toward a Feminist Theory of the State*. Cambridge, MA: Harvard University Press.

Maggenti, M. (1993) 'Wandering through Herland.' In A. Stein (ed.) *Sisters, Sexperts, Queers*. New York: Plume.

Mercer, K. (1992) 'Just Looking for Trouble: Robert Mapplethorpe and Fantasies of Race.' In L. Segal and M. McIntosh (eds) *Sex Exposed: Sexuality and the Pornography Debate*. London: Virago.

Moraga, C. and Anzaldúa, G. (eds) (1981) *This Bridge Called My Back: Writings by Radical Women of Color*. Watertown, MA: Persephone Press.

Morris, M. (1995) *Pink Triangle: The Gay Law Reform Debate in Tasmania*. Sydney: University of New South Wales Press.

Nestle, J. (ed.) (1992) *The Persistent Desire: A Femme-Butch Reader*. Boston: Alyson.

Parnaby, J. (1996) 'Queer Straits.' In Harne and Miller (1996).

Pateman, C. (1988) *The Sexual Contract*. Cambridge: Polity Press.

Penelope, J. (1993) *Lesbian Culture*. Freedom, CA: The Crossing Press.

Peterson, S. (1992) *Gendered States: Feminist (Re)visions of International Relations Theory*. Boulder, CO: Lynne Rienner.

Radicalesbians (1970) 'The Woman Identified Woman.' In Hoagland and Penelope (1988).

Raymond, J. (1986) *A Passion for Friends*. London: The Women's Press.

Rich, A. (1983) 'Compulsory Heterosexuality and Lesbian Existence.' In Abelove, H., Barate, M.A. and Halperin, D.M. (eds) *The Lesbian and Gay Studies Reader*. London: Routledge.

Richardson, D. (ed.) (1996) *Theorizing Heterosexuality*. Milton Keynes: Open University Press.

Robson, R. (1992) *Lesbian (Out)Law: Survival under the Rule of Law*. Ithaca, NY: Firebrand Books.

Rose, H. (1996) 'Gay Brains, Gay Genes and Feminist Science Theory.' In J. Weeks and J. Holland (eds) *Sexual Cultures: Communities, Values and Intimacy*. Basingstoke, Hants: Macmillan.

Rothblum, E. (1993) *Boston Marriages: Romantic but Asexual Relationships among Contemporary Lesbians*. Amherst, MA: University of Massachusetts Press.

Sahli, N. (1979) 'Smashing: Women's Relationships Before the Fall.' *Chrysalis*. 8.

Schwartz, R.L. (1993) 'New Alliances, Strange Bedfellows: Lesbians, Gay Men and AIDS.' In A. Stein (ed.) *Sisters, Sexperts, Queers*. New York: Plume.

Sedgwick, E. Kosofsky (1993) 'Queer Performativity: Henry James's "The Art of the Novel".' *GLQ*. 1/1: 1–16.

Smith, B. (1988) 'Sappho Was a Right-*Off* Woman.' In G. Chester and J. Dickey (eds) *Feminism and Censorship*. London: Prism.

Smith-Rosenberg, C. (1979) 'The Female World of Love and Ritual: Relations between Women in Nineteenth-Century America.' In N.F. Cott and E.H. Pleck (eds) *A Heritage of Her Own*. New York: Simon and Schuster.

Stanley, L. (1982) '" Male Needs": The Problems and Problems of Working with Gay Men.' In S. Friedman and E. Sarah (eds) *On the Problem of Men*. London: The Women's Press, pp. 190–203.

Sullivan, A. (1995) *Virtually Normal: An Argument about Homosexuality*. Basingstoke, Hants: Macmillan.

Thompson, D. (1985) *Flaws in the Social Fabric*. Sydney: Allen and Unwin.

Tsui, K. (1991) 'Breaking Silence, Making Waves and Loving Ourselves: The Politics of Coming Out and Coming Home.' In Allen (1990).

Vaid, U. (1995) *Virtual Equality: The Mainstreaming of Gay and Lesbian Liberation*. New York: Anchor Books, Doubleday.

Walter, A. (ed.) (1980) *Come Together*. London: Gay Men's Press.

Watney, S. (1992) 'Lesbian and Gay Studies in the Age of AIDS.' *NYQ*, 21 (22 March): 42.

Weeks, J. (1977) *Coming Out: Homosexual Politics in Britain from the Nineteenth Century to the Present*. London: Quartet.

Weeks, J. (1991) *Against Nature: Essays on History, Sexuality and Identity*. London: Rivers Oram Press.

Wilkinson, S. and Kitzinger, C. (eds) (1993) *Heterosexuality: A Feminism & Psychology Reader*. London: Sage.

Wilson, A.R. (ed.) (1995) *A Simple Matter of Justice?: Theorizing Lesbian and Gay Politics*. London: Cassell.

Wittig, M. (1992) *The Straight Mind and Other Essays*. Hemel Hempstead: Harvester Wheatsheaf.

11

Lesbians and Psychology: Straightening Us Out?

Celia Kitzinger

When, at the age of seventeen, I began my first sexual relationship with a woman, I read every psychology book I could find. It was the early 1970s, and virtually all the books I consulted told me I was sick. Lesbians were described as jealous, insecure and unhappy. We were the sick products of disturbed upbringings, suffering from unresolved castration anxiety or Oedipal conflicts, pursuing other women in a futile attempt to substitute a clitoris for a nipple as a result of our unresolved weaning problems. I remember particularly two thin blue paperbacks that I read (concealed inside a large glossy book on Byzantine art) behind a pillar in the public library: Donald West's *Homosexuality* and Anthony Storr's *Sexual Deviation*. Both books include sections on the prevention and 'cure' of homosexuality, and both paint a very dismal picture of lesbians and gay men. 'No one in his right mind would opt for the life of a sexual deviant', writes West (1968, p. 12), 'to be an object of ridicule and contempt, denied the fulfilments of ordinary family life and cut off from the mainstream of human interests.' According to Anthony Storr, 'to be a woman who is loved by a man, and who has children by him, is the first and most important aim of feminine existence' (1964, p. 68).

Traditionally, psychological research on lesbianism and male homosexuality has served as a justification for our oppression. From the late nineteenth and early twentieth centuries, when research on homosexuality first started to appear, until the mid-1970s, as much as 70 per cent of psychological research on homosexuality was devoted to the three questions: 'Are homosexuals sick?'; 'How can homosexuality be diagnosed?'; and 'What causes homosexuality?' (Morin, 1977). The vast bulk of this early sexological, psychological, psychiatric and (especially) psychoanalytic writing supported the view that homosexuality was pathological, and this view is still expressed by some mental health practitioners. In a book published in 1980 called *Overcoming*

Homosexuality, a clinical psychologist advances an argument still used by some psychologists today:

> Homosexuality is a symptom of neurosis and of a grievous personality disorder. It is an outgrowth of deeply rooted emotional deprivations and disturbances that had their origins in infancy. It is manifested, all too often, by compulsive and destructive behavior that is the very antithesis of fulfilment and happiness. Buried under the 'gay' exterior of the homosexual is the hurt and rage that crippled his or her capacity for true maturation, for healthy growth and love. (Kronemeyer, 1980, p. 7)

According to psychoanalyst Elizabeth Moberly, lesbians suffer from 'a state of incompletion' which does 'imply pathology' (1983, p. 86) and lesbians supposedly exhibit 'childishness; marked dependency needs; jealousy and possessiveness; a sense of inferiority and depression' (p. 40). The main psychoanalytic training institutions in England have been widely criticized for their assumptions about homosexuality (Ellis, 1994). In 1995 the Association for Psychoanalytic Psychotherapy in the National Health Service (one of the most prominent British organizations) invited as a guest speaker the North American psychoanalyst Charles Socarides whose view is that homosexuals are sick, compulsively driven by their unnatural urges into abnormal forms of sexual behaviour. He has said that homosexuality is a form of 'aberrancy', and 'a revision of the basic code and concept of life and biology', and he recommends conversion therapies to 'cure' homosexuals by changing them into heterosexuals (Jones, 1995).

In sum, psychology has provided a 'scientific' justification for the oppression of lesbians and gay men; psychological 'evidence' has been invoked as a rationale for locking us up in mental hospitals and prisons, breaking up our relationships with our lovers, taking our children away, denying us jobs and blatantly discriminating against us in law and social policy. Psychology as a discipline has been deeply complicit in our oppression.

The 'straight study' of lesbianism was clearly in need of 'modification' – in fact, it needed a thorough overhaul. Lesbians (and gay men) have fought long and hard to create change within the discipline. In many ways they have been successful, and the traditional 'lesbians are sick' perspective is no longer the norm within psychology. In 1973 the American Psychiatric Association, after major disruption to its meetings by lesbian and gay activists, removed homosexuality *per se* as a category from its *Diagnostic and Statistical Manual*. In 1975, the American Psychological Association (APA) adopted the official policy that homosexuality *per se* does not imply any kind of mental health impairment, and urged mental health professionals to take the lead in removing the stigma of mental illness that has long been associated with gay male and lesbian sexual identities. Nine years later, in 1984, the APA approved the establishment of a formal division (APA, Division 44) dedicated to the psychological study of lesbian and gay issues. It is now relatively unusual for explicitly anti-lesbian and anti-gay comments to be made by representatives of psychological bodies, or by acknowledged experts in the field, and rare to find overt references, within Anglo-American psychological writing, to homosexuality as pathology (Morin and Rothblum, 1991). The majority of psychologists are *not* now willing to use techniques designed to change clients' 'sexual orientation' (Hall, 1985, p. 222).

Socarides's message of lesbian pathology was not well received by most psychologists. In addition to the boycotts and demonstrations organized by lesbian and gay groups, two hundred psychotherapists, including nine professors of psychiatry, signed a 'letter of concern' about the continuing stigmatization of lesbians and gays by the psychoanalytic establishment, which was sent to six academic periodicals, to the Royal College of Psychiatrists and to the Health Secretary (Jones, 1995). The uproar caused by Socarides's view finally led the Conservative Government Minister, John Bowis, Under-Secretary for Health, to make a public statement condemning prejudice against homosexuality and praising 'the richness that lesbian and gay people add to our society' (Bowcott, 1995).

Despite these positive developments, it is clear that lesbian (and gay) perspectives in psychology are still subject to ridicule, incomprehension and trivialization. Members of the APA rate the work of Division 44 (the Society for the Psychological Study of Lesbian and Gay Issues) *even lower* in importance and interest than that of the Division for the Psychology of Women. In the UK there is no formally recognized forum within the British Psychological Society for lesbian and gay psychology. Proposals have been turned down by the Society's Council on three separate occasions (Coyle *et al.*, 1995; Comely *et al.*, 1992). Very recently, I co-authored – with a gay man – (Kitzinger and Coyle, 1995) an article about lesbian and gay relationships for the national professional journal, *The Psychologist*. The following two extracts give an indication of psychologists' responses; they were published under the heading 'Are You Normal?':

> I object to the misleading use in a publication of a scientific society of the innocent-sounding word 'gay' when referring to what is the abnormal practice of anal intercourse between males. Secondly, I object to attempts to mislead readers about the epidemiological incidence and prevalence of male and female homosexuality which in statistical-mathematical terms is fortunately still tiny. (Hamilton, 1995, p. 151)

> In their account of lesbian and gay relationships, Drs Kitzinger and Coyle wrote of it being 'usual for heterosexuality to be everywhere flaunted' in the workplace. Do I detect a certain amount of underlying annoyance that at work, as elsewhere, there is, indeed, a normality of

> life for the vast majority of people? It is certainly not a matter of heterosexuality being flaunted – it is simply the ordinariness of life from which homosexuals and lesbians, however much they may wish it were different, are perforce excluded. (Davis, 1995, pp. 151–2)

Although it is true to say that these comments provoked a deluge of letters from psychologists protesting this narrow definition of 'normality' and arguing for the celebration of diversity and difference, it was also significant that those who characterized homosexuality as 'healthy' agreed with those who regarded it as abnormal in opposing the proposal for a formal group within the British Psychological Society:

> [T]he creation of a Gay and Lesbian Section in the Society would itself be the ultimate in homophobic actions, damaging the very cause it seeks to promote. If it is reasonable to believe that homosexual people are not abnormal, but merely different from heterosexual people in respect of one area of their development, namely their sexuality, what sense can it make to group them together as requiring their own global perspective on psychology? To create such a grouping is surely to stereotype homosexual people and to exaggerate differences between them and heterosexual people beyond the sexual domain. (Seager, 1995, p. 295)

As these extracts illustrate, psychology has strenuously resisted lesbians' and gay men's efforts to challenge the discipline. In the face of psychology's opposition, it is remarkable how well we have done. Psychological research on lesbian and gay issues – a large and growing area of the discipline – has now moved well beyond simply arguing the case for homosexuality as a normal variant of sexual behaviour. Instead of justifying ourselves to heterosexuals, most lesbian and gay psychology now sets out deliberately to explore issues relevant to lesbian lives and in lesbians' own interests. Recent texts outlining and defining the field of lesbian and gay psychology (for example, D'Augelli and Patterson, 1995; Greene and Herek, 1994; Garnets and Kimmel, 1993; Gonsiorek and Weinrich, 1991) cover a wide range of topics including:

- coming out as lesbian, overcoming internalized homophobia and developing positive and healthy lesbian identities;
- building healthy lesbian relationships;
- the challenges of lesbian adolescence, mid-life and old age;
- parenting issues for lesbians;
- homophobia and anti-lesbian discrimination;
- mental health issues relating to physical health including HIV, AIDS and chemical dependence;
- cultural diversity among lesbians;

- bisexuality and questions of 'choice', flexibility and flux in sexual identities;
- the development of positive psychotherapeutic models for working with lesbians.

In addition to these 'academic' texts, there are now many popular psychology and self-help books available, written by lesbian psychologists, counsellors and therapists, for lesbian readers (for example, Rothblum and Cole, 1989; Tessina, 1989; Clunis and Green, 1988; Boston Lesbian Psychologies Collective, 1987; Loulan, 1984). All of these start from the idea that lesbians are not 'sick' (at least, not simply by virtue of being lesbian) and they show how many of our psychological problems derive from living in an oppressive society. Lesbian psychologists have also developed and promoted positive models of lesbian psychotherapy with lesbian clients (for example, Falco, 1991). The pervasiveness of therapy and counselling in lesbian communities, and the wide range of psychological books found on lesbian and gay bookshelves combine to suggest that lesbians have indeed created major changes within psychology, and that lesbian psychology is valued and eagerly purchased by lesbians more generally.

At this point, however, I am compelled to introduce a note of pessimism. I *wish* I could say that lesbian psychologists are creating radical change and challenging pyschology's oppressive practices. I *wish* I could say that the practice of psychology by lesbians is fundamentally different from that pursued by heterosexual men and women – that, as lesbians, we necessarily introduce new insights and fresh perspectives. I *wish* I could point to the ways in which psychology as a whole is radically altered by lesbians. Instead, I have to admit that 'lesbian psychology' seems (on the whole) to do little more than 'add lesbians in' to a discipline which is fundamentally individualistic, victim-blaming and politically reactionary. Lesbian and gay psychology was born out of a reaction against a traditional mainstream psychology which defined homosexuality as sick. Its reaction, not surprisingly, was to present evidence for lesbian and gay mental health – and, subsequently, to provide evidence for the pathological nature of anti-gay ('homophobic') individuals. Lesbian and gay psychology has thus been shaped by that which it opposed: it accepted that psychology was in the business of diagnosing the mental health or pathology of individuals and it wanted only to alter the bases upon which those diagnoses were made.

Mainstream traditional psychology is in the business of labelling people as 'sick' and then finding various 'cures'. As lesbians have been among those to be branded in this way by conventional psychological and psychiatric practice, you might think that lesbian psychologists would be especially sceptical of applying diagnostic categories to individual lesbians. Far from it – many lesbian psychologists are now at the forefront of inventing new psychological disorders from which they say we lesbians are suffering. According to traditional psychologists, we were sick simply by virtue of being lesbians. The 'modification' made to this theory by many lesbian psychologists is that we are no longer 'sick' simply because we are lesbians; instead we are 'sick' because we are lesbians living in an oppressive society. Either way, though, we're sick – and in need of the dubious 'cures' offered by therapists.

Take, for example, the term 'homophobia', which is the word lesbian and gay psychology typically uses to describe our oppression. It was psychology which invented this term, back in the early 1970s: the word became widely used only after 1973 when a psychoanalyst, Dr George Weinberg, published a popular book on homosexuality, in which he used the word. The term is a psychological diagnosis: 'phobia' comes from the Greek for 'fear', as in 'claustrophobia' or 'agoraphobia', meaning an irrational fear or dread. Lesbian and gay psychologists have developed scales to measure homophobia (for example, Hansen, 1982; Larsen *et al.*, 1980) and describe homophobes as authoritarian, dogmatic and sexually rigid individuals who have low levels of ego development and suffer from a whole range of personal problems and difficulties in their relationships (Hudson and Ricketts, 1980; Weiss and Dain, 1979; MacDonald and Games, 1974). Not only does this concept reinforce the power of psychology to label people as 'sick' or 'mentally healthy' at will, it also depoliticizes lesbian and gay oppression by suggesting that it comes from the personal inadequacy of particular individuals suffering from a diagnosable phobia.

Worse still, the mental health not only of *heterosexuals* but also of lesbians (and gay men) is threatened by homophobia – not simply because homophobes reject us and hurt us (behaviours which have, according to lesbian and gay psychologists, 'negative mental health consequences' for lesbians and gay men; Garnets *et al.*, 1993, p. 600), but also because we allegedly suffer from something called 'internalized homophobia' ('the oppressor within'; Margolies *et al.*, 1987, p. 229). The idea of internalized homophobia was recently described as a 'central organizing concept for a gay and lesbian affirmative psychology' (Schidlo, 1994, p. 176). Instead of going to heterosexual therapists (like Socarides) to be cured of our homosexuality, now we are supposed to seek out lesbian therapists to be cured of internalized homophobia, which is purported to have a 'deleterious and pathogenic impact on development events in gay people and their psychological functioning' (p. 180) – causing everything from generalized misery to impaired sexual functioning. Accepting oneself as lesbian or gay is characterized as a 'developmental task' or as a 'stressor', and the therapist's task is to help the client come to terms with their real sexual orientation (Greene, 1994, p. 6). This process is made more difficult, according to these psychologists, by internalized homophobia. Therapists working with lesbian and gay clients are advised: 'Always plan to spend a period of therapy time assessing with your client the effects of possible internalized homophobia' (Falco, 1991, p. 29). Of course, it is true that some people are unhappy about being lesbian, just as some people are unhappy about being working-class, or black, but these forms of unhappiness are not 'phobias' or instances of individual pathology; they are perfectly reasonable responses to oppression.

The concept of internalized homophobia is used as an explanation for the many ways in which lesbians allegedly *oppress ourselves*. Unable to accept our own sexuality, riddled with guilt and self-hatred, we deliberately seek out situations in which we can experience pain or failure. In lesbian therapy, clients are helped 'to see all the ways in which they may maintain a victim attitude or provoke and perpetuate their social isolation' (Decker, 1984, p. 41). As one therapist explains:

> It is also possible for the person who is not comfortable with being gay to use coming out as a weapon to hurt herself as well as those she has chosen to 'come out' to. One aspect of the process of guilt on the part of the lesbian may be to develop a need for self-punishment which can be accomplished by alienating herself from family and friends. The fear of family rejection can become a self-fulfilling prophecy. (Groves, 1985, p. 18)

Others make similar points: homosexuals may 'set themselves up for rejection with poorly planned and impulsive disclosure in an environment that is likely to produce a harsh response' (Gonsiorek, 1995, p. 34) and they may 'abandon career or educational goals with the excuse that external bigotry will keep them from their objectives' (p. 33). The idea that lesbians and gay men are psychologically damaged (suffering from internalized homophobia) runs throughout the literature of lesbian and gay psychology. The focus is yet again shifted away from the oppressor and back onto the victims of oppression.

Another psychological diagnosis, invented by lesbian psychologists and applied pretty much exclusively to lesbians, is the label 'merger'. Unlike 'homophobia', this term has not (yet) caught on among lesbians outside psychology (at least, not in the UK), but it is a standard concept in use in lesbian psychology, and has become a catch-all term developed as a pseudo-explanation for virtually everything that can go wrong between lesbian lovers. Lesbian psychologists use the notion of 'merger' to explain why a lesbian wants more (or less) sex than her lover; why she has an 'affair' outside her established couple relationship; why she maintains a close friendship with an ex-lover (or why she doesn't); why she and her lover stay together 'too long' or why they break up. By 'merger' they mean 'a psychological state in which there is a loss of a sense of oneself as individual or separate' (Perlman, 1989, p. 78). In other words, our closeness to our lesbian lovers, our intimacy and involvement with each other, is pathologized. According to lesbian psychotherapists, merger is much more commonly a problem in lesbian than in heterosexual or gay male relationships (Perlman, 1989; Hall, 1985) and one heterosexual woman has even cited 'fear of merging' as 'one of the reasons I remain heterosexual' (Rowland, 1993, p. 77)!

Some lesbian psychologists also pathologize lesbian sexuality. Lesbian couples are supposed to suffer from ISD, which stands for 'Inhibited Sexual Desire' (Nichols, 1987, p. 106) – also known as 'lesbian bed death' (Loulan, 1984) or 'erotophobia' (Nichols, 1987, p. 122). What this means is that lesbians don't have genital sexual activity with their partners as often as they (or their partners, or their therapists) think they should. According to lesbian psychologists, this is often caused by internalized homophobia – that is, lesbians are frightened of admitting to themselves that they desire women sexually, and so they avoid sexual contact. Instead of exploring the social and political framework within which lesbians do or do not feel sexual, do or do not like certain sexual activities, psychologists label us 'sexually repressed'. If we don't like penetration, this is labelled 'vaginismus' (Richardson and Hart, 1980), and therapists like JoAnn Loulan devote three full pages to explaining how someone can train herself to accept larger and larger objects in her vagina. Dislike of oral or anal sex is a 'phobia' (Richardson and Hart, 1980) and according to Laura Brown (1986) 'lesbians suffer from sexual dysfunctions of similar types and etiologies as do many heterosexual women' (p. 99). In branding particular sexual preferences and dislikes as 'dysfunctions' or 'phobias', sex therapists are promoting their own definition of 'correct' lesbian sex, smuggling in covert value judgements under the banner of non-judgementalism. Many lesbian sex therapists (for example, Brown, 1986; Loulan, 1984) recommend the use of pornography or 'erotica' to overcome internalized homophobia, and the use of sadomasochism to 'cure' merger (for example, Nichols, 1987).

Lesbian and feminist writing *outside* psychology is full of discussion and debates about lesbian erotica, sadomasochism, heterosexuality, lesbian friendship and so on. But lesbians writing *within* psychology often write as though these discussions do not exist: their writings are located completely outside the dazzling array of political positions we have adopted, and the arguments we have used to defend or to explain our choices. Instead of taking political positions for (or against) sadomasochism, or pornography, lesbian psychologists advocate it as cure. Ignoring feminist debates about the role of penetration in lesbian sex, lesbian psychologists simply describe those who dislike it as 'phobic'. Rather than focusing on our *reasons* as lesbians for coming out, or staying in the closet, lesbian psychologists diagnose internalized homophobia. In sum, much lesbian psychology simply glosses over the politics of diagnosis just as traditional psychology has always done.

Internalized homophobia, merger, erotophobia and the rest are just labels peddling a particularly individualistic view of the world. They are no more 'real' than are diseases like 'drapetomania' or 'dysthesia aethiopis', both of which were diagnosed by the North American nineteenth-century physician Cartwright (1981). Both diseases were peculiar to slaves: the main symptom of drapetomania was running away from the plantations; dysthesia aethiopis (also know as 'rascality') was caused by idleness and cured by whipping and hard physical labour. More recently, in the 1970s, there emerged a disease known as 'state benefit neurosis', an illness characterized by refusing to take poorly paid employment when more money was available through state benefits. As with both of these examples, the alleged pathological conditions of lesbians do reflect real feelings and behaviours. What is at issue is not whether some nineteenth-century slaves tried to escape, or whether some lesbians are frightened to come out: of course both statements are true. What is at issue is how we want to think about this. If we think about these facts in terms of drapetomania and internalized homophobia we wilfully obscure the social and political realities of oppression.

Lesbian psychology has been developed over the past thirty-five years in response to the specific oppressions of mainstream psychology: its diagnoses, its counter-arguments and its analyses of lesbianism are to a large extent informed by the mainstream psychology which it opposes, adopting the agenda of mainstream psychology (rather than that of lesbian feminism) which the field of lesbian psychology has attempted to 'modify' as an oppressive discipline. This modification (while a great improvement on traditional psychology's treatment of lesbians) leaves intact the individualistic and pathologizing tendencies of psychology in general. This means that, despite all the fears and oppositional tactics of mainstream psychology, lesbians in psychology have proved remarkably little threat to the discipline. We have shown ourselves willing to play by the boys' rules on the boys' terms: we have done no more than tinker with the system, making minor modifications in favour of lesbians, but leaving intact the whole rotten apparatus of diagnosis and cure.

Some lesbians and some psychologists are now very critical of these lesbian modifications to psychology, and are demanding and creating radical alternatives. A *real* lesbian transformation of psychology would do much more than invert and invent diagnostic categories. A *real* lesbian transformation of psychology would expose the political basis of the diagnostic categories themselves. It is my fervent hope that future lesbian intervention in psychology may seek more thoroughly to interrupt the workings of a heteropatriarchally defined discipline – and that our political analysis of psychology may transform it out of all recognition.

References

Boston Lesbian Psychologies Collective (1987) *Lesbian Psychologies: Explorations and Challenges*. Urbana: University of Illinois Press.

Bowcott, O. (1995) 'Tory Minister Praises Gay "Richness".' *Guardian*, 22 June.

Brown, L.S. (1986) 'Confronting Internalized Oppression in Sex Therapy with Lesbians.' *Journal of Homosexuality*. 12: 99–107.

Cartwright, S.A. (1981) 'Report on the Diseases and Physical Peculiarities of the Negro Race.' In A.L. Caplan, H.T. Engelhardt and J.J. McCartney (eds) *Concepts of Health and Disease: Interdisciplinary Perspectives*. Reading, MA: Addison-Wesley.

Clunis, M. and Green, D. (1988) *Lesbian Couples*. Seattle: Seal Press.

Comely, L., Kitzinger, C. Perkins, R. and Wilkinson, S. (1992) 'Lesbian Psychology in Britain: Back into the Closet?' *Feminism & Psychology*. 2/2: 265–8.

Coyle, A., Kitzinger, C., Flynn, R., Wilkinson, S., Rivers, I. and Perkins, R. (1995) 'Lesbian and Gay Psychology Section'. (Letter). *The Psychologist*. 8/4, April 1995: 151.

D'Augelli, A.R. and Patterson, C.J. (eds) (1995) *Lesbian, Gay and Bisexual Identities over the Lifespan: Psychological Perspectives*. New York: Oxford University Press.

Davis, M. (1995) Letter. *The Psychologist*. 8/4, April 1995: 151–2.

Decker, B. (1984) 'Counselling Gay and Lesbian Couples.' *Journal of Social Work and Human Sexuality*. 2(2/3): 39–52.

Ellis, M.L. (1994) 'Lesbians, Gay Men and Psychoanalytic Training.' *Free Associations*. 4/4: 501–17.

Falco, K.L. (1991) *Psychotherapy with Lesbian Clients: Theory into Practice*. New York: Brunner/Mazel.

Garnets, L.D. and Kimmel, D.C. (eds) (1993) *Psychological Perspectives on Lesbian and Gay Experiences*. New York: Columbia University Press.

Garnets, L.D., Herek, G.M. and Levy, B. (1993) 'Violence and Victimization of Lesbians and Gay Men: Mental Health Consequences.' In Garnets and Kimmel (1993).

Gonsiorek, J.C. (1995) 'Gay Male Identities: Concepts and Issues.' In D'Augelli and Patterson (1995), pp. 24–47.

Gonsiorek, J.C. and Weinrich, J.D. (eds) (1991) *Homosexuality: Research Implications for Public Policy*. London: Sage.

Greene, B. (1994) 'Lesbian and Gay Sexual Orientations: Implications for Clinical Training, Practice and Research.' In Greene and Herek (1994).

Greene, B. and Herek, G.M. (eds) (1994) *Psychological Perspectives on Lesbian and Gay Issues Vol. 1. Lesbian and Gay Psychology: Theory, Research and Clinical Applications*. Thousand Oaks, CA: Sage.

Groves, P.A. (1985) 'Coming Out: Issues for the Therapist Working with Women in the Process of Identity Formation.' *Women and Therapy*. 4/2: 17–22.

Hall, M. (1985) *The Lavender Couch: A Consumer's Guide to Psychotherapy for Lesbians and Gay Men*. Boston: Alyson.

Hamilton, V. (1995) Letter. *The Psychologist*. 8/4, April 1995: 151.

Hansen, G.L. (1982) 'Measuring Prejudice Against Homosexuality (Homosexism) among College Students: A New Scale.' *Journal of Social Psychology*. 117: 233–6.

Hudson, W.W. and Ricketts, W.A. (1980) 'A Strategy for the Measurement of Homophobia.' *Journal of Homosexuality*. 5: 357–72.

Jones, J. (1995) 'Minister to Rebuke "Anti-Gay" Disciples of Freud.' *Observer*, 18 June.

Kitzinger, C. (1987) *The Social Construction of Lesbianism*. London: Sage.

Kitzinger, C. (1990) 'Heterosexism in Psychology.' *The Psychologist*. 3/9: 391–2.

Kitzinger, C. and Coyle, A. (1995) 'Lesbian and Gay Couples: Speaking of Difference.' *The Psychologist*. 8/2: 64–8.

Kitzinger, C. and Perkins, R. (1993) *Changing Our Minds: Lesbian Feminism and Psychology*. New York: New York University Press.

Kronemeyer, R. (1980) *Overcoming Homosexuality*. New York: Macmillan.

Larsen, K., Reed, M. and Hoffman, S. (1980) 'Attitudes of Heterosexuals toward Homosexuality: A Likert-Type Scale and Construct Validity.' *Journal of Sex Research*. 16/3: 245–57.

Loulan, J. (1984) *Lesbian Sex*. San Francisco: Spinsters Ink.

MacDonald, A.P. (1976) 'Homophobia: Its Roots and Meanings.' *Homosexual Counseling Journal*. 3: 23–33.

MacDonald, A.P. and Games, R.G. (1974) 'Some Characteristics of Those Who Hold Positive and Negative Attitudes toward Homosexuals.' *Journal of Homosexuality*. 1: 9–27.

Margolies, L., Becker, M. and Jackson-Brewer, K. (1987) 'Internalized Homophobia: Identifying and Treating the Oppressor Within.' In Boston Lesbian Psychologies Collective (1987), pp. 229–41.

Moberly, E.R. (1983) *Psychogenesis: The Early Development of Gender Identity*. London: Routledge and Kegan Paul.

Morin, S.F. (1977) 'Heterosexual Bias in Psychological Research on Lesbianism and Male Homosexuality.' *American Psychologist*. 19: 629–37.

Morin, S.F. and Rothblum, E. (1991) 'Removing the Stigma: Fifteen Years of Progress.' *American Psychologist*. 46: 947–9.

Nichols, M. (1987) 'Lesbian Sexuality: Issues and Developing Theory.' In Boston Lesbian Psychologies Collective (1987), pp. 97–125.

Pearson, G. (1975) *The Deviant Imagination: Psychiatry, Social Work and Social Change*. London: Macmillan.

Perlman, S.F. (1989) 'Distancing and Connectedness: Impact on Couple Formation and Lesbian Relationships.' *Women and Therapy*. 8/1: 77–88.

Richardson, D. and Hart, J. (1980) 'Gays in Therapy: Getting It Right.' *New Forum*. 6: 58–60.

Rothblum, E.D. and Cole, E. (1989) *Loving Boldly: Issues Facing Lesbians*. New York: Harrington Park.

Rowland, R. (1993) 'Radical Feminist Heterosexuality: The Personal and the Political.' In Wilkinson and Kitzinger (1993).

Schidlo, A. (1994) 'Internalized Homophobia: Conceptual and Empirical Issues in Measurement.' In Greene and Herek (1994), pp. 176–205.

Seager, M. (1995) 'Sectioned Off?' Letter. *The Psychologist*. 8/7, July 1995: 295.

Storr, A. (1964) *Sexual Deviation*. London: Penguin.

Tessina, T. (1989) *Gay Relationships for Men and Women: How to Find Them, How to Improve Them, and How to Make Them Last*. Los Angeles: Tarcher.

Weinberg, G. (1973) *Society and the Healthy Homosexual*. New York: Anchor.

Weiss, C.B. and Dain, R.N. (1979) 'Ego Development and Sex Attitudes in Heterosexual and Homosexual Men and Women.' *Archives of Sexual Behaviour*. 8: 341–56.

West, D. (1968) *Homosexuality*. Harmondsworth: Penguin.

Wilkinson, S. and Kitzinger, C. (1993) *Heterosexuality: A Feminism & Psychology Reader*. London: Sage.

Wilkinson, S. and Kitzinger, C. (1996) *Representing the Other: A Feminism & Psychology Reader*. London: Sage.

12

'Friends', Feminists and Sexual Outlaws: Lesbianism and British History

Alison Oram

Since the early 1980s lesbian history has enjoyed a healthy growth in terms of research and publishing in the UK. This has largely been achieved outside academic history departments, by lesbian scholars in women's studies, sociology, English literature and adult education. Despite having had relatively little impact on mainstream history as a discipline, lesbian historians have energetically developed a vital series of debates. We have argued long and hard over who and what we are looking for in the past when we embark on a study of lesbian history – and even more over how we interpret it. Is lesbian history about love between women? Is sexual desire an essential part of the equation? What kinds of evidence do we need to apply the term 'lesbian'? Are we looking for women who refused contemporary notions of femininity – by acting or dressing like men, for instance? Or are we looking for those who strongly identified as women – to the extend of making feminist allegiances and communities?

Consider the following two nineteenth-century examples, which might reasonably be included in any history of lesbianism. In February 1835, the following London police court report appeared in the newspapers:

> A creature in the garb of a man, who at the station-house had given the name of Bill Chapman, was placed at the bar with one Isabella Watson, and complained of for being a common cheat and imposter, and creating a disturbance. Oakley, inspector of the E division, stated that although the thing before them, that called itself Bill Chapman, was attired in man's apparel, he had ascertained that it was a woman. . . . 'I have known her at least ten years, and she always appears in a dress similar to the one she now wears, namely, a hat, smock-frock, trousers or knee-breeches, and until last night I always supposed her to be a man. She is known all over England as a ballad-singer. . . . She travels the country with a woman named Isabella Watson, and they are both known at every race-course and fair as ballad-singers, and

> considered to be man and wife.' The magistrate, very surprised, declared: 'I never saw a figure more like a man, and the voice is manly', and complained that he knew of no law to punish her for wearing male attire. 'It is a case that puzzels [*sic*] me, but I must discharge the prisoner.' . . . The prisoner, who was chewing tobacco, then bowed his head, and walked out of the office with Isabella, who exclaimed, 'Never mind, my lad, if we live a hundred years it will be in this manner.' (Anonymous, 1848, pp. 68–70)

Twenty-five years later, two middle-class feminists met: Octavia Hill, the housing reformer, and Sophia Jex-Blake, one of the women who fought to open the medical profession to women. In May 1860, Sophia proposed a joint holiday in Wales. She recorded in her diary:

> May 17th, Whitsunday – Told Octa about Wales, – sitting in her room on the table, my heart beating like a hammer. That Carry [Sophia's sister] wanted to go to Wales and I too, and most convenient about the beginning of July, so . . . 'Put off my visit?' said Octa. 'No, I was just going to say (slowly) if you wish to see anything of me, you must come too, I think, and not put off the mountains till heaven.' She sunk her head on my lap silently, raised it in tears, and then such a kiss! (Todd, 1918, pp. 85–6)

Are these the women we are looking for in our lesbian past? We can empathize with Isabella's bravado, admire Bill's success at cross-dressing and applaud the long-term survival skills of this female couple living on the margins of society. Similarly we can appreciate the emotional tension and suppressed eroticism between the two romantic friends of the second example. But what, if anything, do they have in common with each other – or indeed, with lesbians in the late twentieth century? Our answers to these questions have been shaped by our political perspectives. As Martha Vicinus (1989) and other historians have observed, lesbian history is all about identity. Women in the past who loved and/or had sex with other women, or who cross-dressed, and who resisted heterosexuality, did not necessarily have a language to describe themselves as 'lesbian', or to claim any particular identity based on their sexuality. They could only understand their desires, behaviour and experiences within the social context of their own times. Recognizing that sexual identities are socially and historically constructed, lesbian historians must engage with diverse groups of women, and be alert to, in Vicinus's (1994) useful phrase, 'lesbian-like' cultures and behaviour.

By investigating the past, we are also 'inventing ourselves', choosing – indeed sometimes 'falling for' – those lesbian ancestors (whether disreputable cross-dressers or acceptable romantic friends) who attract us from the past and who have meaning for us, to construct, justify and extend our present-day lesbian identities. History-writing is always the story of the present rather than an account of the past. The past is crucially important to us in formulating our current identities and politics, both individual and collective, but there can never be one 'true' story of 'what happened' in history. Competing versions of the past reflect different understandings of the world and different interests; dominant white male history-writing has been contested by oppositional histories such as black history and feminist history, as well as by lesbian history. But our writing of lesbian history also reflects a range of lesbian identities. We can see how British lesbian history since the early 1980s has been constructed differently by each group or generation – chronological, sexual and political generations, informed by different theoretical and political positions – in the process of forming an identity.

Indeed, it could be argued that the question is not so much about how lesbians and lesbian politics have altered the discipline of history as about how representations of the past have been used either to support or to attack various positions in lesbian politics. Some of the most spectacular arguments in lesbian politics in the 1980s and 1990s have been informed by or connected with lesbian history. These have included, in the UK, the meaning of feminist politics for lesbians, the acceptability or not of role-playing and butch/femme identities, the self-censorship of lesbian films (the argument over the showing of *She Must Be Seeing Things* at the Lesbian Summer School run by the Lesbian Archive in July 1988) and the lesbian feminist critique of the so-called 'lesbian sexual revolution' (Jeffreys, 1994; Ardill and O'Sullivan, 1989, 1986).

Lesbian history and politics are also closely interconnected because lesbian history in the UK in the 1980s emerged out of grassroots lesbian politics rather than from the academy. Specific projects were established by the lesbian community, including the Lesbian Archive in 1982, and, following a successful Lesbian Studies Working Weekend in London in the summer of 1984, the Lesbian History Group was set up to provide a forum for discussion and research for lesbians inside and outside of the education system. American publications began to be supplemented by British research, such as the Onlywomen Press lesbian history diary for 1984, *Past Participants* (Mohin and Wilson, 1983). Another important pressure was the demand and support for courses in lesbian history in adult education. In the mid-1980s, lesbian history courses offered by the University of London Extramural Centre attracted large numbers of women, and similar courses have continued in later years. These courses stimulated further research, the production of teaching materials, and early publications (Uncovering Lesbian History 1800–1970 Course, 1988). Some research was also carried out in universities in the late 1970s and 1980s, but in a fairly isolated context, and, following the pattern of development of women's studies, was conducted in sociology and English departments rather than in history, which remained male-dominated and largely resistant to women's history, let alone feminist or lesbian history, well into the late 1980s.[1]

Early lesbian history had specific aims which remain valid today. The immediate task was to name and recover lesbians from the past, as individuals, couples and women's networks. This project, which typically took the form of rereading and rewriting women's biographies and collecting oral histories, asserted the existence of lesbians in the past, redeeming them from historical invisibility. At the same time this validated the existence of lesbians today and contributed to the creation of a contemporary identity, as the titles of books and courses from that period like *Not a Passing Phase* and *Inventing Ourselves* (Lesbian History Group, 1989; Hall Carpenter Archives Lesbian Oral History Group, 1989) attest. Associated with this was the desire to challenge the way that contemporary history – including feminist history – continued to erase lesbian history by assuming a heterosexual orientation and life cycle for women in the past, even in the teeth of the evidence. The Lesbian History Group argued that

> The suppression of lesbianism extends beyond the control of contemporary images and information to include control of historical knowledge so that, for instance, the lives of women who were lesbians are rewritten to a more acceptable script which focuses on a man or men. (Lesbian History Group, 1989, p. 2)

But the aim was also to move on from rediscovery to analyse the ways in which ideas about lesbianism (however this was to be defined) had been regulated and suppressed by various social mechanisms in the past, including science, sexology and patriarchal ideologies of heterosexuality. Lesbian history, argued the Lesbian History Group, was '*an approach to history*' which should analyse heterosexuality as a political institution of patriarchal power (Lesbian History Group, 1989, p. 16).

This approach was inspired by lesbian feminist politics of the 1970s and early 1980s, and in particular by the pioneering work of two American writers. Carroll Smith-Rosenberg (1975) was the first to highlight the importance and frequency of love relationships between women in her study of the romantic friendships of nineteenth-century bourgeois women. Extensive bonds and networks between single women, married women, cousins and sisters were to be found in a 'female world of love and ritual'. Adrienne Rich (1980) developed the concept of the transhistorical 'lesbian continuum', which potentially included most women, and which referred to a whole range of 'women-identified experience' – intense emotional ties, caring, nurturing, sexual desire and 'bonding against male tyranny'. Work in the UK at the same time used a broadly similar framework, defining lesbianism in feminist terms as an act of resistance to male power involving female autonomy and the building of relationships and community between women (Faraday, 1985). This perspective linked lesbians with other women rather than conceptualizing them as a marginal or deviant group. It also rejected a definition of lesbianism centred on genital sex between women as being too limited, as well as impractical for the purposes of historical research. Lesbian historians at this time and since set out to challenge the 'compulsory heterosexuality' of contemporary society and its historiography.

Continually inspired by lesbian politics, lesbian history has been profoundly shaped by the political debates of the 1970s, 1980s and 1990s. Particular brands of lesbian politics have become heavily inscribed in lesbian history. The focus in transatlantic lesbian history has moved from a lesbian feminist emphasis on the model of romantic friendship (initiated by Smith-Rosenberg (1975) and Faderman (1981) and discussed in more detail below) towards a 'pro-sex' re-evaluation (some would argue glorification) of sexual desire, dress codes and butch/femme role-playing, whether in the 1950s or the eighteenth century (Donoghue, 1993; Kennedy and Davis, 1993; Nestle, 1987, 1981). Martha Vicinus in 1989 criticized both these models as ahistorical: 'Too often the current fashion in appropriate behaviour [is] used to judge the past. . . . Now roles are in, romance is out; what will be next year's correct lesbian stance?' (p. 172). It may be too simplistic to *directly* map these political differences – is lesbianism about sexual desire or resistance to patriarchy? – on to the academic debates, but they have certainly been influential. As lesbian history has moved into the 1990s, these political differences have also intersected with shifting academic interests and paradigms, particularly from cultural studies. Academic institutions have opened up (albeit to a still limited extent) to gay and lesbian studies, following the intellectual challenge of feminist and lesbian scholarship, accompanied by a postmodern concern with issues of 'difference' and diversity.[2] The central part of this chapter will therefore outline and discuss the main debates in British lesbian history in this changing political and intellectual context.

From passionate friendship . . .

The debate over romantic friendship was popularized by Lillian Faderman's book *Surpassing the Love of Men*, first published in 1981 and still the only general survey of the lesbian history of white women in Europe and the USA. Her archetype of lesbianism was the nineteenth-century romantic friendship – love between women in the broadest sense. In their feminist identification and community networks, these women looked remarkably like lesbian feminists of the 1970s and early 1980s. 'I venture to guess that had the romantic friends of other eras lived today, many of them would have been lesbian feminists; and had the lesbian feminists of our day lived in other eras, most of them would have been romantic friends' (Faderman, 1981, p. 20). In their middle-class milieu, she argued, such friendships were socially acceptable and even valued. Faderman further asserted that sex between women was culturally unthinkable and therefore an unlikely possibility before the late-nineteenth-century sexologists brought 'the Fall'. The late nineteenth century offered new opportunities for women's economic independence and hence strengthened women's ability to choose such pair-bonds, but also witnessed increased attacks on these autonomous New Women. Broadly speaking, the Faderman lesbian feminist approach was the one adopted, though not entirely uncritically, in the mid-1980s by the group of British lesbian historians associated with the Lesbian Archive and the Lesbian History Group, who emphasized that sex between women was just one possible element, and perhaps not the most important, in lesbian identity (Lesbian History Group, 1989, pp. 6–17; Faraday, 1985; Jeffreys, 1985).

Lesbian feminist history presented passionate friendship in different ways: as an integral part of a feminist woman-centred life, as part of a 'lesbian continuum' and as a prototype of 1970s and 1980s lesbian feminism. In the later 1980s, this led to increasingly sophisticated research, as historians investigated further aspects of romantic friendship such as the changing historical context of such friendships and the boundaries of their social acceptability. They found that fresh versions of romantic friendship were forged by late-Victorian feminists, often linked together through friendship networks and political interests. Evidence of eroticism and the tentative development of 'lesbian-like' sexual identities have also been explored in the context of lesbian networks and women's communities. In some respects this is an extension of the biographical approach – finding networks of women, often writers and artists, who were friends, partners and lovers. Vicinus (1985) showed how nineteenth-century women's communities could be an escape route from the limitations of family life for middle-class women, offering the opportunity for useful work in a respectable environment. Within these communities female friendships, some powerful and erotic, could flourish. By the turn of the century, more radical groups such as the suffragettes might directly discuss sexuality, albeit generally understood as heterosexuality. This overlap with the history of feminism has been intriguing, if also frustrating. Liz Stanley's work on the suffragette Emily Wilding Davison illustrates some ways in which inevitably patchy evidence of important friendships, and their tokens of affection and love, can be read as lesbian-like behaviour (Bland, 1995; Auchmuty, 1989; Stanley, 1988; Vicinus, 1985).

From the mid-1980s the lesbian feminist approach to history was increasingly critiqued as downplaying the significance of eroticism and sexual expression in lesbian history and identity. The challenge came from two sources – politics and the academy. Politically, the Faderman model was challenged by the increased sexualization of lesbian culture, as the lesbian feminist ideal of women-loving-women living in feminist communities was criticized as moralistic and anti-sex.[3] Joan Nestle (1981), one of the founders of the New York Lesbian Herstory Archives, wrote in the early 1980s reaffirming butch/femme role-playing as an important and positive feature of lesbian identity in recent history. In the UK, debates about sexual practice, including lesbian sadomasochism, polarized the lesbian community (Jeffreys, 1994; Ardill and O'Sullivan, 1989, 1986). Academically, Faderman's thesis that romantic friendship (and therefore lesbian history) was largely about emotional bonding rather than sexual relationships between women was challenged by further research into romantic friendship and especially by the discovery and publication of the diaries of Anne Lister (Whitbread, 1988). Anne Lister was a rare example of an early nineteenth-century woman from the gentry class who wrote explicitly, though in coded form, about her sexual relationships with other women, recognized her sexual desires and forged an individual lesbian identity for herself, despite having few role models (Clark, 1996). Interestingly, there was some scepticism from British lesbian feminist historians about the veracity of the diaries when they were first published, showing how deeply accepted (and acceptable) the asexual romantic friendship version of lesbian history was at that time.

In the early 1990s, Lisa Moore (1992) and Emma Donoghue (1993) (both from a literary studies background) insisted on reading lesbian sex in history, even within romantic friendship. Using other contemporary texts alongside the Anne Lister diaries, Moore demonstrated the tensions and contradictions within the early nineteenth-century category of romantic friendship. While love between women could represent chastity, virtue and asexuality, it might also be attacked and prohibited as hinting at female homosexuality. In her discussion of a substantial and varied body of published texts from the period, including novels, plays, ballads, erotica, court cases and medical literature, Emma Donoghue argued that a language of sexual desire and passion between women did exist in English culture of the seventeenth and eighteenth centuries. Contemporary women – at least in some sections of society – could obtain this knowledge from a variety of references to Sapphism, tribadism, cross-dressing and passionate female friendship, and although perceived as transgressive and sinful, this did amount, she asserted, to evidence of a lesbian culture.[4]

. . . To sexology: sad or glad?

The classic lesbian feminist historiography of romantic friendships, feminist networks and women's communities argued that they were thoroughly disrupted by the patriarchal forces of late-nineteenth-century sexology.

The writings of Havelock Ellis and other sexologists, powerfully grounded as scientific discourses, set down the origins of lesbianism (or 'female inversion' as it was often termed), and classified its various forms. This, argue historians such as Sheila Jeffreys (1985) and Margaret Jackson (1994), pathologized love between women, established lesbianism as a deviant sexual category and attempted to enforce heterosexuality on women by emphasizing the dangers of celibacy and female friendship. Other historians, including Liz Stanley (1992), have taken issue with this interpretation of the evidence and put forward a revisionist account of this period. They argue that Ellis described what was already there – self-identified lesbian networks and subcultures – and show that the work of more radical sexologists, such as Edward Carpenter, was welcomed and taken up by some women, enabling them to describe their nascent (and varied) lesbian identities.

The debate among lesbian historians about sexology is illustrated by the different approaches to the publication and trial of Radclyffe Hall's *The Well of Loneliness* as a significant watershed in lesbian history. Published in 1928 and successfully prosecuted for obscenity, the work has often been described as the classic lesbian novel of the twentieth century. Its cultural and political meanings as a text are undoubtedly immense. But arguably its importance has been overemphasized; it needs to be seen in the context of other contemporary books about lesbianism and the widespread social anxieties about women's sexuality and independence in the interwar years (Faraday, 1985; Doan, forthcoming). Some lesbian historians have argued that *The Well of Loneliness* should be seen as an extension of the negative influence of sexology (on which it was partly based), since it propagated a powerful but limited model of lesbian identity as congenital inversion, with inevitable suffering, and (if the poor afflicted invert did find a partner) involving fixed butch/femme role-playing (Jeffreys, 1985; Faderman, 1981). In so far as *The Well* was the subject of a widely publicized trial for obscenity, it created a public debate about the problem and threat of female inversion to society. Rosemary Auchmuty and other historians have shown how, from the 1930s, expressions of love and friendship between women (and indeed schoolgirls) were more tightly controlled, both textually in fiction and in women's real lives (Oram, 1996, chapter 6; Auchmuty, 1992; Johnson, 1989).

But this new interwar visibility of sexual relationships between women could also be argued to have had positive effects on lesbians' lives. An alternative approach, first spelled out as long ago as the early 1980s by Sonia Ruehl (1982), used Foucauldian theory more directly to argue that *The Well* can be seen as initiating a reverse discourse which helped lead to the creation of a lesbian identity and subculture. Ruehl showed how Radclyffe Hall shifted Ellis's ideas about female inversion from a medical-psychological discourse to a literary-fictional discourse. In speaking as a lesbian herself, Hall made a powerful and politically courageous intervention on behalf of all female inverts (asking for society's tolerance), and her book contributed to a new lesbian identity. She opened up a space for other lesbians to speak for themselves, and eventually, argued Ruehl, through the establishment of a lesbian politics and community, to challenge the negative medical category of female homosexuality.

Issues of difference in lesbian history

The 1980s debates on identity also raised questions about differences – of 'race', class and sexual practice – among women and among lesbians. How can we write a lesbian history which takes into account the ways that sexual identities intersect with the other dominant social categories of class and race, as well as with gender? Early lesbian history tended to imply that romantic friendship was the model for middle-class women's relationships, while cross-dressing (and especially passing) was the main paradigm for working-class women. Although this assumption has since been revised, there remains the problem that much lesbian history uses only the most accessible sources, especially published texts such as novels and diaries, by and about middle-class women. There is also a certain fascination with the glamour and powerful presence of twentieth-century upper- and middle-class women, and the certainty that here was a documented lesbian community (De Salvo and Leaska, 1992; Souhami, 1988). Records of working-class women's lives tend to be more indirect, and working-class women are more often represented by others than themselves, whether in newspaper articles about odd or passing women or sensationalist books and commentary. (One important exception to this generalization are the letters and diaries of two turn-of-the-century working women, Ruth Slate and Eva Slawson, which document love and friendship between the two of them and with other women (Thompson, 1987).) Partly because very few 'professional' historians are working on lesbian history, these more difficult sources are neglected, despite the fact that they would be very fruitful for exploring the currently fashionable questions about representation.

British historians have yet to follow the lead of the USA in analysing 'race' and ethnicity in the historical construction of lesbian identity, in the way that Kennedy and Davis (1993) have used oral history to examine class and racial divisions within the changing lesbian bar communities of Buffalo, New York. It has been those groups which have taken an oral history and life-story approach to British lesbian history which have most explicitly tried to address the diversity of lesbian experience and record the stories of those who have been marginalized – black and ethnic minorities, disabled and working-class lesbians (Brighton Ourstory Project, 1992; Neild and Pearson, 1992; Hall Carpenter Archives Lesbian Oral

History Group, 1989). However, these publications have not, on the whole, gone further and used the collected accounts to begin an analysis of how race and class have structured lesbian experience. Research into lesbian history should be able to show how the construction of particular forms of imperial, racial and gender identity has served to privilege specific sexual identities and marginalize others. For example, the turn-of-the-century feminists who refused marriage and chose like-minded female companions were attacked for emptying the Empire's cradles of good middle-class stock, as well as for their aberrant sexuality (Bland, 1995; Moore, 1992).

Cultural studies and lesbian history

Much of the current academic work on lesbian history in the UK is not conducted within the discipline of history at all, but in related fields such as English literature and within cultural studies generally. In English literature, the turn to history in recent years, and the 'new historicist' criticism, emphasize the lack of distinction between historical and literary texts, while feminist and lesbian criticism has generated an important and growing body of work on lesbian writing from the past (for example, Griffin, 1993; Hobby, 1991). This has been paralleled in historiography in the current debates about representation, language and discourse ('the linguistic turn'), manifested in women's history by Joan Scott's (1986) call to feminist historians to investigate the discursive construction of gender, gender identities and gender relations. The emphasis on questions about representation and meaning in the interdisciplinary field of cultural studies more generally has also lent itself to the exploration of issues around sexuality, often examining cultural products from the past such as written and visual texts, film and television and the popular press.

These disciplinary shifts, coupled with changing ideas in lesbian and feminist politics, have opened up new approaches to lesbian history, exploring the cultural existence and meanings of lesbian sexuality in the past. 'Lesbian-like' sexualities have been represented in specific and varying ways by the dominant culture, whether in popular cultural forms such as eighteenth-century ballads or in scientific discourses such as twentieth-century sexological theories. A number of writers have demonstrated the significance of the idea of lesbian sexuality in cultural texts and the cultural imagination of the late modern period, as discussed above (Donoghue, 1993; Moore, 1992; White, 1990). Work in cultural studies has also shown us how to look for the many ways that lesbians in the past have created identities from the knowledge and meanings available to them (Rolley, 1990). To fully understand their lives, we also need to use 'conventional' feminist historical work to contextualize how ideas about femininity and sexuality could be negotiated, and how they intersected with class, ethnicity and occupation in any particular period.

This need for detailed scholarly archival research in lesbian history – rather than applying theories and deriving conclusions using only the most accessible texts – signals that there are some dangers as well as benefits associated with the location of lesbian history within cultural studies. Cultural studies approaches may be dominated by an overly Foucauldian interpretation of the history of sexuality, which may not be supported by empirical research (Clark, 1996). The recent enthusiasm for queer theory in cultural studies can also lead to specifically lesbian history, and in particular a feminist awareness of the position of lesbians as women in a male-dominated society, being effaced (Vicinus, 1994; Auchmuty *et al.*, 1992).

Lesbians and history

So, has lesbian history made a difference to 'history'? It certainly *should* have done, for a number of reasons. First of all, lesbian history reveals the tenuous nature of *heterosexuality* for women. Feminist histories of women's sexuality have shown the changing patriarchal construction of women's sexual 'nature'. The classic example of this is the mid-nineteenth-century notion that respectable women did not experience sexual desire, followed by the twentieth-century rediscovery of middle-class women's sexuality – but only within marriage, and with the aim of marital stability and motherhood (Bland, 1995; Jackson, 1994; Jeffreys, 1985). Lesbian history has sought to show that lesbian sexuality has always existed in different forms, *challenging* dominant heterosexuality, whether in the power of romantic friendship (especially when coupled with women's economic independence) or by cross-dressing women subverting the norm of heterosexual marriage, as 'female husbands'.

These issues are of wide importance to all historians, who have to accept, for example, that passionate friendships may have been of greater emotional or sexual importance to Victorian women than their relationships with their husbands. Categories of 'experience', however powerfully inscribed in dominant understandings, are historically *specific*. Mainstream historians must acknowledge that these include ideas about sexuality and gender, as well as categories which more obviously change over time and are less often assumed to be essentialist, such as class. Further historiographical questions are also posed for lesbian historians themselves. What choices did 'lesbians' have in the past? How did women understand their actions if they engaged in lesbian sexual practices? Was there the possibility of creating a lesbian identity, as Anne Lister sought to do, and what might this mean (Clark, 1996; Donoghue, 1993)?

Lesbian history should also have an important place in historiography because it throws into sharp relief the way history is constructed from contemporary political positions rather than having an independent existence as 'past facts'. History-writing is not about the past but about the present. Early lesbian history assumed its project was to find lesbian foremothers, but, as discussed above, these largely appeared in our own image. Lesbian history *does* challenge mainstream histories, but has gained only an insubstantial foothold in the conventional institutions of history. In the USA, lesbian and gay history has become increasingly academically respectable through the growth of women's history and social history, on the one hand, and pressure from the lesbian and gay movements on the other. However, this process is far less advanced in the UK, and even if gay studies has gained a niche (at least in academic publishing) there is a question mark over the extent to which it includes a distinct lesbian perspective (Auchmuty *et al.*, 1992). Even in the radical margins of mainstream history, lesbian history has a relatively small presence. Reflecting the earlier discussion, lesbian history is more likely to be found in women's studies, literary and cultural studies journals than in history journals, including women's history journals. And while the number of higher-education courses in women's history and the history of sexuality continues to grow, it is difficult to assess the extent to which lesbian history is included.

The relationships between lesbian history and women's history in the UK has been a fairly cautious and distant one. While feminist history recognizes the social construction of women's sexuality, and the way this shifts over time, women tend to be seen as subject to dominant masculine constructions of sexuality rather than as having much agency of their own. Furthermore, the tendency of feminist historians to assume that marriage was the normal or typical experience of women in the past means that there has been comparatively little recognition of women's partnerships and friendship networks (though more research has been published in recent years) and that a whole series of questions about single women's experiences (just one place where lesbian history might appear) is avoided. This also ignores the evidence which shows that the 'total' experience of marriage is a contemporary one – there was a very high proportion of single women in most periods in the past. However, some feminist historians have taken seriously the need to integrate lesbian history perspectives with those of women's history. These include, for example, Lucy Bland (1995) in her work on feminism and sexuality at the turn of the century, Philippa Levine (1990) on Victorian women's friendship networks and June Purvis (1992) writing on methods and sources in women's history.

In contrast to the limited success of lesbian history in the academy, the idea of lesbianism in the past remains a significant and constant reinvention in popular cultural forms, including both mainstream and lesbian-generated popular culture. The television dramas *Portrait of a Marriage* and *Oranges Are Not the Only Fruit*, shown in the early 1990s, reflect a contemporary cultural fascination with lesbianism and a need to investigate it, in the process constructing particular kinds of historical lesbian characters – the upper-class patrician butch in the costume drama tradition, the plucky heroine of the Northern working-class kitchen-sink genre. Meanwhile novels from women's presses have served a lesbian readership, including Ellen Galford's (1984) *Moll Cutpurse* and Caeia March's (1988) *The Hide and Seek Files*, both centring on working-class cross-dressing women. This indicates a desire by lesbian communities to create a heritage and an identity rooted in the past as well as created in the present. Lesbian biography is also an important genre. Non-academic lesbian history remains overwhelmingly biographical in nature (Collis, 1994), while mainstream biography – of Vita Sackville-West and Daphne du Maurier, for example – shows it is now acceptable to discuss a subject's lesbian past (Glendinning, 1984; Forster, 1994).

It is still important to know who we were in the past, and to make that knowledge more widely available. British lesbian history needs to pursue the rich theoretical and textual questions which have recently been opened up in cultural studies. But as well as this, it would be fruitful to retrieve and strengthen a political thrust in lesbian history by maintaining strong links with lesbian communities, feminist politics and women's studies, in all their diversity and ecleticism. And lesbian history also needs (despite the theoretical challenges) to maintain a strong sense of 'real lesbian lives' in the past, however imagined, for only then can we make meaningful links with the present, which is the purpose and joy of writing history.

Notes

1. This was due to a number of factors: women's studies as a new interdisciplinary field of study which paved the way for lesbian studies and lesbian history was developed mainly in sociology departments from the early 1980s (as indeed was women's history). Sociologists were undertaking the theorization not only of gender but also of sexuality from this time. This was also a period of interest in women's role in literary history (particularly of the nineteenth century), and a tradition of lesbian studies was being established in literary studies that followed the work of Jeannette Foster, Lillian Faderman and others. (It was also, perhaps, easier to seek out the lesbian as a figure of representation in literature, rather than as a specific concrete figure in history.) Despite the growth of radical history-writing (for example, labour and Marxist history) in the 1960s and 1970s, history departments tended to be threatened by, and resistant to, women's history for many years, though the subject was taught in some polytechnic history courses from the 1970s.
2. At the same time as feminism and gender studies problematized assumptions about gender and sexuality, lesbian and gay scholars have increasingly 'come out' and challenged the last respectable bastion of prejudice in the academy – homophobia. Following feminist theory, postmodernism has also drawn attention to issues of difference, identity and marginality.

3. There were a number of factors contributing to this. One strand of 1970s lesbian feminism, revolutionary feminism, demanded that all feminists should give up men and become political lesbians, committing their emotional and political energies to other women (though lesbian sexual engagement was not compulsory). Never likely to be accepted as a pragmatic feminist politics, there was a backlash against this version of lesbianism and feminism from both heterosexual feminists and many feminist lesbians. At the same time, there was an increasing exploration by lesbians and feminists of other ways of understanding sexual desire, especially through feminist rereadings of psychoanalytic theory. Contemporary feminist debates about pornography and censorship also problematized idealized models of female sexuality, while in the broader context, the failure of 1970s feminist politics to speedily change the world was highlighted by the 1980s shift towards individualism and consumerism.
4. In fact Lillian Faderman herself, in her later book on American lesbian history, revised her views on romantic friendship, presenting evidence of sexual relationships between late-nineteenth-century romantic friends and conceding that many early-twentieth-century lesbians found sexology useful, since it enabled them to claim a specific identity.

I would like to express my warm thanks to Rosemary Auchmuty, Cosis Brown, Anna Clark, Gabriele Griffin and Annmarie Turnbull for their comments on this chapter.

References

Anon. (1848; first published 1835) *Sinks of London Laid Open: A Pocket Companion for the Uninitiated.* London: J. Duncombe.

Ardill, S. and O'Sullivan, S. (1986) 'Upsetting an Applecart: Difference, Desire and Lesbian Sadomasochism.' *Feminist Review.* 23: 31–57.

Ardill, S. and O'Sullivan, S. (1989) 'Sex in the Summer of '88.' *Feminist Review.* 31 (Spring): 126–34.

Auchmuty, R. (1989) 'By Their Friends We Shall Know Them: The Lives and Networks of Some Women in North Lambeth, 1880–1940.' In Lesbian History Group (1989).

Auchmuty, R. (1992) *A World of Girls.* London: The Women's Press.

Auchmuty, R., Jeffreys, S. and Miller, E. (1992) 'Lesbian History and Gay Studies: Keeping a Feminist Perspective.' *Women's History Review.* 1/1: 89–108.

Bland, L. (1995) *Banishing the Beast: English Feminism and Sexual Morality 1885–1994.* London: Penguin.

Brighton Ourstory Project (1992) *Daring Hearts: Lesbian and Gay Lives of 50s and 60s Brighton.* Brighton: Queenspark Books.

Clark, A. (1996) 'Anne Lister's Construction of Lesbian Identity.' *Journal of the History of Sexuality.* 7/1: 23–50.

Collis, R. (1994) *Portraits to the Wall: Historic Lesbian Lives Unveiled.* London: Cassell.

De Salvo, L. and Leaska, M.A. (eds) (1992) *The Letters of Vita Sackville-West to Virginia Woolf.* London: Virago.

Doan, L. (forthcoming) *The Boyish Aesthetic: Fashioning Sapphism in the 1920s.*

Donoghue, E. (1993) *Passions between Women: British Lesbian Culture 1668–1801.* London: Scarlet Press.

Faderman, L. (1981) *Surpassing the Love of Men: Romantic Friendship and Love between Women from the Renaissance to the Present.* London: Junction Books.

Faderman, L. (1991) *Odd Girls and Twilight Lovers: A History of Lesbian Life in Twentieth-Century America*. London: Penguin.

Faraday, A. (1985) 'Social Definitions of Lesbians in Britain, 1914–1939.' Unpublished PhD thesis, University of Essex.

Forster, M. (1994) *Daphne du Maurier*. London: Arrow Books.

Galford, E. (1984) *Moll Cutpurse: Her True History*. Edinburgh: Straumullion Co-operative Ltd.

Glendinning, V. (1984) *Vita: The Life of V. Sackville-West*. London: Penguin.

Griffin, G. (1993) *Heavenly Love?: Lesbian Images in Twentieth-Century Women's Writing*. Manchester: Manchester University Press.

Hall Carpenter Archives Lesbian Oral History Group (1989) *Inventing Ourselves: Lesbian Life Stories*. London: Routledge.

Hobby, E. (1991) 'Katherine Philips: Seventeenth-Century Lesbian Poet.' In E. Hobby and C. White (eds) *What Lesbians Do in Books*. London: The Women's Press.

Jackson, M. (1994) *The* Real *Facts of Life: Feminism and the Politics of Sexuality c. 1850–1940*. London: Taylor and Francis.

Jeffreys, S. (1985) *The Spinster and Her Enemies: Feminism and Sexuality 1880–1930*. London: Pandora Press.

Jeffreys, S. (1994) *The Lesbian Heresy: A Feminist Perspective on the Lesbian Sexual Revolution*. London: The Women's Press.

Johnson, P. (1989) '"The Best Friend Whom Life Has Given Me": Does Winifred Holtby Have a Place in Lesbian History?' In Lesbian History Group (1989).

Kennedy, E. Lapovsky and Davis, M. (1993) *Boots of Leather, Slippers of Gold: The History of a Lesbian Community*. London: Routledge.

Lesbian History Group (1989) *Not a Passing Phase: Reclaiming Lesbians in History 1840–1985*. London: The Women's Press.

Levine, P. (1990) *Feminist Lives in Victorian England*. Oxford: Basil Blackwell.

March, C. (1988) *The Hide and Seek Files*. London: The Women's Press.

Mohin, L. and Wilson, A. (1983) *Past Participants: A Lesbian History Diary for 1984*. London: Onlywomen Press.

Moore, L. (1992) '"Something More Tender Still Than Friendship": Romantic Friendship in Early Nineteenth Century England.' *Feminist Studies*. 18/3: 499–520.

Neild, S. and Pearson, R. (1992) *Women Like Us*. London: The Women's Press.

Nestle, J. (1981) 'Butch-Femme Relationships: Sexual Courage in the 1950s.' *Heresies*. 12: 21–4.

Nestle, J. (1987) *A Restricted Country*. London: Sheba.

Oram, A. (1996) *Women Teachers and Feminist Politics 1900–39*. Manchester: Manchester University Press.

Purvis, J. (1992) 'Using Primary Sources When Researching Women's History from a Feminist Perspective.' *Women's History Review*. 1/2: 273–306.

Rich, A. (1980) 'Compulsory Heterosexuality and Lesbian Existence.' *Signs*. 5: 4.

Rolley, K. (1990) 'Cutting a Dash: The Dress of Radclyffe Hall and Una Troubridge.' *Feminist Review*. 35: 54–66.

Ruehl, S. (1982) 'Inverts and Experts: Radclyffe Hall and the Lesbian Identity.' In R. Brunt and C. Rowan (eds) *Feminism, Culture and Politics*. London: Lawrence and Wishart.

Scott, J. (1986) 'Gender: A Useful Category of Historical Analysis.' *American Historical Review*. 91: 1053–75.

Smith-Rosenberg, C. (1975) 'The Female World of Love and Ritual: Relations between Women in Nineteenth Century America.' *Signs*. 1/1: 1–18.

Souhami, D. (1988) *Gluck: Her Biography*. London: Pandora Press.

Stanley, L. with Morley, A. (1988) *The Life and Death of Emily Wilding Davison*. London: The Women's Press.

Stanley, L. (1992) 'Romantic Friendship? Some Issues in Researching Lesbian History and Biography.' *Women's History Review*. 1/2: 193–216.

Thompson, T. (ed.) (1987) *Dear Girl: The Diaries and Letters of Two Working Women 1897–1917*. London: The Women's Press.

Todd, M. (1918) *The Life of Sophia Jex-Blake*. London: Macmillan.

Uncovering Lesbian History 1800-1970 Course, 1985-86 (1988) *For Those Who Would Be Sisters: Uncovering Lesbian History*. London: Birkbeck College, University of London.

Vicinus, M. (1985) *Independent Women: Work and Community for Single Women 1850–1920*. London: Virago Press.

Vicinus, M. (1989) '"They Wonder to Which Sex I Belong": The Historical Roots of the Modern Lesbian Identity.' In D. Altman, C. Vance, M. Vicinus and J. Weeks, *Homosexuality, Which Homosexuality?* London: Gay Men's Press, pp. 171–98.

Vicinus, M. (1994) 'Lesbian History: All Theory and No Facts or All Facts and No Theory?' *Radical History Review*. 60: 57–75.

Whitbread, H. (1988) *I Know My Own Heart*. London: Virago.

White, C. (1990) '"Poets and Lovers Evermore": Interpreting Female Love in the Poetry and Journals of Michael Field.' *Textual Practice*. 4/2: 197–212.

13

Queering the Master Discourse: Lesbians and Philosophy

Margrit Shildrick

When I first agreed to produce this chapter I imagined, naively as it turns out, that there would be no difficulty in outlining a large and well-acknowledged body of lesbian work within philosophical discourse, nor in naming a respectable band of lesbian academics. The more I thought about it, however, both in terms of my own trajectory and that of other aberrant philosopher friends, the more apparent it became that I was mistaken. For one thing, it is by no means clear what exactly is meant by philosophy. A review of any number of feminist texts would show that the disciplinary boundaries recognized by the masculinist tradition have been stretched by feminists to encompass almost any 'high' theory such that the distinction between philosophy and cultural studies, or philosophy and politics, for example, is extremely flexible. It is indicative of the change effected by feminism that Routledge's 'Gender and Women's Studies' catalogue simply conflates feminist theory and philosophy. And then, more disturbingly, a similar difficulty arises around the category of lesbian. Who would or wouldn't count, I wondered? And what are the credentials for a lesbian philosopher? When are we writing as women, and when as lesbians? Does 'it' show in my work if the subject to hand makes no mention of sexuality, let alone lesbianism, and may indeed focus on the abstract intricacies of Kantian moral theory, for example? Is there a lesbian perspective that will somehow seep into our work regardless of the issue to be addressed? Now, the two difficulties I mention are of the same order: they are both concerned with issues of identity, of how we settle questions of sameness and difference. As I shall argue, what really matters about lesbian interventions into philosophy is that rather than resulting in a distinct body of work, the point is precisely that they disrupt both signifiers to the extent that the comfortable – but ultimately sterile – security of each term is opened up to productive new possibilities.

Western philosophy as a discipline is – to its true disciples – the master discourse, the one that supposedly precedes and guarantees all other bodies of knowledge. It is the one that reflects not only on knowledge itself (epistemology) but also on the nature of the knowing subject (ontology), and the one that grounds the superiority of the male over the female, while all the time professing gender neutrality. Abstract transcendent thought has long been taken as the mark of the highest intellectual capacity, the capacity to operate as pure mind untrammelled by such mundane considerations as the body. And that is just one in a series of exclusions on which philosophy depends. Let's be clear: if the convention has no place for the body, it certainly has no place for sex. And as it happens no place for the non-male, non-white, non-heterosexual others whom it does not, indeed cannot, recognize as full subjects. The ideal subject of philosophy need never be theorized as such; it is defined simply by its differences and exclusions, by all those who fail to make the grade by reason of their grossly corporeal immanence, or their embodied difference. The form of mainstream western philosophy is, in consequence, not simply inherently patriarchal, in that men are represented as mind, women as body, but also heterosexist, racist and imperialist. And by the same token the practitioners of that philosophy are equally dominated by white western heterosexual men, pretending all the time to be neutral, objective and impartial (Lloyd, 1984). Worse still they claim to speak for and about all of us, or at least about all of us who are able or prepared to renounce our difference and claim identity with the impersonal disembodied universal subject. And for those who don't or won't, the alternative has long been silence.

Against such a failure to recognize or give voice to difference, radical feminists have long waged a political struggle to find a place of our own. Where the emphasis of reformist or liberal feminism has centred on a drive for equality which effectively covers over difference and relies on the claim that women are just like men in all significant ways, more radical approaches treat women as a class in opposition to men. Liberation depends then on overturning or reversing the power relations between the two. For lesbians, however, the elevation of women to an oppositional category that defies the embrace of universal Man is not necessarily a difference that makes much difference. The gendered binary that results – male:female – is no less homogenizing and in-different than the single standard. From a somewhat shaky start in the 1970s and the early 1980s, feminism has slowly and reluctantly ('kicking and screaming' as Donna Haraway (1990) puts it) come to recognize the political and personal inadequacy – indeed inherent violence – of a simple gender split that pays no attention to the specificities of ethnicity, age, class, able-bodiedness, sexuality and so on that mark each of our lives. We are never just women, any more than we were ever Man, and though we may choose to operate under that sign it is at the expense of silencing and excluding afresh a series of more nuanced oppressions. Lesbians were among the first of the other others to protest that while challenging the male domination expressed in the gender binary might be a prime goal of women's liberation, it would leave untouched other equally entrenched oppressions. The struggle to put heterosexism on the agenda alongside sexism predictably broke up the cosy illusion of universal sisterhood, and forced both straight women and lesbians to confront the differences between them.

All this has happened as a result of the material frustrations and disappointments of the women involved, and in a sense, theory merely serves to formalize an explanation after the event. Nonetheless, it has too a predictive character which makes clear that lesbians and other others must do some radical rethinking if they are to avoid simply perpetuating a series of equally devastating splits. What is at stake is the notion of identity, and the way in which sameness and difference are deployed to secure or contest particular political contexts. The either/or character of identity – either you are the same as me, or you are 'other' – is not one that can long stand up to either theoretical or practical scrutiny. The appeal of identity is to a sense of givenness, to a fundamental truth residing within the clearly marked boundaries of a closed category. But to call myself a lesbian simultaneously names one incredibly influential aspect of my lived experience, *and* enacts a series of exclusions that do violence not only to those others who are not me but also to other aspects of myself with respect to ethnicity, class and so on. As Judith Butler puts it: 'In the act which would disclose the true and full content of that "I", a certain radical concealment is thereby produced' (1991, p. 15). In other words, I am never just a lesbian, but nor does parading additional signifiers solve the problem. Of course, I can be more specific and name myself as a white-middle-class-lesbian-feminist-of-working-class-origin-with-a-cat without making the slightest dent on the closure of identity. On the contrary, the move is one that seems to secure the boundaries around the truth of my being even more firmly than before. The problem is that although all those aspects may indeed be significant factors, they are not necessarily fixed in the way that identity would seem to imply. Moreover, the more specific my self-description, the more I become identical only with myself. In other words, the idea of identity as something which unites us with those who share attributes – and with whom we might then make common cause – is entirely lost.

So, what then is meant by the category lesbian philosophy? Does it signal an identity descriptive of the woman, or of the philosophy? We may all 'know' that many of the most admired, desired and influential women philosophers are dykes, but that is as much a matter of social gossip as of a well-considered analysis of their intellectual output. Moreover, although there are now a substantial number of books and articles which contest the heterosexual normativities of mainstream philosophy, that, in itself, is no sure guide to the sexuality of their authors. As Claudia Card, editor of the robustly named *Adventures in Lesbian Philosophy*, carefully puts it:

> These articles exemplify the search for wisdom in and about lesbian activity, experience, choices, relationships, communities, perspectives and ideals. . . . Yet the reader should not take it that a particular contributor identifies herself as a lesbian, or aligns herself with any sexual or erotic social identity, unless she says so. (1994, p. xiii)

Nonetheless, the act of coming out is invested with enormous significance for lesbians, and whatever the intellectual objections to the concept of identity may be we all go on wanting to experience those moments of mutual acknowledgement. The danger is that in claiming a common difference to the mainstream, we simply perpetuate the structure of the heterosexual/ homosexual binary in which the first term sets the standard for what is the norm. The lesbian perspective becomes – just like the non-western perspective – simply the difference that secures the unity and primacy of the dominant term. Not only does it imply that lesbians can and do have a specific and unique standpoint, but that this standpoint is necessarily defined in relation to the very centre that it might wish to oppose.

The development of lesbian philosophy over the period in which women in general have struggled to make a place within the discipline has, by and large, mirrored the vicissitudes of feminist theory. Early inroads were almost entirely pitched in terms of what I have called the lesbian standpoint. It represents not simply the desire to mobilize an alternative voice within philosophy, but also the belief that it offered something morally and politically superior to the dominant discourse. The claim is that the universalist pretensions of the dominant voice do not reflect the experience and knowledge of marginalized groups, and that in being outside the mainstream, those groups have a clearer grasp on reality. And just as women in general want to mark their distance from the discourse evolved by men, so lesbians stand yet further apart as a distinct identity group. Put crudely, standpoint theory seems to suggest that the more marginalized or excluded a group, the greater its capacity to escape the ideological distortions propagated by the self-interested centre. And it results, it seems to me, not in any greater capacity for self-reflection, but in a rather smug claim to knowing better. Here is how Sarah Hoagland describes the 'singular vantage point' of the lesbian:

> It affords her certain freedom from constraints of the conceptual system; it gives her access to knowledge which is inaccessible to those whose existence *is* countenanced by the system. Lesbians can therefore undertake kinds of criticism and description, and kinds of intellectual invention, hitherto unimagined. (Conference paper quoted in Frye, 1989, p. 77)

Lucky us! So, how in practice has this lesbian standpoint intervened in philosophy?

The most successful areas of enquiry – as for feminist philosophy in general – are in the fields of epistemology and ethics. Both lend themselves to a standpoint approach which claims a superior, more adequate understanding of the true and the good. The difficulties of such an approach are many, but the most pertinent to my own rejection of standpoint is its reliance on an identity category that buys into uniform difference rather than a multiplicity of differences. It is not that the various adherents do not embark on long enquiries into the meaning of the word lesbian, but that however wide or narrow the definitions turn out to be, the one common feature is that there is a stable distinction between lesbian and heterosexual. An individual woman may of course cross and recross the invisible line, moving from one identity to another, but what doesn't change is the certainty that there is a specific community of interest on either side. The book *For Lesbians Only: A Separatist Anthology* (Hoagland and Penelope, 1988) which takes in several philosophical papers is a potent illustration of that trend. What will be expressed by lesbian philosophy, then, must stand apart not only from masculinist discourse but from heterosexual feminist texts as well. So, for example, where numerous feminist papers have been written in response to Carol Gilligan's (1982) assertion that women speak with a different moral voice, there is a yet more specific and parallel take-up of that idea in journals such as *Lesbian Ethics* (1984–present) and the short-lived *Gossip* (1986–8), as well as in books by Hoagland (1988) and Card (1991). And though there may be a constant emphasis on how wonderfully varied 'we' are, there is nevertheless an assumption of a fundamental sameness that I find deeply claustrophobic.

Of the very few texts, like those mentioned above and the recent *Adventures in Lesbian Philosophy*, which place themselves entirely outside the mainstream, it is taken as self-evident that lesbians just will do philosophy differently. And, as Card explains, that generally means 'reflect[ing] philosophically upon the lesbian data of everyday experience' (1994, p. xi). Thus her collection covers such topics as creativity, the sex wars, community and responsibility, all of which are well-trodden paths within feminist writing, but are given here the additional spin of a lesbian perspective. What you don't get, and this is true of the standpoint field in general, is a lesbian spin on Aristotle or Kant or Hegel. There is, in other words, alongside an opening up the boundaries of philosophy to include more political and cultural questions, a very clear rejection of, or disinterest in, the dead white males who form the backbone of the convention. This exclusion, interestingly, doesn't seem to extend to living or recently dead white males, so that Derrida, Deleuze, Foucault and Levinas, for example (none of whom evidence any real awareness of lesbian lives), do occasionally creep in round the edges. More usually, however, standpoint theorizing directs itself towards the analysis of areas of explicitly lesbian agency and may make no reference at all to male-authored texts. And though it shifts the parameters of philosophy to take on new concerns, it simultaneously abandons others. In short, standpoint cannot be said to have broadened the scope for lesbian philosophers themselves.

The impetus to take up an oppositional standpoint is undeniably strong when the choice seems to be between the inaudibility of speaking within the mainstream which authorizes only a male/heterosexual voice, or adopting a position of defiance. The immediate problem is that by defining a differential take on issues in philosophy, lesbians are not so much making inroads into the discourse as entrenching themselves in their difference. If it were simply a matter of constructing an alternative body of work with free movement between the two, there would be an undeniable gain, but that is to ignore the operation of power. The dominant discourse not only has centuries of tradition behind it but also the ongoing support of the male social order in which the intellectual and abstract remain the domain of men. In consequence, the lesbian standpoint may result not in pluralizing the concerns of philosophy, but rather in an evacuation of the field which leaves it even more firmly in the grasp of hegemonic forces. Of the names most strongly associated with an explicitly non-normative standpoint – Julia Penelope, Claudia Card, Jeffner Allen, Sarah Lucia Hoagland, Joyce Trebilcot, Marilyn Frye, and others – only a very few seek currency beyond the confines of what is seen to be directly *about* women. The restriction is largely self-chosen, and as Trebilcot remarks:

> academic philosophy . . . is essentially oppressive, in part because most of its practitioners following tradition assume that they have a right to determine how other people should think and act. Why would a dyke want to be associated with such an enterprise? (1994, p. 36)

There is, in consequence, little reason for powerful heterosexual males professing a masculinist discourse to feel in the least bit challenged. And it's noticeable, too, that my list is of North American women only, which suggests that the British establishment is even more entrenched and conservative. Despite a far greater familiarity with my home territory, I can think of no British women who define themselves as lesbian philosophers, though there are plenty of dykes in the discipline. In a recent issue of *Women's Philosophy Review*, Joanna Hodge bemoans the invisibility of that presence and suggests that 'the male domination of the profession leads to a splitting along a gay/straight line between women who go into women's studies, cultural studies and queer theory on the one side, and women who stay in philosophy on the other' (1995, p. 5). In other words if you want to talk theoretically about gay issues – and indeed to a large extent women's issues – then you relocate to other disciplines. Even standpoint seems too radical for the establishment.

Now, although I greatly deplore the very practical inability of women to find a place *as lesbians* within the institution of philosophy – by which I mean academic departments, mainstream journals, student textbooks, and so on – we are not, I believe, thereby on the outside of philosophy itself. Though the Anglo-American establishment may continue hanging on to its classical and analytical tradition, it is in any case being swiftly overtaken by a whole new set of considerations that disrupt the cosy club of living and dead white heterosexual males. The challenge comes not so much from discontented identity groups like women, gays and lesbians, people of colour and others who have all experienced the silencing of exclusion, as from the disruptive influence of what are broadly termed poststructuralist and postmodernist modes of enquiry. In explicit contradistinction to the politics of identity, such approaches work precisely by deconstructing oppositional difference and demonstrating that the boundaries between categories are both permeable and unstable. The distinctions between male and female, straight and gay do not, of course, cease to be of relevance, but instead of mapping out fixed or even essentialist differences, they are seen to represent a spectrum of incalculable possibilities ranging from discursive convenience to politically efficacious performances. The main point is that however firmly secured the opposing identities may seem to be, they are at most provisional, and are always open to deconstruction and transformation. Moreover, it is not simply that the dominant are engaged in a process of self-definition by the continual exclusion of what is other; the others too repeat the move in their own grasping for identity.

The major implication of what is in itself a philosophical project to rethink the metaphysics of subjectivity and identity is that to address the issue of lesbian interventions in philosophy becomes highly problematic. It is no longer a question of defining the characteristic features of a woman's life that might entitle her to speak as a lesbian, but rather a recognition that even in its own stereotypes, lesbian desire is always excessive to the binary norms of phallocentric culture. It is, in other words, no easy matter for a postmodernist to write *as* a lesbian *or* about what Card calls 'lesbian data'. That is not to say of course that there are not very many women committed to post-conventional methodologies who do nonetheless conduct their philosophy under the lesbian signifier. But the point is that their approach, in being less determined by a putative lesbian identity, may escape the exclusionary moves, even smug superiority, associated in my mind at least with an uncontested assumption of community interest. What I want to suggest as a new motivating force for engaging profitably with philosophy at all is that it is the very undecidability, the absence of a defined counter-category, that enables the postmodern lesbian to queer the certainties of the master discourse. So the real question is not whether lesbians are apparent in philosophy, or whether there is any body of specifically lesbian-identified work, but rather in what ways does the disruption emanating from an ex-cessive/ex-centric perspective take effect? What is at stake in *queering* the discourse is not the turn towards an alternative and rival set of values and concerns, but the intervention that changes everything.

To explain more coherently what I mean by excess, I want to outline what I see as three possible lesbian responses to the phallogocentrism of philosophy. The first, which I have already rejected as inadequate, is essentially a reversal of the relations of power. Though it mounts a challenge to heterosexism, it does so only by substituting its own privileged epistemology. What is left intact is what Luce Irigaray calls the economy of the same, by which meaning and value are variably assigned to sameness and difference, but are yet dependent on a single standard. In other words, difference is only recognized as one face of the binary *A* and ***not-A***. The genders, male and female/not-male, are constructed only within a heterosexual matrix that has no place for either the material experience or discursive meaning of the lesbian. As Monique Wittig summarizes it:

> [the straight mind] speaks of . . . *the* difference between the sexes, *the* symbolic order, *the* Unconscious, Desire, *Jouissance*, Culture, History, giving an absolute meaning to these concepts when they are only categories founded upon heterosexuality, or thought which produces the difference between the sexes as a political and philosophical dogma. (1992, pp. 27–8)

Against such rigidity a second position has been developed in which French women philosophers, such as Wittig and Irigaray, have played a central role. Their project is to make a place for the feminine that is not part of the masculine:feminine binary, and inevitably that has spoken most clearly to and for lesbians. Wittig is explicit in her elevation of the lesbian as a figure outside the gender binary, while Irigaray, though naming such figures only as female, nevertheless writes lyrically of the sexual desire of those women as having nothing to do with the phallic economy.

What is immediately striking about Wittig's approach is that it is the complete opposite of the politically inclusive Anglo-American feminist claim that every woman can be a lesbian. Where Adrienne Rich (1986) provided the intellectual grounding for such a move with her notion of the 'lesbian continuum', the ultimate in non-specific shared sisterhood, Wittig contests that same monolithic category of women, and declares: 'Lesbian is the only concept I know of which is beyond the categories of sex (woman and man), because the designated subject (lesbian) is *not* a woman, either economically, or politically, or ideologically' (1992, p. 20).

Wittig's powerful challenge to modernist notions of knowledge, nature, history and gender is undermined, however, by her own turn to an equally foundational pure lesbian identity which seems somehow to be outside both the material and discursive relations of our cultural context, as though – as Judith Butler puts it – it were 'conceived as radically unconditioned by heterosexual norms' (1990, p. 121). In contrast, what the work of Butler, and other postmodernists, shows is that all that Wittig has done by opposing woman and lesbian is to reiterate the binary structure in a different way. It is not in the end so very different from the essentializing modernist move of claiming lesbianism as a counter-identity.

Luce Irigaray's position is often seen as not dissimilar, in that her work has long laboured under accusations of essentialism. There is undoubtedly some currency in the usual defence that Irigaray uses essentialism strategically (notably Whitford, 1991), but it is equally possible to argue that her turn to the (lesbian) body is both discursive and speculative, and at the same time materialist, without buying into biological essence. In any case, Irigaray, unlike Wittig, is explicit that the feminine she envisages does not yet exist except as a figure on the horizons of aspiration. Moreover, although she is clear that such a woman exceeds – particularly in her *jouissance* – what she calls the 'hom(m)osexual'[1] economy in which everything circulates around the single male standard, she is equally insistent that women must find a place in a reconceived Symbolic. There can in other words be no nostalgic return to a pure and pre-existent female imaginary. The recovery of the m/other in texts such as *Speculum of the Other Woman* does not, then, parallel the move in the work of Wittig that Judith Roof critiques as a turn to lesbian metanarrative 'founding itself in the imaginary of the great goddess' (1994, p. 61). Rather it is an attempt to bring into being the mother-other, mother-matter, other-lover (Irigaray, 1985b, *passim*).

What concerns Irigaray above all is the recuperation of the (not-yet) feminine as the other of the other, as the speaking position which exceeds the binary of modernist gender difference, and yet practises a radical sexual difference. Her method – and this is what marks her work as 'lesbian' – is to find a language in which to express the distinctive morphology (and *jouissance*) of the female body, of the two lips which differ in themselves and which are excessive to the isomorphic standard of the phallus: 'Between our lips, yours and mine, several voices, several ways of speaking resound endlessly, back and forth. One is never separable from the other. You/I: we are always several at once' (Irigaray, 1985a, p. 209). The image of women's desire as radically different, as uncontained by and unrepresented in the Symbolic, pervades Irigaray's early work, emphasizing not the alternative discourse of lesbianism as such, but rather the multiple possibilities of the sexuality of women among themselves. And far from moving towards an essentialist image of the biological, it shows corporeality to be interactive and dynamic. The body towards which Irigaray gestures is determined by no one form and no one sexuality. It is always plural, fluid and unbounded; a body that is not yet realized but which expresses the material powers of the distinctly feminine as it is excluded by, and, more importantly, escapes the closure of the binary.

In quite diverse ways, both Wittig and Irigaray take on the task of writing sexual difference and sexuality outside the phallocentric power of the logos by introducing a third term. I don't mean to suggest that either, and particularly not Irigaray, necessarily sees that as effecting a new closure, but there is a sense in which the deconstruction of the binary goes no further. In contrast – and this is the third response to phallogocentrism – the work of Judith Butler, perhaps the best-known and most influential woman philosopher claimed as a lesbian, makes that deconstruction the take-off point rather than the end of her project. As with much feminist postmodernism, Butler's work is intellectually sexy – a very long way from the somewhat worthy claims to lesbian superiority evidenced by standpoint – but it is also deeply serious. Butler is at the forefront of those who use the (non)category of queer to radically disrupt not simply the presence and authority of the hom(m)osexual economy, but also to problematize the attribution of *any* identity, sexual or otherwise. While making quite plain the direction of her own sexual preferences, Butler says of the marker 'lesbian': 'I would like to have it permanently unclear what precisely that sign signifies' (1991, p. 14). And unlike Wittig, and indeed the standpoint theorists in their more modernist analysis, she does not see lesbianism as outside the dominant discourse, but as intrinsic to it.

There are two related issues at stake in the postmodernist approach to the authority of the speaking subject, and both should give pause to all but the most intransigent demands for lesbian philosophers to practise an identity politics. The first point, as Foucault has made clear, is that to have a subject identity is to be subjected (1980, p. 97), to be constructed as what one ostensibly 'is' by a series of disciplinary and regulatory controls, to invite constant surveillance and policing.[2] In such a model the question of self-determined agency is highly problematic, and the efficacy of philosophical interventions at very least constrained. Moreover, the whole project of deconstruction is directed towards undermining the modernist concept of full self-presence wherein the speaking/knowing subject is fixed, bounded and delimited by what it is not. The claim is that the predication of self-definition on a faith in the certainty of sameness and difference as the supposed guarantee both of the self/other distinction, and by derivation of the stability of categories such as sex, gender and sexuality, is highly precarious. Above all, what deconstruction shows – and this is the second point – is that those boundaries are always permeable and leaky, and that at very most identity is provisional. Far from being unified, 'identity always contains the specter of non-identity within it' (Fuss, 1989, p. 103). To function, then, as a discrete entity the subject must enact what Butler calls 'a radical concealment'. She goes on:

> it is always finally unclear what is meant by invoking the lesbian-signifier, since its signification is always to some degree out of one's control, but also because its *specificity* can only be demarcated by exclusions that return to disrupt its claim to coherence. (1991, p. 15)

It makes no sense, then, to hope that the identity of lesbian as a distinct category can be taken up as the disruptive force within phallogocentric discourse, for what is being argued is that identity is both necessarily produced by and productive of the modernist episteme. In consequence, it is the very *refusal* to take up the position of the lesbian subject that queers the master discourse. The seriously playful emphasis given to concepts such as the lesbian phallus in recent work (de Lauretis, 1994; Butler, 1993) is evidence of the counter-commitment to make full use of the risky but productive slide between categories and identities. Moreover, to expose the failure of both Freudian and Lacanian psychoanalytic models to account adequately for lesbian desire is not so much to propose the recovery of a repressed alterity, as to explore the fantasmatic structure of identity in general.

To a large extent, the disinclination of Butler and other postmodernist philosophers to put lesbian identity into play as a positive term is justified by the assertion that as a figure of difference it can never be wholly subversive. What queer theory proposes instead is a disruption that enacts agency in the plasticity and performativity of (be)coming lesbian where desire is neither straight or gay. The question of whether this is sufficient for a politics that makes a difference here and now is less easily settled. The popularity in academia of queer theory as opposed to lesbian studies is motivated less, I think, by intellectual considerations than by the former's openness to appropriation by the boys. Nonetheless I remain convinced that though the deconstruction of lesbian identity as the site of unitary experience and political meaning is a necessary move, the deployment of the catachrestic lesbian signifier enables a transgression of the binaries and boundaries of the master discourse. The fear that without an identity as a point of contact and coalition we will remain on the margins of influence might be replaced by the understanding that the project is to decentre everything. Lesbianism is never simply coincidental with academic practice. The purpose of our interventions cannot be to elevate a new and elitist purism, but to seek out points of interaction. As Liz Grosz puts it:

> the question is not am I – or are you – a lesbian . . . [but] what it is that together, in parts and bits, and interconnections, we can make that is

> new, exploratory, opens up further spaces, induces further intensities, speeds up, enervates and proliferates production. (1995, p. 184)

The proposal is one for a textual erotics, a reconfiguring of concepts and ideas through the medium of lesbian desire. And that, stripped as it is of the ambivalent burden of identity, is our chance to queer the master discourse.

Notes

1. The term 'hom(m)osexual' plays on the signifiers of both maleness and sameness. It describes a discourse dominated by men, and reflective only of the masculine.
2. Most older lesbian feminists will understand precisely what this means from the period of overt conflict between sex radicals and anti-porn groups. To call oneself a lesbian in either context involved, for a time, the ability to produce the right credentials on demand.

References

Butler, J. (1990) *Gender Trouble: Feminism and the Subversion of Identity*. London: Routledge.

Butler, J. (1991) 'Imitation and Gender Insubordination.' In D. Fuss (ed.) *Inside/Out: Lesbian Theories, Gay Theories*. London: Routledge.

Butler, J. (1993) 'The Lesbian Phallus and the Morphological Imaginary.' In J. Butler, *Bodies that Matter*. London: Routledge.

Card, C. (ed.) (1991) *Feminist Ethics*. Kansas: University Press of Kansas.

Card, C. (ed.) (1994) *Adventures in Lesbian Philosophy*. Bloomington, IN: Indiana University Press.

de Lauretis, T. (1994) *The Practice of Love: Lesbian Sexuality and Perverse Desire*. Bloomington, IN: Indiana University Press.

Foucault, M. (1980) *Power/Knowledge: Selected Interviews and other Writings, 1972–77*. Brighton: Harvester Press.

Frye, M. (1989) 'To See and Be Seen: The Politics of Reality.' In A. Garry and M. Pearsall (eds) *Women, Knowledge and Reality*. London: Unwin Hyman.

Fuss, D. (1989) *Essentially Speaking: Feminism, Nature and Difference*. London: Routledge.

Gilligan, C. (1982) *In a Different Voice: Psychological Theory and Women's Development*. Cambridge, MA: Harvard University Press.

Gossip: Journal of Lesbian Feminist Ethics, 1986–8.

Grosz, E. (1995) 'Refiguring Lesbian Desire.' In E. Grosz, *Space, Time and Perversion*. London: Routledge.

Haraway, D. (1990) 'A Manifesto for Cyborgs: Science, Technology and Socialist Feminism in the 1980s.' In L. Nicholson (ed.) *Feminism/Postmodernism*. London: Routledge.

Hoagland, S.L. (1988) *Lesbian Ethics: Toward New Value*. Palo Alto, CA: Institute of Lesbian Studies.

Hoagland, S.L. and Penelope, J. (eds) (1988) *For Lesbians Only: A Separatist Anthology*. London: Onlywomen Press.

Hodge, J. (1995) 'Feminist Politics and the Philosophy Establishment: Conference Report.' *Women's Philosophy Review*. 14: 4–5.

Irigaray, L. (1985a) *This Sex Which Is Not One*. New York: Cornell University Press.

Irigaray, L. (1985b) *Speculum of the Other Woman*. New York: Cornell University Press.

Lesbian Ethics. 1984–present.

Lloyd, G. (1984) *The Man of Reason: 'Male' and 'Female' in Western Philosophy*. London: Methuen.

Rich, A. (1986) 'Compulsory Heterosexuality and Lesbian Existence.' In *Blood, Bread, and Poetry: Selected Prose 1979–1985*. New York: Norton.

Roof, J. (1994) 'Lesbians and Lyotard: Legitimation and the Politics of the Name.' In L. Doan (ed.) *The Lesbian Postmodern*. New York: Columbia University Press.

Trebilcot, J. (1994) 'Not Lesbian Philosophy.' In Card (1994).

Whitford, M. (1991) *Luce Irigaray: Philosophy in the Feminine*. London: Routledge.

Wittig, M. (1992) 'One Is Not Born a Woman' and 'The Straight Mind', both in *The Straight Mind*. Hemel Hempstead: Harvester Wheatsheaf.

14

Sexuality and Computing: Transparent Relations

Linda Stepulevage

Feminist studies of women's under-representation in the computing field have found that girls and women are discouraged, uninterested, excluded or deficient in the skills and knowledge required. In this chapter, I focus on one of the main approaches used to explain women's relationship to computing, and its social construction as a masculine site of knowledge, skills and high-status employment. In these analyses, women are seen to struggle to maintain an identity that is locally appropriate to their situation as women in a male domain. Implicit in these analyses is an assumption that the struggle is within heterosexual social norms. What is missing from the analysis so far is a consideration of the interrelationship between computing and gender and heterosexuality. In this chapter, I take a lesbian perspective (grounded in white working-class Italian-American roots) and explore three questions regarding the gendered construction of computing. First, I examine why, even though some women take computer science, and some women work as professionals in computing, a discourse of women's invisibility persists in feminist research and teaching. Second, I explore how a social construction of computing as masculine and associations between 'the masculine' and 'the lesbian' may keep some women out of computing while motivating others towards it. Third, I question whether 'the hacker', a dominant social construction in computing, may differently affect heterosexual women and lesbians who are thinking of entering the field.

Studies on women's positioning in the domain of computing tend to be grounded in a perspective of gender that implicitly assumes heterosexuality. I refer to this perspective as hetero-gendered, that is, one in which gender is socially constructed as a masculine/feminine dualism, embedded in heterosexuality. In exploring these three questions I want to show how a feminist analysis of the social construction of computing that takes hetero-gender relations into account can contribute to an understanding of how the field retains existing power relations. I hope this analysis can inform feminist strategies for challenging existing relations of technology and, as articulated by Henwood (1993), inform more marginal and radical feminist theorizing for the creation of new knowledges and positive changes in the conditions of women's lives. I start by situating computer science as a discipline and tracing aspects of women's invisibility in it. Then I discuss two pieces of research based on conventional computer science courses, one at a new university in England, the other in Norway, in order to explore how the social construction of computing as masculine affects women. Finally, I discuss computing as a site for lesbians.

Computer science and women's under-representation/invisibility

As Perry and Greber (1990) note, much educational research on women's under-representation forgets the point that just because computing exists and women can develop expertise in it, does not mean that an education or profession in computing is desirable. However, some feminists do present a strong case for women gaining expertise in computing, whether as potential designers, producers or critics of new technological developments (see Green *et al.*, 1993). This chapter will concern itself with the women who do enter computer science courses and/or those in the computing profession.

Analyses that examine the discipline of computing and the design of computer-based work systems (for example, Bodker and Greenbaum, 1993) draw on the body of feminist work that explores the paradigm of reason, universality and abstraction within modern western science (Rose, 1994; Harding, 1986). The abstraction basic to the construction of science and computing as disciplines allows their study and practice to ignore the social and cultural contexts within which they are located. Computing, having applied as well as pure science aspects, always entails technology, both use of computers and knowledge and skills in programming. Earlier work highlighted the gendered character of technology itself (for example, van Oost, 1992) and gender-technology relations as a site of struggle repeatedly appropriated for masculinity (Cockburn, 1992).

The literature discussing women's under-representation in computing (for example, Cole *et al.*, 1994; Mahony and Van Toen, 1990; Kvande and Rasmussen, 1989; Griffiths, 1988) points to many barriers to account for imbalances in the number of women in technology, but it also notes that some women actively resist entry. Studies about schooling have identified the issues as inequality of access to IT and masculine gender bias in course design, teacher attitudes, teaching style, expectations and assessment, and a focus on the technology without a critical perspective (Cole *et al.*, 1994). Studies that deal with computing in higher education explain women's low participation in computer science in terms of its construction as a male domain that actively excludes women (for example, Kvande and Rasmussen, 1989). One aspect of some of the research relates to the grounding of computer science in science and mathematics. The decontextualized approach taken in computer science courses, embedded in a scientific paradigm, apparently acts as a major deterrent; and it is reported that women prefer to study computing when it is embedded in a social context, that is, the number of women students rises as courses move further from science and mathematics bases towards the social sciences (Mahony and Van Toen, 1990). Another factor in some analyses is the dominant discourse of the hacker within computer science. Weizenbaum (1976) and Turkle (1985) write about hacker cultures that embody obsession, isolation, competition and discovery. Mahoney and Van Toen describe the image of the male computer boffin as asocial at best, antisocial at worst and solitary rather than people-orientated. The construction of the computer hacker as a social deviant and a rebel may have a particular resonance for some lesbians.

Men's numerical dominance in the computing profession is well documented (for example, Tijdens, 1991). Feminists have written about the gendering of computing as masculine on a symbolic level early in its development (van Oost, 1992) and on its social construction, more recently, in the office (for example, Grundy, 1994). Sundin (1995) has written about the flexibility of computing, wherein its meaning varies according to local workplace relations (see also Lie, 1995). In this analysis gender and technology are not static, but rather cultural processes which 'are subject to negotiation, contestation and, ultimately, transformation' (Henwood, 1993, p. 44).

Computer science has been a problematic area for feminists not only because of exclusion questions but also in terms of participation. Perry and Greber note that at a conference convened to explore links between the humanities, social sciences and computer science feminist computing professionals 'felt to varying degrees, that the women's movement had tacitly excluded them, as if by working in such a traditional masculine field they had forfeited their right to be considered as women and as sisters' (1990, p. 90). A survey of women's studies courses in the UK shows that development of knowledge and skills in the design and implementation of computer-based systems within a feminist context is offered as part of the programme in only one undergraduate women's studies degree. It is an open question as to whether the absence of computing in women's studies is an active decision based on a political stand in relation to computing, a *fait accompli* as a result of the interests and/or experience of those offering the programme, or an omission due to its construction as a masculine domain within education.

Gender and heterosexuality in computing

A key concern evident in studies of women in computing is how 'women are asked to exchange major aspects of their gender identity for a masculine version without prescribing a similar "degendering" process for men' (Wajcman, 1993, p. 23). This concern leaves women only one alternative, to become 'masculine'. Byrne applies a 'sex-normal' taxonomy in her study of the position of women in Australia in science and technology. Computer science is classified as 'sex-normal' for men and non-traditional or 'sex-abnormal' for women. This classification system reconstitutes a relationship between women and computing that works against the author's intention of developing policies for changing the situation. Byrne echoes earlier explanations regarding women's disinterest in science and technology disciplines. She notes that their image 'as objective, detached or destructive switches off girls and "androgynous" boys' (1993, p. 167). There is no parallel 'androgynous' position for girls who are switched on. Implicit in these explanations is an essentialist construction of women as hetero-gendered.

In approaching the culture of technology as masculine, feminists can logically assert: 'If technological competence is an integral part of masculine gender identity, why should women want to go into a field that privileges and admires the stereotypes of the obsessional and antisocial hacker and the techno-freak who uses his technical mastery as a form of macho posturing?' (Mahony and Van Toen, 1990, p. 326). This sort of question points to hetero-gender relations that constrain women, even though the analyses do not identify the constraint as such.

The problem is that if women are to keep their feminine gender identity, they must remain 'other' in relation to men. The logical extension of this relation is that women must be vigilant in their performance of heterosexuality, or at least should not transgress the boundaries of the local heterosexual culture, otherwise they lose their identity as women. In her study of women in science, Thomas provides a clear example of this dualism in the one woman student she identified as 'the exception'. The exceptional student's rejection of feminine performance is interpreted in the study as 'a taking on of masculine values' (1990, p. 126). These analyses, grounded in hetero-bipolarity, present any women who moves outside what is locally deemed to be 'normal' as deviant. A linkage of biological sex, gender role, gender identity and sexual object choice is implicit, and deviance from gender role indicates deviance from heterosexuality (Phelan, 1993). Phelan goes on to warn that this analysis sometimes leads to the conflation of feminism with lesbianism, that is, if you do not behave as a girl/woman should, you are on the road to becoming a lesbian. In my analysis I do not intend to conflate feminism and lesbianism; the individual sexualities of any women in the case studies discussed below are not the main issue. Rather, I use the concept of lesbian positioning to begin to unpick the gender-computing relationship.

Analyses of computing as gendered are incomplete in that they do not expose the constraint for women of a continual maintenance of hetero-gendered relations. My teaching within a women's studies programme provides illustrations of how heterosexual relations constitute computing as a masculine domain. For example, one student started the semester with confidence in her skills in the use of some software applications and much enthusiasm about gaining more expertise in computing. For the first few weeks, she engaged with database theory and worked on data analysis and design, but then I noticed a dramatic reversal. She began to talk of the material being too difficult. Her loss of confidence was evident in her decision to redo work she had already completed successfully rather than moving on. At one point she complained that she didn't know what she was doing, then that her male partner had told her the work was too advanced for her to learn, and that even the men in his office who work with computers were unfamiliar with the theory she was trying to apply in her design of a database. This continual renegotiation within hetero-gendered positions points to a key question: does investment in heterosexuality implicate some women in colluding un/consciously in a discourse of computing that excludes them?

Lesbian perspective

The explanations in the literature about why so few women choose computing, when moving beyond straightforward access issues, usually deal with the social construction of women's needs, wants and preferences within heteropatriarchy. Kitzinger documents how this construction contributes to the invisibility of lesbians and gay men. Common responses in her classes, when she refers to lesbians, are 'Lesbians and gay men are just like heterosexuals'; 'We don't discriminate'; 'We treat everyone exactly the same' (1993, p. 10). This treating everyone the same is practised in the feminist literature on computing. It usually means treating everyone as if they are heterosexual. That the world of lesbians and gay men is profoundly different is beginning to be documented and discussed (see Wilton, 1995). That it is a difficult place for students in higher education is clear from a survey of lesbian and gay students at thirty-five institutions in the UK (Fahey, 1995). About 40 per cent of the respondents reported peer isolation, verbal abuse and pressure to conform to heterosexual norms (p. 18).

All women move within a profoundly heterosexist world, and some women, namely lesbians, negotiate relationships outside it as well. Lesbians have become used to interrogating what is assumed for others as the accepted way to be.[1] Those of us who identify as lesbians have had to invent or fashion ourselves out of 'a whole network of identity and power relations' (Phelan, 1993, p. 775). The very process of 'becoming' lesbian in a hostile world can offer insights that may be invisible to many heterosexuals. It leads to the conclusion that theory and practice predicated upon heterosexuality as the absolute norm and universal referent cannot be adequate (Wilton, 1995, p. 14). In the specific studies I explore in the next section, I use a lesbian perspective to provide insights into two questions about the relationship between women and computing. The first one is a common question – why aren't more women in computing? The other is less familiar – how does a hetero-gender discourse affect the positioning of the women who are there?

As I found in my past experience as a programmer and systems designer, and currently as a tutor, there are women who are keen to gain expertise in computing. In most social construction studies, however, it is usually the women who consider computing as something alien who are implicitly taken as the norm. This disregard for the women who have a different sort of relationship to computing could be related to its inevitable siting in a masculine domain, with hetero-gendered relations as the accepted norm. In studying the 'other' women in computing, I ask if the discipline might serve as an amenable locality for lesbians.

Conventional computer science courses

Turkle (1985) looked at the ways of thinking embodied in a hacker's relationship with his machine. A recent equivalent to the 'deviant' hacker is 'Webmaster' who constructs and customizes Websites. In an article on this new media position, we are given a description of one of this new breed, a programmer called Taylor 'who lives in the grungey East Village, has dyed red hair, a goatee and tattoos' (McElvogue, 1996, p. 2). The social construction of the hacker is one that continues to occupy an intersection of the masculine and the deviant. This image helps explain why some women do not take up computing, but how does it affect women who have chosen conventional computer science courses? A study conducted by Rasmussen and Hapnes (1991) explores exactly this. They looked at undergraduates taking a conventional computer science course and examined the dominant hacker discourse in relation to women students, who were in the minority on the course. Their study revealed that women students' anxiety regarding the course came from a concern to be seen as 'normal', as living 'a normal life' outside computer science. Operating within the confines of what the women students initially perceived as a hacker culture, they were relieved to find men who led 'normal' lives. It is implied, though not directly stated or explored in this research, that what is meant by 'normal life' is heterosexual socializing and conventional family life. The women students maintained their position by leading their 'normal' life while at the same time carrying out their studies and making choices that fitted in with their interests. In problematizing the hackers or 'key pressers' as deviant, the women reinscribe their hetero-gendered identity in relation to the 'normal' men on the course. The deviants, however, operating within what they considered to be a dominant discourse for computer science, typify a position that is masculine in opposition to their feminine positioning.

The hackers are constructed by these women as having a twilight life or, in fact, no life outside computing. They are portrayed as solitary, obsessed, isolated, indulging in a deviant relationship with a machine. This is in contrast to how the hackers see themselves: as eccentric, different, special, daring, but not as solitary and/or social misfits. As a group they socialize together and enjoy physically signifying their difference through their clothing, hairstyles, etc. While these 'key pressers' are in the minority numerically, Rasmussen and Hapnes explain that they represent the dominant culture because dominant groups among teachers and male students share their values, and there is a lack of alternative values and perspectives. This dominant culture is steeped in masculinity.

Research exploring women's contradictory location in masculine domains explains women's positioning in terms of a struggle to maintain the feminine (for example, Thomas, 1990). But looking deeper into the constitutive dynamic of hetero-gender relations, another dominant constituent can be identified, that of sexuality. Two aspects are relevant: socially, the necessity of maintaining a position through relations that imply heterosexuality, and, subjectively, the danger of stepping out of these relations and becoming 'another'. The 'options' are put most bluntly when women do enter male-dominated fields. Thomas (1990) describes them as requiring women to be a) more feminine, b) like a man, or c) better than a man (see also Byrne, 1993). According to Maddock, 'In any highly segregated culture, women are left with two options, either rebel or conform to the roles allocated to them . . . either be a "man" and desexualized, a bullying "school mam" or pander sexually to male interests' (1994, p. 108). In her discussion of lesbian identity, Phelan (1993) notes that oppressed groups (in this case women) do not have agency to authorize or deny a given identity in society. It is a well-documented association for women that being employed in 'men's work' means continual work at reproducing femininity if you are concerned not to be seen as 'masculine' (Sheppard, 1989). Rasmussen and Hapnes's study provides overt documentation of this: one of the hackers is reported as commenting that 'the female students in computer science looked so female, dressed up like women in restaurants or as if going to a celebration'; he continues, in other departments you can find 'girls who are more like one of the boys' (1991, p. 1111). The ascription of deviance to women not performing their expected local heterosexual role is historically documented by van Oost. She describes how, in a 1950s study of labour relations made prior to the organizational shaping of computer jobs, a researcher described 'a number of unmarried female managers'. The researcher notes that 'married men with children' complained about 'the lack of warmth in [these women's] style of leadership'. His explanation for their behaviour is the women's 'diligence and devotion to duty developed out of compensation of missed life-chances' (1991, p. 416).

Although deviance from local gender roles should not be conflated with lesbianism, the threat of being labelled lesbian is used to keep women in their place (Sheppard, 1989, p. 154). Another conflation, from a heterosexual perspective, is that of lesbian and feminist. Epstein and Johnson report that a fear of women starting women's studies courses is that 'they will be taken for lesbians' (1994, p. 204). In her study of women working in three different organizations, Cockburn found that in the two less progressive ones lesbians were pathologized and said to differ fundamentally from 'women' or people from ethnic minorities because lesbianism is associated with choice (1991, p. 92). The position of gender deviant is especially dangerous for women who need and/or want to maintain a secure footing as heterosexual in a male-majority area such as computing. In reading Rasmussen and Hapnes's study with its highlighting of an abnormal/normal polarity in addition to a masculine/feminine one, the construction of hackers bears a striking resemblance to some common constructions of lesbian identity. Wilton describes four commonalities in the definitions of 'a lesbian', two of which are especially relevant to my analysis: lesbians as pseudo-males, and as a 'sorry state to be in' (1995, p. 30). Hackers are represented as solitary people, whose life outside computer science is non-existent because it is invisible. The hacker construction thus has parallels with that of women who do not perform heterosexuality, the women whose social relations are invisible or hidden, and therefore abnormal in the context of Rasmussen and Hapnes's study. Analysis of their study from a lesbian position highlights gender relations that need unpicking when examining women's positioning in male-dominated areas like computing.

The second example I use is based on data from a research project I carried out with Sarah Plummeridge into women's experience on the first year of a conventional computer science course in one of England's new universities (Stepulevage with Plummeridge, 1996). The limited participation of women students and staff and the interviews we carried out are explored in this example. While male domination in computing was acknowledged in the interviews we did with students and staff participating in the research project, the women students we spoke to did not consider their learning situation as oppressive. Women students, in the minority, were critical of the pedagogy and structure of the course, but not the content. Women tutors associated with the course were openly supportive of women students. They gave them their time outside of class and made no secret of their 'campaign' for more women students. One of them made women's high achievements well known to students as a whole. The women students we interviewed spoke constructively about the role of women tutors, and expressed positive views about the possibility of women-only learning situations. On the other hand, these students expressed no need to meet together as women on the course and told us they experienced no sex discrimination from male fellow students. One of the students said, ' . . . the guys, no, people treat you based on the amount of knowledge you've got, how much you know, they're not sexist and that kind of thing'. While acknowledging male domination and sexism towards women in computing generally, it seemed to us that they did not wish to identify themselves as women who were having such experiences on this course. In her discussion of associations between masculinity and computing, Griffiths notes how women and men might not wish to confine themselves in gender categories for a variety of reasons, for example, to avoid stereotyping or an awareness of the existence of sexism (1988, p. 146). For the women students, it might lead to a shift from their position as individuals to one which highlights their gender identity and opens up the possibility of being identified as 'feminine', that is, as incapable of being computer scientists.

Our research revealed the women students' agency in maintaining their hetero-gender position as women on this computer science course. In interviews, the women stated that they preferred men as friends. As researchers, we observed that they sat and conferred with men or sat on their own in workshop classes, but not with women. Both they and the tutors we interviewed told how the women students spent time with tutors and asked questions whenever they needed clarification about material or assessment work.[2] Looking at the women students' performance within its hetero-gendered confines, we pinpointed advantageous spaces for women. They asked questions of tutors, exposing their lack of understanding and need for help without losing face, unlike the men students who told us that they didn't expect tutors to give them this sort of support and did not ask for it. The women worked at developing their computer knowledge and skills while at the same time performing gender that is implicitly heterosexual in order to maintain their positioning in a professional area that they described as male-dominated.

The aspect of the project significant to this chapter concerned the participation of the women, both staff and students, in the research. They did not see their identity as 'women' as a barrier to success in an environment in which they were very much in the minority; however, their relations with us as researchers led us to believe otherwise. In thinking about the women's limited participation, I began to consider how the project's focus on gender might have contributed to their (un)availability for interviews, as it required an explanation of the position of women – therefore, themselves – in 'a man's world'. This may have made the research project a dangerous location, pointing implicitly to a further confining identity that may be at issue, that of 'feminist'. The women might not have wished to identify with or as feminists because feminist, by extension, means lesbian. This layer of analysis acknowledges the entwining of heterosexuality with gender.

Butler (1990) analyses gender identity as assumed and taken for granted, but also as a regulator, enforcing the norm of heterosexuality. For the women on this course, their regulated gender identity could be read as heterosexual, and a project critically examining gender becomes a potentially dangerous situation for them and one in which they may position themselves outside an acceptable gendered location. They may become identified as 'women' in relation to other women, rather than to men. Instead of being seen according to technology-gender stereotypes, they may begin to be seen as challenging to the content of the course; rather than being seen as incapable of working as computer scientists, they may, after critical reflection, see themselves as unwilling to become conventional computer scientists.

Our experience of the interview process provided a demonstration of how threatening an alternative location can be, even though, as noted earlier, individual sexual identity was not at issue. We completed interviews with the participating men students and tutors by mid-semester; this proved unproblematic as we were exploring a location in which their gender identity was associated with dominance within the gender-technology relation. We found it difficult to set dates with both women students and tutors, however, and this involved extensive negotiation and persuasion. Meetings, therefore, took place late in the semester or at its end. The women students kept putting their appointments on hold due to prior arrangements, pressure of work, etc. This ultimately resulted in only one of the five women students agreeing to a taped in-depth interview, to which she brought along a man friend who remained throughout the session. A second women student met with the interviewer in a public place, over coffee in the canteen. We experienced similar problems with the women tutors. The two participating women staff found it almost impossible to make time. One tutor finally agreed to a telephone conversation after the semester had ended. The other invited the interviewer to her shared office, which remained a public space where she talked amid continual interruptions from staff and students. At best, these four women can be seen as needing to perform locally acceptable versions of 'woman student or tutor' in order to survive within the course. At worst, they were demonstrating deeply homophobic attitudes in relation to a private meeting with a woman researcher who identified herself as interested in gender issues and who therefore might be lesbian.

These two research studies point to another level of analysis in theorizing women's relation to computing besides that of an assumed hetero-gender positioning. Articulating a hetero-gender level in which heterosexual relations can be seen to constitute gender relations shows women must, to varying degrees and depending on their own subjectivities, reinscribe their relationship to men in order to participate in computer science courses. To be a woman in computer science can require active reinforcement of a hetero-gendered identity, no matter what your sexuality. An exclusive focus on the contradictory positioning of women in this masculine field and how they hold on to their 'feminine' gender identity leaves some questions regarding hetero-gendered relations unexplored. The next section discusses women in computing who may experience the oppression of heteropatriarchy, but who do not regard their participation in a masculine domain as threatening to their identity.

Lesbians and computing: parallels and intersections

In England and the USA, computing has been portrayed as an area of exciting career opportunities and unlimited technological potential. It has also been portrayed as an arena where ability means more than who you are. The hacker, on one hand, is portrayed as socially inadequate and abnormal, but on the other as a rebel and challenger of the system. Hacking is seen as a discourse in which women have no place for various reasons, particularly because of its machine orientation, its lack of sociability, its time and resource demands. Hackers are not in the majority in computing, however. Hacking represents the extreme end of a continuum of the computer person as 'different' as well as 'male'. Sometimes the difference is evident in the culture of departments responsible for computing. Cockburn, for example, describes a computing division in one organization as anti-hierarchical and anti-procedural in spirit, giving people some freedom (1991, p. 57). It is the possible relevance of computing in terms of career potential and the opportunity for difference that I explore next.

In a study that asked sixty 'non-heterosexual' women to recall their secondary schooling years, Dunne (1992, pp. 88–90) discusses how many of the women were concerned with their need for economic independence, that is, life without a man. She reports that two-thirds of those women who did not expect to marry looked forward to a professional career or a job that offered career possibilities. Just under half of these women were attracted to what are described as masculine jobs and/or areas of study, for example, construction, engineering, etc. The occupations of the sample reflected this, with the highest proportion of those in paid employment working in qualified science and technical occupations, including computing. In this research, masculine-gendered jobs/subject areas were directly linked to the potential for economic independence. Indeed, the vast literature on women and employment confirms that there is an intersection between professional careers, high salaries and men.

Does the gendering of professional computing jobs as masculine also have significance in relation to lesbians? Hall (1989) notes that computer-related jobs are particularly popular with lesbians. She explains this as an example of a coping strategy characterized by a neutralizing of gender so that sexuality is less likely to come into focus. In the case of computing, it is a combination of masculine technology with feminine keyboard work that provides such a de-gendered or neutralized position (p. 135). As feminist studies show, masculine associations with computing are common. The feminine association with keyboards, however, is less relevant today as the computer is more of a flexible artefact. There may be other reasons why computing may provide a neutralized position for lesbians. The 'difference' of people in computing and their association with things abstract and therefore unfathomable might act as a neutralizer, with 'unfeminine' women at present still falling within an acceptable borderline of 'different' as long as the proportion of women in the profession remains low and jobs are still available for men. The possibility of difference, then, may make computing a viable education and employment option for lesbians.

For lesbians personally, computing may offer a locality in which the pervasiveness of hetero-social life is diminished. While not necessarily hackers, who are assumed to have no life outside a deviant relationship with a machine, computer people are constructed as being outside the borders of 'normal' socializing. The area is portrayed as one in which there is less pressure to appear as a 'normal' person with a 'normal' life or social skills. The possibility of a well-paid professional career provides the prospect of economic independence. The promise of new and unlimited horizons, echoed by the women and men students we interviewed in our research project, may also have resonance for some lesbians, invisible and/or oppressed as we are now. The possibility of working on your own becomes the possibility of working away from a constantly hetero-normalizing environment and the requirement to negotiate within it. The possibility of studying in the abstract becomes the possibility of studying without the need to analyse heterosexual images, relations and contexts.

Economic, cultural and social factors all play a role in the construction of this subject area as a potential location for lesbians, but other factors remain a deterrent. Computing is intertwined with destructive and oppressive policies and practices in the military, government, industry and culture, for example, weaponry and surveillance. As Perry and Greber (1990) note, vigilance is required if one works in computing.

Conclusions

By considering the significance of heteropatriarchal relations in the masculine construction of computing, a richer analysis of the positioning of both lesbians and heterosexual women is possible. One of the many aspects that needs to be considered is how the current hetero-gender order is held in place in computing. By understanding how the practice of heterosexual relations contributes to the gender-technology relation as a conservative force, women can develop more comprehensive strategies for challenging and transforming the power and control elements of these relations.

The development of skills and knowledge for social change in computing, however, needs a counter-cultural context where groups of women have the opportunity for 'mind expansion' (Schulman, 1995). Harding proposes that science is parallel to the arts rather than the humanities, with the sciences allowing no equivalent to critical 'humanist' work (1993, p. 52); this adds another facet to explanations of the dominant philosophy of science. Her proposal also opens up the option for creativity, craft, skill and the prospect of a science committed to positive consequences for oppressed groups of people. Conventional computer science courses like those I have cited will not allow this counter-cultural context, so it is important that alternative locations, like women's studies courses, do so. The social construction of computing as masculine needs to be critically analysed as a trick designed to constrain women within a hetero-gender discourse that maintains women's exclusion, rejection and/or disinterest. Feminists need to critically study gender-technology relations and to develop skills and knowledge in computing so that they can intervene, subvert and create new knowledge in community with other politically committed women already in computing.

Notes

Thanks to Carmel Keeley for critical comments on drafts of this paper.

1. Wilkinson and Kitzinger (1993) explore taken-for-granted heterosexuality and demonstrate the difficulty of examining heterosexual identity for women academics who practise these relations.
2. Thomas discusses women students' perceptions of a sexual element in staff's greater willingness to chat to them than to men students (1990, pp. 127–8).

References

Bodker, S. and Greenbaum, J. (1993) 'Design of Information Systems: Things Versus People.' In Green *et al.* (1993).

Butler, J. (1990) 'Gender Trouble, Feminist Theory and Psychoanalytic Discourse.' In L. Nicholson (ed.) *Feminism/Postmodernism*. New York: Routledge.

Byrne, E. (1993) *Women and Science: The Snark Syndrome*. London: Taylor and Francis.

Cockburn, C. (1991) *In the Way of Women: Men's Resistance to Sex Equality in Organizations*. London: Macmillan Education.

Cockburn, C. (1992) 'The Circuit of Technology: Gender, Identity and Power.' In R. Silverstone and E. Hirsch (eds) *Consuming Technologies*. London: Routledge.

Cole, A., Conlon, T., Jackson, S. and Welch, D. (1994) 'Information Technology and Gender: Problems and Proposals.' *Gender and Education*. 6/1: 77–85.

Dunne, G. (1992) 'Difference at Work: Perceptions of Work from a Non-Heterosexual Perspective.' In H. Hinds and J. Stacey (eds) *Working Out: New Directions for Women's Studies*. London: Taylor and Francis.

Epstein, D. and Johnson, R. (1994) 'On the Straight and the Narrow: The Heterosexual Presumption, Homophobias and Schools.' In D. Epstein (ed.) *Challenging Lesbian and Gay Inequalities in Education*. Buckingham: Open University Press.

Fahey, W. (1995) 'Discriminating Students.' *Young People Now*. (March): 18–19.

Green, E., Owen, J. and Pain, D. (eds) (1993) *Gender by Design? Information Technology and Office Systems*. London: Taylor and Francis.

Griffiths, M. (1988) 'Strong Feelings about Computers.' *Women's Studies International Forum*. 11/2: 145–54.

Grundy, F. (1994) 'Women in the Computing Workplace: Some Impressions.' In A. Adam, J. Emms, E. Green and J. Owen (eds) *Women, Work and Computerization: Breaking Old Boundaries – Building New Forms*. Amsterdam: Elsevier.

Hall, M. (1989) 'Private Experiences in the Public Domain: Lesbians in Organizations.' In J. Hearn, D. Sheppard, P. Tancred-Sheriff and G. Burrell (eds) *The Sexuality of Organization*. London: Sage.

Harding, S. (1986) *The Science Question in Feminism*. New York: Cornell University Press.

Harding, S. (1993) 'Comments on Anne Fausto-Sterling's "Building Two-Way Streets".' *National Women's Studies Association Journal*. 5/1 (Spring): 49–55.

Henwood, F. (1993) 'Establishing Gender Perspectives on Information Technology.' In Green *et al.* (1993).

Kitzinger, C. (1993) 'Not Another Lecture on Homosexuality.' *Young People Now*. (March): 10–11.

Kvande, E. and Rasmussen, B. (1989) 'Men, Women and Data Systems.' *European Journal of Engineering Education*. 14/4: 369–79.

Lie, M. (1995) 'Technology and Masculinity.' *European Journal of Women's Studies*. 2/3 (August): 379–94.

McElvogue, L. (1996) 'Webmasters of the Universe.' *Guardian Online*. (22 February): 2–3.

Maddock, S. (1994) 'Women: A Force for Democracy.' In J. deBruijn and E. Cyba (eds) *Gender and Organizations: Changing Perspectives*. Amsterdam: VU University Press.

Mahony, K. and Van Toen, B. (1990) 'Mathematical Formalism as a Means of Occupational Closure in Computing – Why "Hard" Computing Tends to Exclude Women.' *Gender and Education*. 2/3: 319–31.

Perry, R. and Greber, L. (1990) 'Women and Computers: An Introduction.' *SIGNS*. 16/1: 74–101.

Phelan, S. (1993) '(Be)Coming Out: Lesbian Identity and Politics.' *SIGNS*. 18/4: 765–90.

Rasmussen, B. and Hapnes, T. (1991) 'Excluding Women from the Technologies of the Future?' *Futures*. (December): 1107–19.

Rose, H. (1994) *Love, Power and Knowledge: Towards a Feminist Transformation of the Sciences*. Cambridge: Polity Press.

Schulman, S. (1995) *My American History: Lesbian and Gay Life During the Reagan/Bush Years*. London: Cassell.

Sheppard, D. (1989) 'Organizations, Power and Sexuality: The Image and Self-Image of Women Managers.' In J. Hearn, D. Sheppard, P. Tancred-Sheriff and G. Burrell (eds) *The Sexuality of Organization*. London: Sage.

Stepulevage, L. with Plummeridge, S. (1996) 'The Deconstruction of Computer Science as Science.' University of East London Working Paper Series.

Sundin, E. (1995) 'The Social Construction of Gender and Technology.' *European Journal of Women's Studies*. 2/3 (August): 335–53.

Thomas, K. (1990) *Gender and Subject in Higher Education*. London: Society for Research into Higher Education and Open University.

Tijdens, K. (1991) 'Women in EDP Departments.' In I.V. Eriksson, B.A. Kitchenham and K.G. Tijdens (eds) *Women, Work and Computerization*. Amsterdam: Elsevier.

Turkle, S. (1985) *The Second Self: Computers and the Human Spirit*. New York: Touchstone.

van Oost, E. (1991) 'The Process of Sex-Typing of Computer Occupations.' In I.V. Eriksson, B.A. Kitchenham and K.G. Tijdens (eds) *Women, Work and Computerization*. Amsterdam: Elsevier.

van Oost, E. (1992) *The Masculinization of the Computer: A Historical Reconstruction*. Lulea, Sweden: Forum.

Wajcman, J. (1993) 'The Masculine Mystique: A Feminist Analysis of Science and Technology.' In B. Probert and B. Wilson (eds) *Pink Collar Blues: Work, Gender and Technology*. Melbourne: Melbourne University Press.

Weizenbaum, J. (1976) *Computer Power and Human Reason: From Judgment to Calculation*. San Francisco: W.H. Freeman and Co.

Wilkinson, S. and Kitzinger, C. (eds) (1993) *Heterosexuality: A Feminism & Pyschology Reader*. London: Sage.

Wilton, Tamsin (1995) *Lesbian Studies: Setting an Agenda*. London: Routledge.

15

Healing the Invisible Body: Lesbian Health Studies

Tamsin Wilton

Lesbian health studies has been until very recently a form of grassroots community praxis. In the last few years its insights and demands have slowly begun to trickle into the formal academic arena, as social changes make it incrementally more possible for lesbian academics and practitioners to be 'out', and as the impact of HIV brings the question of sexuality within the remit of health studies. It is therefore not yet possible to critically engage with 'lesbian health studies' as a mature academic discipline, only to attempt a tentative overview of this newly prolific but scattered field and to outline possible directions for future development. Yet the expanding discipline of health studies offers an arena within which lesbian issues may be incorporated and supported in both an academic and a vocational context. This is one disciplinary area where academic intervention, whether by lesbians or by heterosexuals, may have directly positive consequences in the daily lives of lesbians.

Current policy has moved towards training health care professionals in a higher education framework and often within higher education institutions. An important characteristic of this shift has been the emphasis on the social sciences as an integral part of the training. The term 'health studies' is generally used to designate the sociology of health and health care with varying health policy and health psychology content. Midwives, nurses, physiotherapists, radiographers and other students of the professions allied to medicine (PAMS) now receive at least an introduction to psychology, sociology and basic social policy.

Health studies is often engaged in an uneasy relationship with the more clinical components of PAMS training, since its emphasis on the social factors which contribute to health and illness challenges the biomedical model which presents disease as a purely biological process in isolation from social factors such as poverty, marginalization or cultural norms. It is clearly important that nurses, midwives and others should understand at least some of the social factors which may restrict or enhance the wellbeing of their patients/clients or which influence their own professional lives. It can be both enlightening and radicalizing to understand the complex intersections of racism, class, gender, dis/ability and age in the field of health and health care.

Yet health studies, while offering a forum for challenging stereotypes about ethnicity, gender, class, etc. (stereotypes which may be particularly damaging in a health care context) generally fails to incorporate issues around sexuality and sexual identity. Moreover, when sexual identity *is* covered, discussion tends to focus on gay men and is all too often largely subsumed under the topic of HIV/AIDS (for example, Savage, 1987). Lesbians remain invisible as a client group whose needs require specific consideration.

Alliances and strategies

The political and social movements for women's liberation and gay liberation have been little better than the mainstream in foregrounding lesbian health. One of the most positive achievements of feminism has been a burgeoning and energetic focus on women's health, reflected in the mushrooming of well-woman clinics, a national and international network of women's health initiatives and the popularity of women's health courses at both an academic and community level (Doyal, 1995; Health Education Authority, 1993; Smyke, 1991; Workers' Educational Association, 1986). Yet lesbian health continues to be marginalized or ignored even within this specifically feminist context. The ravages of the HIV pandemic mean that the energies of queer communities have been directed to the health needs of gay and bisexual men. This is right and proper, but it has meant that lesbian health has, once again, received relatively little attention. To constitute lesbian health studies as an autonomous entity (as I believe we must) mounts a challenge to allopathic medical science, whose record regarding lesbians makes nonsense of any claim to scientific rigour or objectivity, to mainstream health studies and to the women's health movement, which has consistently failed to address lesbian health.

Yet, although lesbian health needs to be recognized as an autonomous field of study, practice and activism, it makes little sense to isolate it either from health studies or from women's health. This is partly to forestall the risk of ghettoization, but also because studying lesbian health brings to health studies an intellectual rigour which it currently lacks. It is not only a question of 'adding on' lesbianism to an otherwise incomplete laundry list of social variables which influence health and health care. The intersections of gender and the erotic in the very notion of lesbianism offer some powerful insights into theoretical questions at the heart of health studies.

'Lesbian health' is a phrase that elegantly encapsulates the dynamic and unstable relationship between health – generally seen as a property of bodies – and the social. After all, what sense does it make to speak of lesbian health? What needs to be said about the health of women who choose other women for their lovers which could not be said about all women? Does my digestion function differently, my liver develop a peculiar shape, the composition of my blood change because I am a lesbian? Do the physical acts known as 'lesbian sex' have physiological consequences for the lesbian body? And if such questions are as nonsensical as they seem, *why* has the medical profession invested time and resources in trying to pin down a lesbian physiology?

Doctors creating unicorns: the medical construction of the lesbian body

The whole notion of what it means to 'be' a lesbian is complex and fraught with contradiction; perhaps never more so than at the heart of postmodern queer culture in the urban centres of anglo culture, where lesbian boys and lipstick lesbians alike may enjoy sexual liaisons with fairies and faggots while still laying claim to an intact lesbian identity. The cultural and sexual fractures which characterize this particular way of being lesbian certainly complicate any notion that there could be such a thing as a 'lesbian body', or indeed 'lesbian health'. Yet mainstream straight medical science has expended much time and money on trying to establish empirically that there is, indeed, such a thing as a recognizably lesbian body. What is going on?

Bear with me while I take liberties with literature. Many of you will recognize these words of Shylock's:

> I am a Jew. Hath not a Jew eyes? Hath not a Jew hands, organs, dimensions, senses, affections, passions? Fed with the same food, hurt with the same weapons, subject to the same diseases, healed by the same means, warmed and cooled by the same winter and summer, as a Christian is? If you prick us, do we not bleed? If you tickle us, do we not laugh? If you poison us, do we not die? (*Merchant of Venice* III. 1 53–60)

Shakespeare's point is, of course, that although the Jewish body is indistinguishable in shape, function and needs from the Gentile body, the social imperatives of anti-Semitism render this homology – here characterized as a shared humanity – pretty much irrelevant in Renaissance Venice. Similarly, anti-lesbian hostility and lesbian oppression do not depend on bodily difference. Yet, in a culture which is so dominated by the scientific paradigm, and in which the medical profession exerts enormous (albeit contested) power, there is an imperative to locate 'difference' – such as Jewishness or lesbianism – in the body. It has been an important part of the liberation struggles of women, black people and queers to demonstrate that medical science has invested much time and energy in locating the stigmata of difference in the body in the interests of social control, and in so doing has provided a (pseudo)scientific foundation for prejudice and discriminatory behaviour. In the context of homosexuality, the underlying assumption has been that sexual desire and affection for members of one's own sex represent a malfunction of gender (Wilton, 1995; Savage, 1987). Lesbians have been subject to the taxonomic frenzy of medical researchers, who have measured our weight, our waists, our body hair, the size of our breasts and nipples, the length of our clitorises, our height, our hormones, our ability to whistle, the dimensions of our pelvic bones and the thickness of our wrists, in an attempt to distinguish the lesbian body from the heterosexual female body (Ruse, 1988; Henry, 1950) and demonstrate its inherent similarities to the (heterosexual) male body. On the basis of the (contradictory) findings from such experiments, researchers conclude that 'lesbians tend to be more "solid" than heterosexuals', and that we tend to look older than our age, 'sometimes strikingly so' (Griffiths, 1974, p. 550). As the machinery of the medical gaze has become more technologically sophisticated, the search for the physiological markers of homosex has shifted from the grossly anatomical to the hormonal to the neuronal to the chromosomal (Wilton, 1995). Of course, lesbian and gay activists and academics have been closely involved in the struggle to publicly discredit this dubious research enterprise (Powell, 1995; McIntosh, 1968).

Two points to note about such experiments are, first, that they are not regarded as in any way eccentric – this is 'normal' medical science at work – and, second, that the researchers in question are quite cheerful about drawing generalizations from very small samples, something which would be unacceptable in almost any other context. The conclusion that lesbians are 'solid', for example, was drawn from a British study of forty-two subjects.

While being rightly critical of such evidence of the touching, childlike faith which certain medical professionals so clearly demonstrate in the existence of a lesbian body, it is important not to conclude that lesbian health is an oxymoron. Constructionism offers a useful intellectual and strategic intervention in this irrational and politically driven 'scientific' project, and lesbian health studies offers an appropriate and accessible forum for the debate between constructionism and neurogenetic determinism. However, successfully challenging the idea of a recognizably lesbian body (even one which can only be seen with a scanning electron microscope!) is not at all the same thing as claiming that lesbians do not exist. Lesbian-ness is not located in the body, it is not a somatic property (Wilton, 1995; McIntosh, 1968). There are, nevertheless, specific and important issues concerning the health and health care of lesbians which need the attention of researchers and health care professionals, and they tend to cluster at the dynamic interface between the body and the society which gives that body meaning.

Feminists looking the other way

We have a women's health movement. Women's health, indeed, is one of the success stories of feminism, yet it has failed lesbians badly, both in a self-identified feminist context and in its incorporation into the mainstream. The British Health Education Authority's *Women's Health Guide* (Furedi and Tidyman, 1994) contains in its 347 pages *two sentences* on lesbians, and has a particularly unhelpful definition of lesbianism: '"Lesbian": where women are attracted to other women'. Sexual partners are referred to as 'he' throughout, and issues of particular concern to lesbians are utterly ignored. An important gesture would have been to title the book *A Heterosexual Women's Health Guide.*

The inclusion of lesbian issues on the women's health agenda seems to have a built-in time lag, and change is ongoing. The Boston Women's Health Book Collective (1971) responded to criticism by greatly enlarging the section on lesbian health in the revised edition of *Our Bodies Ourselves*, and many important books and other resources on women's health now incorporate at least some lesbian issues (Doyal, 1995; HEA, 1993; WEA, 1986). Yet this inclusion is at best patchy.

Lesbian health activism

Frustrated by the continued failure of the women's health movement to address lesbian health, lesbians have responded by establishing specialist lesbian services such as the lesbian genito-urinary medicine (GUM) clinics in London or the lesbian health group Lesbewell in Birmingham. A new generation of lesbian health activists, primed with sophisticated political tactics learned from working in AIDS activist organizations like ACT UP (AIDS Coalition to Unleash Power), began organizing to promote lesbian health to policy-makers (Schulman, 1994), and the inter-sectorial response to the HIV pandemic gave lesbians in some countries an opportunity to focus attention on lesbian sexual health needs.

In 1990 the Fourth International Congress on Women's Health Issues was disrupted by lesbians protesting at the failure to include lesbian issues. Lesbian delegates demanded that a future issue of *Health Care for Women International* be devoted to lesbian health care, and there was such a high demand for the resulting issue that it was subsequently republished as a book. Yet, even in this instance, a recalcitrant heterosexism informed the outcome. Phyllis Noerager Stern, recounting these events in her preface to the book, addresses her reader with the assurance that 'You will be outraged, as I am, at the prejudice, mistreatment and downright ignorance held by even college-educated nurses! No wonder women are reluctant to come out as lesbians – it's dangerous out there' (1993, p. xii). Well, thanks for telling me! But this is a serious point. The assumption that the entire readership of *Health Care for Women International* is heterosexual leaves a nasty taste in the mouth. It is also significant that other journals – *Hypatia, Discourse, Feminist Review, Textual Practice, Signs,* etc. – have invited lesbian or gay guest editors to edit their special queer issues, while *Health Care for Women International* remained content with a heterosexual editor.

Lesbians, what lesbians?

Perhaps the most important project of a specifically lesbian health studies is to make lesbians visible as both providers and users of health care services. It has become taken for granted within feminist discourse that lesbians are 'invisible', that is, that the oppression of lesbians is characterized by and expressed in heterosexuals ignoring or denying lesbian existence, and by the erasure of traces of that existence from the historical record (Donoghue, 1993; Wilton, 1995). 'Lesbian invisibility' is hardly a straightforward notion currently, with the (seemingly) acceptable face of lesbianism looming at us from every television screen, magazine cover, paperback novel or T-shirt (Clark, 1993). Countering the raucous homophobia of the gutter press, the big guns of serious journalism – the *Guardian,* the *Observer,* the *Independent,* even the *Sunday Times* – all seem to have turned queer-friendly, publishing sympathetic articles about everything from sadomasochism to fag hags, body piercing to lipstick lesbians. Hardly a month goes by without an established mainstream magazine asking us 'Do lesbians have more fun?' (*New Woman*, January 1993), 'Are you going through a lesbian phase?' (*Cosmopolitan*, October 1992) or 'Does Jeanette Winterson thinks she's God?' (*Vanity Fair*, February 1995). Even the staid *She* (April 1995) recently carried an article on 'How lesbians feel about love, sex and motherhood', and a suggestive lesbian chic has long been a staple of glam fashion photography. Whatever we are nowadays, invisible we ain't.

Yet the bubbly superficialities of popular culture mean very little in terms of the legislature or social policy. Around the world, it is still the case that lesbians (and gay men) lack the full protection of the law which heterosexuals take for granted. In the UK, for example, it is still perfectly legal to discriminate against lesbians and gay men in employment or the provision of public services such as education, housing and health care. Moreover, legislation continues to be introduced, both in the USA and the UK, which directly discriminates against lesbian and gay citizens.[1] The question of lesbian invisibility must be seen in this political context. While lesbian existence has long been and continues to be ignored, denied or trivialized, making lesbians 'vanish' in the interests of male power, this intersects in complicated ways with the question of passing in order to survive. It is passing together with its corollary, coming out, which determines the particular paranoias of homophobia and which enables the confident ignorance which constitutes heterosexism to continue. The anxious imperative to identify and codify a 'lesbian body' exists because it is (usually) only possible to know that a woman is a lesbian if she wants you to know. This simple fact makes a sexual identity a very different question from, say, the question of gender. For a man to 'pass' as a woman involves painstaking hard work, the ingestion of hormones, voice training and/or surgery. Even then, the performance rarely bears close scrutiny. For lesbians it is not 'passing' as straight which demands hard work, but being recognized as who we are. Heterosexism – that hegemonic world-view which confidently assumes that God or nature designed women *for* men and that 'woman' *means* 'sexually available to men' – is not easy to challenge with the meagre individual resources of clothing, hairstyle and body language, especially when counter-cultural signifiers are continually co-opted by the commercial and pop-cultural mainstream.

The cultural miasma of hegemonic heterosexism makes it all but impossible to be acknowledged as a lesbian. Moreover, unquestioned institutional heterosexism has resulted in a health and social care infrastructure which both assumes and mandates heterosexuality for women (Wilton, 1995; Robertson, 1993). Thus, coming out carries grave and very real dangers, especially for lesbians who are in the vulnerable position of 'patient' or 'client'. Having your sexuality known in the wrong quarters may mean losing your job, your housing or your children, and research has indicated that fear of possible consequences is one factor which strongly inhibits lesbians from being out to health care professionals (Graham, 1993; Rosser, 1993; Stevens, 1993). This is an urgent problem in health care ethics. For while accurate information about a woman's sexuality may be useful or even essential if she is to receive effective and appropriate care, storing such information on her medical records may expose her to serious risk.

Research into lesbian health and health care: a brief summary

As is the case for lesbian issues more generally, most research into lesbian health care to date comes from the USA and, to a lesser extent, Canada (James *et al.*, 1994; Platzer, 1993), where large and relatively privileged lesbian communities are located. The notion of 'relative privilege' in this context is far from straightforward. It is important to recognize that such research is entirely dependent on the courage and tenacity of individual lesbians, who always have to struggle for resources, institutional support or recognition.

The stigma assigned to lesbian-ness means that lesbian health is a topic which appears relatively recently in the literature; articles before the mid-1970s are very rare. Anyone demonstrating an interest in lesbian concerns was and is likely to have their own sexuality called into question, and since the consequences of that were (and are) potentially grave, the choice to foreground lesbian issues has never been a free and easy one for lesbian or non-lesbian researchers (Plummer, 1992, 1981; Ponse, 1978). Indeed, Ken Plummer (1981) has suggested that stigma would have effectively prevented the social sciences from recognizing the existence of lesbians and gay men altogether, were it not for the gay and lesbian liberation movement.[2] And, like so many of the new social movements (Graham, 1993) – anti-racism and feminism to name but two – the gay liberation movement as we know it today in the West originated in the USA. This means that lesbian health has a relatively strong presence in health research in the USA where a substantial lesbian and gay health care movement has grown directly out of political activism, in much the same way as the women's health movement grew out of feminist activism.

In their history of the gay/lesbian health movement in the USA, Deyton and Lear point to the 'longstanding, pervasive and intense hostility of mainstream health services and practitioners towards the issue of homosexuality in general and to homosexual men and women in particular' (1988, p. 15). Although struggling against this general hostility, and against the quite terrifying forces of the religious right (Schulman, 1994), the issue of lesbian and gay health care is more effectively foregrounded in the USA than anywhere else in the world. There is a National Lesbian and Gay Health Foundation (NLGHF), both New York and San Francisco have created civic offices for lesbian and gay health concerns and the American Public Health Association has a Gay Public Health Workers' Caucus. Indeed, there are lesbian and gay caucuses or committees on all the major health professional organizations, and there has been a Gay Nurses Alliance, an adjunct of the American Nurses Association, since 1973 (Deyton and Lear, 1988; Vachon, 1988). Motivated by newly confident lesbian energy, large-scale research projects have been undertaken into lesbian health; the problems faced in these projects say much about the social position of lesbians, and perhaps offer important warnings for anyone trying to undertake similar research elsewhere.

A five-year national lesbian health care survey was instigated through the NLGHF and ran from 1983 to 1988. Unsurprisingly, funding was the first major hurdle. The initial data-collection phase of the project was funded by feminist and community organizations (the Ms Foundation for Women, the Sophia Fund and the Chicago Resource Centre), and the inevitable shortfall made up by donations from individual lesbians.[3] Analysis of the data from almost 2,000 returned questionnaires was delayed until the National Institute of Mental Health agreed to fund analysis by graduate assistants at the Survey Research Laboratory at Virginia Commonwealth University, in return for a preliminary report focusing on the mental health of lesbians (Ryan and Bradford, 1988). In their account of the survey, Ryan and Bradford write:

> It is perhaps a metaphor for the barriers in undertaking lesbian research to report the difficulties in inputting the survey data, once actual data were obtained. Four data keypunch firms were hired and with the exception of the last one, each reneged on their work, eventually refusing to complete the questionnaires and returning them to the Survey Research Lab, unentered. The last company stated that their keypunchers had walked off the job because they were afraid of getting AIDS from handling the questionnaires. (pp. 30–1)

Despite the refusal of mainstream funding bodies to recognize lesbian health as a valid area of enquiry, and of widespread anti-lesbianism bordering on the hysterical, a slowly growing body of research in lesbian health and health care has come out of North America. Findings indicate that anti-lesbianism, especially on the part of health professionals, is a major factor in lesbian health and in lesbian access to health care services. The Michigan Lesbian Health Survey, funded by the Michigan Organization for Human Rights initially to study lesbians and AIDS (MOHR, 1991), collected data from 1,681 lesbians across the state of Michigan. These data, confirming the results of earlier, smaller surveys (see Stevens, 1993, for a full review of the literature), showed that health care providers assume all their clients to be heterosexual, are ignorant, biased or hostile about lesbians, believe lesbians to be at a high risk of contracting HIV,[4] and all too often treat lesbian clients badly or even try to 'cure' them of being lesbian. Other surveys found that, for example, 64 per cent of registered nurses had negative attitudes to gays and lesbians (Young, 1988) – including pity, disgust, repulsion, unease, embarrassment, sorrow and fear – that 34 per cent of nurse educators believe lesbians are disgusting and 17 per cent of them think lesbianism is a disease (Randall, 1989), and that a small number of health care professionals refuse to treat lesbians at all (Harvey *et al.*, 1989).

The Michigan survey also affirmed the findings of other surveys that lesbians, forced to develop strategies for survival in the face of this degree of hostility, respond by managing their interactions with health care professionals in specific ways, all of which have potentially negative implications for their health or the effectiveness of their health care. Ten American studies, in agreement with the findings of the Michigan survey, indicate that the majority of lesbians may simply not come out to health care professionals (reported in Stevens, 1993). The results of this enforced secrecy may include alienation, additional stress and fear, poor self-esteem, inappropriate advice or treatment or even misdiagnosis (Rosser, 1993). Research has also indicated that some lesbians hesitate to use allopathic health care services and may delay seeking treatment or instead seek treatment and health advice from alternative/complementary practitioners or even from lesbian friends in order to avoid the hostility of mainstream health carers (Stevens and Hall, 1990, 1988; Zeidenstein, 1990; Saunders *et al.*, 1988; Glascock, 1983, 1981; Reagan, 1981; Chafetz *et al.*, 1974).

Lesbian readers may wonder whether there is any point in research which seems to say nothing new. After all, much of the above is familiar to lesbians who live with such problems on a daily basis. However, the significance of formal studies which empirically demonstrate what the 'average' lesbian knows from personal experience is greater than it seems. Most health care professionals like to believe that they are unprejudiced in their treatment of all clients, and it takes formal research studies published in academic journals to disabuse them. Such findings indicate, simply, that the anti-lesbianism of the health care system restricts women's health care choices and drastically limits both the options available to them and the quality and effectiveness of the care they receive. Most health care professionals would agree that this is unacceptable.

This body of research also offers supportive evidence to counter the claims of those who insist that they have never met a lesbian in the course of their professional practice. It is all too clear from the literature that it is simply not safe for lesbians to disclose their sexuality to allopathic professionals. The reported responses of health care professionals to a patient or client disclosing her lesbian-ness include: forced psychiatric treatment, overt hostility, anxiety, less willingness to touch, mental health referral, excessive curiosity, demeaning jokes, breached confidence, denial/exclusion of partners, attempts to cure lesbianism, embarrassment, rejection, voyeurism, coolness, rough physical handling, judgemental care, shock, pity, ostracism, invasive questioning, fear, mistreatment of partners, derogatory comments, pathological assumptions, refusal of obstetrical health care, misdiagnosis and general discrimination (summarized in Stevens, 1993). Not untypical is the experience of a British lesbian who

> had suffered for a long time with lumps in her breasts and other worrying symptoms. One specialist finally stumbled on the fact of her lesbianism. He subsequently wrote to her GP saying that her problem was hormonal: as a lesbian she had 'an enlarged clitoris' and 'body hair'. In actual fact, just to put the record straight, she had neither. He wanted to prescribe hormonally: fortunately her more enlightened GP disagreed. (Hemmings, 1986, p. 68)

While the kind of social change needed to eradicate such attitudes is a daunting prospect, every health service user is entitled to well-informed and appropriate behaviour from the professionals involved in their care. This means that training and higher educational programmes for health care professionals have a clear obligation to provide their students with the information and skills which they need to enable them to carry out their responsibilities to their lesbian clients professionally and effectively.

Research in the UK

There is a small but rapidly growing body of work on lesbian health in the UK. The Royal College of Nursing's Lesbian and Gay Nursing Issues Working Party, after a familiar struggle for recognition, has undertaken a continuing large-scale national project researching the health care experiences of lesbians and gay men, and members of the working party have been publishing important articles in the nursing press since 1990 (James *et al.*, 1994; Platzer, 1993, 1992, 1990; Rose, 1993; Rose and Platzer 1993). The RCN has published a statement on the nursing care of lesbians and gay men (Royal College of Nursing, 1994). Clearly, there is always a risk that lesbian issues will be marginalized within this mixed agenda, something which is further complicated by the fact that many health care professionals have only recognized the inadequacy of the services they offer to gay men in the light of the HIV/AIDS pandemic.[5]

There is, however, an exciting and productive explosion of research specifically into lesbian issues. Research is ongoing at London's lesbian GUM clinics – the Audre Lorde and the Sandra Bernhard – into lesbian sexual health (Farquahar and Kavanagh, personal communication, 1994). Lesbian graduate students around the nation are choosing lesbian health as the subject for their Masters' or doctoral research (Godfrey, 1994). As well as publishing in academic and practitioner journals, *Dykenosis*, the newsletter of the Birmingham group Lesbewell, offers a forum for sharing research findings among the growing lesbian health research community. Data from such research, unsurprisingly, support and reinforce the findings of work from the USA. It is the ignorance and anti-lesbianism of health care professionals – doctors, midwives, nurses, clinical researchers, their trainers and educators – which, in the context of a society deeply hostile to lesbians, gives rise to the many problems faced by lesbians whether seeking or providing health and social care.

I cannot stress too strongly that such work is precarious and vulnerable, and that all too often it remains unpublished and unacknowledged. It remains almost impossible to get research into lesbian health funded,[6] so it is only in the context of postgraduate study that much of it even gets done. The limitations of working in this way are obvious. Institutional hostility, lack of appropriate and informed support from supervisors, isolation and great personal stress are common (all have been reported by postgraduate students I have worked with), and theses and dissertations all too often gather dust in university libraries, while others struggle to reinvent the same wheel time and time again.

What are the issues?

Reviewing the literature makes it clear that there are areas where research into lesbian health is currently needed. I would like to end this chapter by highlighting some areas for future development, both in terms of practical research and in terms of incorporating lesbian health studies into practitioner training and higher education curricula. In terms of research my (tentative) suggestion is that lesbian health researchers and activists should be demanding research into some or all of the following:

1. Lesbian sexual health, including HIV/AIDS and cervical cancer, specifically the mechanics and incidence of the sexual transmission of disease between women (O'Sullivan and Parmar, 1992).
2. The lesbian-specific epidemiology of certain diseases – for example, breast cancer, which appears disproportionately to affect lesbian women (de Pinho, 1994; Rosser, 1993).
3. The health consequences of survival in a social environment hostile to lesbians, including questions relating to alcohol and other substance ab/use, depression and suicide, eating disorders and stress-related illness (Deevey and Wall, 1993; Erwin, 1993).
4. Interactions between lesbian service users and health professionals, including the history of medical homophobia, the current failure to provide respectful and appropriate care for lesbians, and the lack of attention paid to lesbian issues in the training of staff (de Pinho, 1994; Platzer, 1993; Rosser, 1993; Stevens, 1993).
5. The extent to which the biological events of the female life cycle may impact differentially on lesbian and non-lesbian women. The menarche, menstruation, so-called 'pre-menstrual syndrome', menopause, pregnancy, miscarriage, abortion, ageing and bereavement are likely to have specific psychological and social implications for lesbians (Wilton, forthcoming).
6. The extent to which ignoring the existence of lesbians leads to poor research design, flawed conclusions and bad science in health research generally (Rosser, 1993).
7. The difficult issue of 'passing', or what is commonly called 'lesbian invisibility'. This question underpins and inflects all the others. It both characterizes and delineates the social field in which lesbian health is located.

Yet all the knowledge in the world will make no difference to lesbians unless those responsible for their health care – including health education, health promotion, primary health care, acute services, long-term care and terminal care – have the information, skills and attitudes they need to provide an appropriate and professional service to lesbians. It is shameful that lesbian health studies continues to exist only where lesbian students or teachers are in the position to ensure that time is allocated to it. Rather, it should be an integral part of the training of all health and social care professionals, at every level.

Notes

1. The infamous Section 28 of the 1988 Local Government Act, which prohibits local authorities from 'promoting' homosexuality and the 'teaching in any maintained school of the acceptability of homosexuality as a pretended family relationship' is an important case in point. The discrimination against 'pretend families' legitimated by the Section has particularly nasty consequences for lesbian mothers, who considerably outnumber gay male parenting couples.
2. To which I would want to add that the Women's Liberation Movement was certainly as important, if not more important, for lesbians.
3. This parallels the situation in the early years of the HIV pandemic, when medical research in the USA, repeatedly denied federal funding, was paid for by energetic fundraising in the gay community (Shilts, 1987).
4. In fact sex between women is an extremely inefficient means of transmitting HIV.
5. In the context of HIV/AIDS, health care professionals are having to work with more 'out' gay men than ever before. This is partly due to the numbers of gay men who need care, and partly because HIV obliges gay men to be open about their sexuality to their medical carers. This is not to deny the huge costs that gay men have borne as a result, in terms of abuse, pain and misery, but simply to note that they have become immeasurably more visible as users of services.
6. My own attempts to get funding from a key national funding body for a project investigating lesbian sexual health were thwarted at the first hurdle. During an 'informal' pre-application chat a representative of the funding body in question kindly told me that there was no chance whatsoever that my proposal would be considered because it would be impossible for me to 'find a significant number of lesbians'. In such ways is lesbian invisibility (non-viability!) reflected and perpetuated.

References

Boston Women's Health Book Collective (1971) *Our Bodies Ourselves*. New York: Simon and Schuster.

Chafetz, J., Sampson, P., Beck, P. and West, J. (1974) 'A Study of Homosexual Women.' *Social Work*. 19: 714–23.

Clark, D. (1993) 'Commodity Lesbianism.' In H. Abelove, M.A. Barale and D.M. Halperin (eds) *The Lesbian and Gay Studies Reader*. London: Routledge.

Deevey, S. and Wall, L.J. (1993) 'How Do Lesbian Women Develop Serenity?' In P. Noerager Stern (1993).

de Pinho, H. (1994) 'Placing Lesbian Health Issues on the Policy Agenda.' Paper presented to Reproductive Health Priorities Conference, Johannesburg, June.

Deyton, B. and Lear, W. (1988) 'A Brief History of the Gay/Lesbian Health Movement in the USA.' In M. Shernoff and W. Scott (eds) *The Sourcebook on Lesbian/Gay Healthcare*. Washington, DC: National Lesbian and Gay Healthcare Foundation.

Donoghue, E. (1993) *Passions Between Women: British Lesbian Culture 1668–1801*. London: Scarlet Press.

Doyal, L. (1995) *What Makes Women Sick? Gender and the Political Economy of Health*. London: Macmillan.

Erwin, K. (1993) 'Interpreting the Evidence: Competing Paradigms and the Emergence of Lesbian and Gay Suicide as a "Social Fact".' *International Journal of Health Services*. 23/3: 437–53.

Furedi, A. and Tidyman, M. (1994) *Women's Health Guide*. London: Health Education Authority.

Glascock, E.L. (1981) 'Access to the Traditional Health Care System by Nontraditional Women: Perceptions of a Cultural Interaction.' Paper presented at the annual meeting of the American Public Health Association, November, Los Angeles.

Glascock, E.L. (1983) 'Lesbians Growing Older: Self-Identification, Coming Out and Health Concerns.' Paper presented at the annual meeting of the American Public Health Association, November, Dallas.

Godfrey, J. (1994) Unpublished MA dissertation, University of the West of England in Bristol.

Graham, H. (1993) *Hardship and Health in Women's Lives*. London: Harvester Wheatsheaf.

Griffiths, P.D. (1974) 'Homosexual Women: An Endocrine and Psychological Study.' *Journal of Endocrinology*. 63: 549–56.

Harvey, S.M., Carr, C. and Bernheine, S. (1989) 'Lesbian Mothers: Health Care Experiences.' *Journal of Nurse-Midwifery*. 34/3: 115–19.

Health Education Authority (1993) *Every Woman's Health: Information and Resources for Group Discussion*. London: HEA.

Hemmings, S. (1986) 'An Overdose of Doctors.' In S. O'Sullivan (ed.) *Women's Health: A Spare Rib Reader*. London: Pandora.

Henry, G. (1950) *Sex Variants: A Study of Homosexual Patterns*. London: Cassell.

James, T., Harding, I., and Corbett, K. (1994) 'Biased Care?' *Nursing Times*. 21 December: 28–30.

McIntosh, M. (1968) 'The Homosexual Role.' Reprinted in K. Plummer (ed.) (1981) *The Making of the Modern Homosexual*. London: Hutchinson.

Michigan Organization for Human Rights (MOHR) (1991) *The Michigan Lesbian Health Survey* (Special Report).

O'Sullivan, S. and Parmar, P. (1992) *Lesbians Talk (Safer) Sex*. London: Scarlet Press.

Platzer, H. (1990) 'Sexual Orientation: Improving Care.' *Nursing Standard*. 13 June: 38–9.

Platzer, H. (1992) 'Chipping Away at Change.' *Nursing Standard*. 16 September: 46–7.

Platzer, H. (1993) 'Nursing Care of Gay and Lesbian Patients.' *Nursing Standard*. 13 January: 34–7.

Plummer, K. (1981) 'Building a Sociology of Homosexuality.' In K. Plummer (ed.) *The Making of the Modern Homosexual*. London: Hutchinson.

Plummer, K. (1992) 'Speaking its Name: Inventing a Lesbian and Gay Studies.' In K. Plummer (ed.) *Modern Homosexualities: Fragments of Lesbian and Gay Experience*. London: Routledge.

Ponse, B. (1978) *Identities in the Lesbian World: The Social Construction of Self*. Westport, VA: Greenwood Press.

Powell, V. (1995) 'Demonstrators Halt Gay "Cure" Doctor.' *Pink Paper*. 5 May: 1.

Randall, C.E. (1989) 'Lesbian Phobia among BSN Educators: A Survey.' *Journal of Nursing Education*. 28: 302–6.

Reagan, P. (1981) 'The Interaction of Health Professionals and their Lesbian Clients.' *Patient Counselling and Health Education*. 3/1: 21–5.

Robertson, M. (1993) 'Lesbians as an Invisible Minority in the Health Services Arena.' In P. Noerager Stern (1993).

Rose, P. (1993) 'Out in the Open.' *Nursing Times*. 28 July: 9–11.

Rose, P. and Platzer, H. (1993) 'Confronting Prejudice.' *Nursing Times*. 4 August: 14.

Rosser, S.V. (1993) 'Ignored, Overlooked or Subsumed: Research on Lesbian Health and Health Care.' *National Women's Studies Association Journal*. 5/2 (Summer): 183–203.

Royal College of Nursing (1994) *The Nursing Care of Lesbians and Gay Men: An RCN Statement*.

Ruse, M. (1988) *Homosexuality: A Philosophical Inquiry*. Oxford: Basil Blackwell.

Ryan, C. and Bradford, J. (1988) 'The National Lesbian Healthcare Survey: An Overview.' In M. Shernoff and W. Scott (eds) *The Sourcebook on Lesbian/Gay Health Care*. Washington, DC: National Lesbian and Gay Health Foundation.

Saunders, J.M., Tupac, J.D. and MacCulloch, B. (1988) *A Lesbian Profile: A Survey of 1,000 Lesbians*. West Hollywood: Southern California Women for Understanding.

Savage, J. (1987) *Nurses, Gender and Sexuality*. London: Heinemann.

Schulman, S. (1994) *My American History: Lesbian and Gay Life during the Reagan and Bush Years*. London: Cassell.

Shilts, R. (1987) *And the Band Played On: People, Politics and the AIDS Epidemic*. New York: St Martin's Press.

Smyke, P. (1991) *Women and Health*. London: Zed Books.

Stern, P. Noerager (1993) 'Preface' to P. Noerager Stern (ed.) *Lesbian Health: What Are the Issues?* London: Taylor and Francis.

Stevens, P.E. (1993) 'Lesbian Health Care Research: A Review of the Literature from 1970 to 1990.' In P. Noerager Stern (1993).

Stevens, P.E. and Hall, J.M. (1988) 'Stigma, Health Beliefs and Experiences with Health Care in Lesbian Women.' *Image: Journal of Nursing Scholarship*. 20/2: 69–73.

Stevens, P.E. and Hall, J.M. (1990) 'Abusive Health Care Interactions Experienced by Lesbians: A Case of Institutional Violence in the Treatment of Women.' *Response to the Victimization of Women and Children*. 13/3: 23–7.

Vachon, R. (1988) 'Lesbian and Gay Public Health: Old Issues, New Approaches.' In M. Shernoff and W. Scott (eds) *The Sourcebook on Lesbian/Gay Health Care*. Washington, DC: National Lesbian and Gay Healthcare Foundation.

Wilton, T. (1993) 'Queer Subjects: Lesbians, Heterosexual Women and the Academy.' In M. Kennedy, C. Lubelska and V. Walsh (eds) *Making Connections: Women's Studies, Women's Movements, Women's Lives*. London: Taylor and Francis.

Wilton, T. (1995) *Lesbian Studies: Setting an Agenda*. London: Routledge.

Wilton, T. (forthcoming) *Good For You: A Handbook on Lesbian Health and Wellbeing*. London: Cassell.

Workers' Educational Association (North West District) and Health Education Council (1986) *Women and Health: Activities and Materials for Use in Women's Health Courses and Discussion Groups*. London: WEA/HEC.

Young, E.W. (1988) 'Nurses' Attitudes towards Homosexuality: Analysis of Change in AIDS Workshops.' *Journal of Continuing Education in Nursing*. 19/1: 9–12.

Zeidenstein, L. (1990) 'Gynaecological and Child-Bearing Needs of Lesbians.' *Journal of Nurse-Midwifery*. 35/1: 10–18.

16

Linguistics: The Impenetrable Paradigm, or Where Were You Two When They Passed Out the Penes?

Susan J. Wolfe and Julia Penelope

For almost two centuries, linguists have considered their discipline a science. Some of the branches of the discipline – acoustic phonetics, for example – can be considered physical sciences, while the majority of them fit squarely among the social sciences. Research in linguistics has therefore proceeded within identifiable scientific paradigms, its researchers using established methodologies, building on the findings of the past. Like other scientists, a linguist solves a problem in four stages. First, she identifies and defines the problem. Second, she studies previous literature bearing on the problem. Next, she collects data. Finally, she draws conclusions about the data, stating them as hypotheses that future researchers can test. It is always possible that her findings may call into question the theories of her predecessors or perhaps even contribute to a shift in the paradigm itself.

We (Julia and Susan) began our work in linguistics in the mid-1960s, years before either of us would call herself a feminist, and a decade before Susan would identify as a lesbian. Both of us were undoubtedly drawn to linguistics because of its methodology: we are both puzzle-solvers, drawn to crossword puzzles, jigsaw puzzles and other pastimes that require us to identify patterns, fit pieces together and work toward solutions, albeit solutions constructed by others. We started out as English majors, a respectable path into linguistics, a field restricted to graduate studies at that time. The work expected of us in English classes indeed resembled the fitting together of jigsaw puzzles: the pieces were precut, the picture predesigned. We were, after all, literature students when the close readings of the New Critics were the rule. We quickly learned its techniques, and became bored.

Linguistics was new to English departments in the 1960s and early 1970s. There were three linguists in the department at the University of Texas at Austin and three at the State University of New York at Stony Brook, where we received our respective doctorates. Linguistics was exciting then: a new theory, transformational-generative grammar (TGG), was taking over the discipline in the USA. An outgrowth of the structural school that had preceded it, TGG promised powerful new descriptions of language structures and the nature of language, and insight into the workings of the human mind through the discovery of linguistic universals. If literary criticism seemed to offer little opportunity to do anything new, TGG offered us the opportunity to contribute to a new theory of human language.

We began our research with high hopes. We would practise good science, contributing to our discipline, adding to the pool of knowledge. Other linguists would acknowledge our work, and we would receive the rewards academia offers. Certainly neither of us set out to do linguistics within a feminist or lesbian paradigm. As linguistics students within English departments, our research raised eyebrows only because the TGG paradigm was still a new one. Julia's dissertation constructed a linguistic theory of lyric poetry, in which she analysed only the works of male poets; Susan's examined the structure of relative clauses in Old English. Neither dissertation was an apparent prelude to linguistic research informed by a lesbian perspective.

One characteristic of TGG that appears to belie its categorization as a science is its reliance on the competence/performance distinction first articulated by Ferdinand de Saussure. The grammatical models developed by TGG linguists describe competence (the internalized knowledge of ideal native speakers) not performance (the sentences speakers actually produce). Although Noam Chomsky, the 'sire' and principal patriarch of TGG, initially held that the distinction existed to rule out such performance errors as stammering and false starts, the focus on competence has in practice ensured that leading theorists, for the most part men who may or may not be native speakers of English, have felt free to draw conclusions about English based on their own intuitions, and then to generalize these 'insights' to other languages.

By contrast, each of us learned to draw our data from real uses of English. Since Susan chose to work in historical syntax and Julia in stylistics, we collected our data from the prose written by others. As unremarkable as this may seem to scholars in other scientific disciplines, this methodology placed us on the margins of TGG linguistics even as we used its syntactic theories. When we found data which disconfirmed a hypothesis of an important linguist – that is, one by Chomsky or those trained by him at the Massachusetts Institute of Technology, or trained by any of his students – the conclusions in our work were bound to be ignored, dismissed as descriptions of usage (performance).

The direction our work, together and separately, has taken has been based on our observation of data, data which other linguists had not adequately accounted for. Julia's research into terms for sexually promiscuous women, for example, was spurred on by a casual joke made by a male student in her Modern English Grammar course at the University of Georgia in the early 1970s, a course for which the textbook was Jacobs and Rosenbaum's *English Transformational Grammar* (1968).

She had been teaching Jacobs and Rosenbaum's version of syntactic features, features which are supposed to account for the distinct forms of English pronouns, for example, as well as the contexts in which they appear. In their account, a noun phrase, *Alice's father*, will subsequently be replaced by *he*, and not *she* (with the presence of the female proper name), because the noun *father* has the feature <+masculine>, and so does *he*. After Julia's explanation of Jacobs and Rosenbaum's features, the student asked jokingly, 'Then how would the common noun *whore* be marked?' The student had a valid point: such 'syntactic' features appeared to work perfectly well as long as linguists stuck to proper nouns and kinship terms. How, indeed, was an 'autonomous' grammar going to account for the pronouns used to substitute for a host of common agentive nouns (*doctor*, *nurse*, *miner*, *secretary*)? As Julia reflected on the student's comment, she realized that *whore*, like many other terms for promiscuous women, would have to carry a <+feminine> feature in order to be replaced by *she*, as it actually is; not only were noun phrases containing such terms regularly replaced by *she*, but males in comparable roles and occupations were explicitly designated as such by speakers: *male prostitute*, *male hustler*.

Julia started her research by collecting over 220 terms used to label women who did or did not engage in sexual intercourse and constructed a semantic field illustrating the relationships among these terms. She established semantic features which distinguished among them and created a semantic field illustrating their relationships. An outgrowth of this research was her work on common nouns in English, which demonstrated that other nouns of agency are typically considered to be masculine, with male referents; when used to refer to women, the nouns must be overtly marked (*female astronaut*, *woman doctor*). Collectively, her work reveals that the English lexicon is split into two unequal parts, with most nouns referring to humans assigned the feature <+masculine>, and those nouns referring to humans as sexual beings largely marked as <+feminine>, used persistently as pejoratives (Penelope, 1977a, 1977b, 1978, 1990).

Similarly, Susan, while teaching a course in introductory linguistics at the University of South Dakota, covered an Esperanto problem designed to train students to look for suffixes with functions unlike those of English suffixes. Esperanto marks its parts of speech with suffixes, so that all nouns end in *-o* and all adverbs in *-e*. Linguists consider Esperanto to have natural gender (gender based on biological sex) rather than grammatical gender (the categorization of nouns based on linguistic features). She was stunned to discover that Esperanto, lacking grammatical gender, simply considers any noun with a human referent to be either generic or male, depending on context. All female nouns are derived from male nouns by means of adding the suffix *-in*, a method derived from German.

Esperanto is an invented language, one created by combining characteristics of several European languages in order to overcome cultural biases and to serve as a vehicle for international communication. Susan saw that one bias had been built into it, however: the assumption that men are the human norm. Even Esperanto kinship terms are masculine generics: *patro* means both 'parent' and 'father', while *mother*, *patrino*, is marked by an affix. She then collected data from natural European languages other than English, each said to have grammatical gender, and found that their nouns were patterned in the same manner as English nouns: agentive nouns were nearly always masculine, and referred to males, except for nouns denoting roles and professions reserved for women (terms for 'prostitute', 'manicurist' and 'receptionist', for example). She examined previous accounts of grammatical gender, and found that linguists and grammarians were generally oblivious to the similarity between 'natural gender' in English and 'grammatical gender' in other European languages (Wolfe, 1980b). Together with Julia's work, her research demonstrates the cultural biases that have determined gender in European languages and have also shaped linguistic and grammatical descriptions of gender.

Both of us have done research that calls into question the favourite pretensions of linguistic theory. Julia has published widely on agentless passive constructions, showing how speakers and writers use them to manipulate others (Penelope, 1975a, 1975b). Canonical TGG explanations of such passives derive them from underlying active sentences, by means of rules linguists describe as 'neutral' between speakers and hearers; that is to say, hearers unerringly retrieve meanings carefully preserved by rules they share with speakers. Analysing sentences like 'Children deserve to be spanked', Julia shows that the agents inferred by hearers are determined by the assumptions they bring to interpreting sentences, assumptions based on their knowledge of the 'real' world – the world outside linguistics (Penelope and Wolfe, 1977, 1978; Penelope, 1990). Susan has published a number of articles on linguistic reconstructions of prehistoric Indo-European culture, demonstrating the ways in which assumptions of prehistoric male supremacy have skewed linguists' interpretations of the data they find (Wolfe, 1980a, 1980c, 1984, 1986, 1993).

Thus our work began to critique the treatment of women in general, and occasionally lesbians in particular, in languages. Once we compared our conclusions to the descriptions offered by grammarians and the explanations offered by linguists, our critique of the field itself followed. The problems we perceived may well have been more obvious to us than to others. As lesbians, we know that patriarchal culture and all its discourses have been constructed in order to exclude us, occasionally through open attack but more often through omission; we are not surprised that those writing about language would fail to notice when this occurs.

These insights need not have sprung from a lesbian perspective on linguistics. The second and third steps in solving a problem in linguistics require that prior research and data be scrutinized, after all; the problems suggested to us by the data we observed might, in theory, have been obvious to any trained linguist seeking objective solutions to problems. Why should asymmetries based on sexual difference exist in the English lexicon? Why do comparable asymmetries appear in languages with 'grammatical gender'? What does the similarity between English and these languages suggest about the long-held distinction between natural and grammatical gender?

Because many of the problems we have investigated centre on sex and gender, the conclusions we have drawn consider the social and cultural contexts in which language occurs. We did not begin with the assumption that sexism and other biases figure in the rules and patterns of languages; we found that they did. Once we had determined that sexism, homophobia and other prejudices were factors in determining the directions languages would take, we questioned the fact that other linguists' explanations had not taken such factors into account.

But our critiques were also bound to go unnoticed. Not only have we worked outside the inner circle of linguists – both as students and as professional linguists – but we have considered language data as socio-cultural phenomena. TGG linguists consider studies of language and sex/gender to be peripheral, as part of socio-linguistics rather than linguistics 'proper'. Like psycholinguistics, socio-linguistics is considered to be a form of 'hyphenated linguistics', its prefix demonstrating hybridization. TGG, like other structural approaches to languages, regards the components of languages as 'autonomous', structured by linguistic factors and divorced from the cultures in which they are spoken. Explanations of data that tie languages to cultures are irrelevant to the chief business of linguistics, which is constructing increasingly abstract (mathematical) models that account only for sentences made up by linguists or borrowed from philosophers of language, such as the ubiquitous '*Have you stopped beating your wife?*'

Perhaps it is the case that, as women and lesbians, we are all too aware that little that 'happens' in a patriarchal culture is 'autonomous'. If language is a matter of convention and males hold the power in a culture, they will determine language as they determine all other conventions capable of sustaining their control. If our position in a patriarchal culture makes us sceptical of facile conclusions that all too often appear to transcend culture, it is because we have found that such conclusions are completely enmeshed in the culture of their researchers. So-called native-speaker intuitions are particularly suspect when they emanate from the linguist describing a language. In this case, scientific objectivity is a near impossibility.

As lesbians, however, we exist on the periphery of patriarchal culture. Unable to find a way to describe our childhood experiences of the world, lacking a vocabulary to describe ourselves to ourselves, we had groped for a notion of self, only to find ourselves objects of pity, ridicule or condemnation. Views of the world others consider to be objective have often excluded us. Once we discovered that we were not as others described us, we were prepared to challenge other assumptions that seemed unassailable, the cultural givens. Common sense and the received wisdom passed on to us by others assured us that heterosexuality and marriage were normal, the only possibility. If we were willing to call institutionalized heterosexuality a lie, why would we balk at questioning the concept of linguistic autonomy?

If we have observed linguistics and language data from the unique perspective of lesbian researchers, we nonetheless hoped that our findings would be adopted by other linguists. The problems we identified and the hypotheses we advanced would, we hoped, serve to modify the ways in which linguistic enquiries proceeded. Each of us believed that language could be approached empirically, objectively; if many of the linguistic studies we found were riddled with patriarchal bias, we assumed that our work could serve as a corrective.

We have been disappointed. Our research has made little or no impact on linguistics, synchronic or diachronic. Some have made use of it in their classrooms, and continue to request reprints. Other linguists outside the field of TGG, such as Dwight Bolinger, have adopted some of our conclusions, and feminists like Mary Daly and Sarah Lucia Hoagland have made use of it in their own work. Some writers have felt free to appropriate it without citing it because they, unlike us, have established reputations in the field. But most linguists have simply ignored it.

Furthermore, we are, as far as we know, the only known lesbians in the field. Linguistics, unlike philosophy and literary criticism, lacks a lesbian presence. In fact, though women have entered the field in large numbers since the 1970s, their comparative absence well into the twentieth century has guaranteed that the majority of its leading theorists continue to be men. Non-lesbian feminists who have published important work on sexism in language and sex differences in language use began by adopting the interpretations of their male predecessors. Now, though many question the findings of earlier linguists, none suggest that these findings challenge the tenets of structural linguistics (including TGG) or historical linguistics.

Challenges to the concept of linguistic autonomy have usually come from those working on language acquisition and/or language change because their work has a pragmatic focus and they, too, describe actual patterns of use. Such researchers have suggested that the data they observe cannot be accounted for by autonomous grammars. But they have not succeeded in deflecting linguists from the general tendency to regard language as something that happens outside of human intentions either, primarily because linguists dismiss such research as 'applied' linguistics. Never will the taint of practical use befoul the purity of theory!

Lesbian perspectives brought to bear on existing linguistic paradigms, particularly those which insist on the objectivity of their methodology and the autonomy of language(s), could help to cause a paradigmatic shift. Lesbians are less inclined to ignore anomalous data in favour of elegant solutions, perhaps because we are anomalous ourselves within patriarchy. Problems which have been dismissed or ignored as irrelevant might be seen to be central, evidence of cultural ordering of knowledge through language – perhaps through language structures as well as lexicons. (This view, now unfashionable in linguistic circles, is a weak version of a hypothesis advanced by Benjamin Lee Whorf, a chemical engineer who worked as an underwriter for Hartford Fire Insurance Company.)

But the lesbian subversion of linguistic theory remains no more than a remote possibility. We are still 'all dressed up with no place to go'. Today's practising linguists have abandoned the hope of providing insights into the workings of the human mind, leaving the search to philosophers and psychologists. Likewise, the connections between language and culture are of more interest to anthropologists than to TGG linguists. In the field as it now exists, our findings are as anomalous as we are. We do not publish in *Language* (the major linguistics journal in the USA) or in other leading journals in linguistic theory; our work, if it did appear in such places, would be out of context and, therefore, unintelligible. We publish in journals that encourage 'interdisciplinary' research and that have made themselves the 'home' of other maverick linguists (such as the dispossessed old guard of the structuralist school). We are not invited to present at meetings of the Linguistic Society of America or at major research universities. Unheard and invisible among linguistic theorists, neither of us is likely to subvert the paradigms men have constructed.

References

Penelope (Stanley), J. (1975a) 'Passive Motivation'. *Foundations of Language*. 13: 25–39.

Penelope (Stanley), J. (1975b) 'The Stylistics of Belief.' In D.J. Dieterich (ed.) *Teaching about Doublespeak*. Urbana, IL: National Council of Teachers of English, pp. 175–87.

Penelope (Stanley), J. (1977a) 'Gender-Marking in American English.' In A.P. Nilsen, H. Bosmajian, H. Lee Gershuny and J.P. Stanley (eds) *Sexism and Language*. Urbana, IL: National Council of Teachers of English, pp. 43–74.

Penelope (Stanley), J. (1977b) 'Paradigmatic Woman: The Prostitute.'

In D.L. Shores and C.P. Hines (eds) *Papers in Language Variation*. Birmingham, AL: University of Alabama Press, pp. 303–21.

Penelope (Stanley), J. (1978) 'Sexist Grammar.' *College English*. 39/7: 800–11.

Penelope (Stanley), J. (1990) *Speaking Freely: Unlearning the Lies of the Fathers' Tongues*. New York: Teachers College Press.

Penelope (Stanley), J. and Wolfe (Robbins), S. (1977) 'Forced Inference: Uses and Abuses of the Passive.' *Papers in Linguistics*. 10/3–4: 299–311.

Penelope (Stanley), J. and Wolfe (Robbins), S. (1978) 'Agent Recoverability and Truncated Passives.' *Forum Linguisticum*. 2/1: 33–46.

Wolfe, S. (1980a) 'Amazon Etymology.' *Sinister Wisdom*. 12: 15–20.

Wolfe, S. (1980b) 'Gender and Agency in Indo-European Languages.' *Papers in Linguistics*. 13/2: 773–94.

Wolfe, S. (1980c) 'Linguistic Problems with Patriarchal Reconstructions of Indo-European Culture.' *Women's Studies International Quarterly*. 3/2–3: 227–37.

Wolfe, S. (1984) 'The Reconstruction of Proto-Indo-European Kinship.' *North Dakota Quarterly*. 52/1: 67–76.

Wolfe, S. (1986) 'On Terms of Consanguineal Kinship in Proto-Indo-European.' *Papers in Linguistics*. 19/4: 425–47.

Wolfe, S. (1993) 'Reconstructing PIE Terms for Kinship and Marriage.' *Word*. 44/1: 41–51.

Index